The ANATOMY & DEVELOPMENT
of the
SPORTS PROTOTYPE
RACING CAR

Ian Bamsey

Foulis

Haynes

A **Foulis** Motoring Book

First published 1991

Published by:
Haynes Publishing Group
Sparkford, Nr Yeovil
Somerset BA22 7JJ, England

Haynes Publications Inc
861 Lawrence Drive, Newbury Park,
California 91320, USA

A catalogue record for this book is
available from the British Library

ISBN 0 85429 829 0

Library of Congress Catalog Card Number
91-74067

Editor: Robin Read
Layout: Jill Moulton
Typeset in Frontiera medium 9/10pt. and
printed in England by
J. H. Haynes & Co. Ltd.

Contents

HISTORICAL NOTE

What is a 'Sports Prototype'?

The World Sports Car Championship was created in 1953. Even then there was no clear cut definition of a sports car: was it a two seater road car designed primarily for performance or was it a Grand Prix car with mudguards? The rule makers undoubtedly saw it as the former but found it hard to legislate against the latter, given that it was felt there had to be provision for 'prototypes' of future models. After all, was not sports car racing intended to 'improve the breed'?

1962

In 1962 the World Championship was reserved for homologated GT cars in an attempt to solve this dilemma. However, the organisers of the classic sports car races did not want to lose the spectacle of sports-racing cars such as the Maserati Birdcage and the Ferrari Testa Rossa. Thus was born 'Experimental GT'. At the same time the mid engine revolution was in full swing and quickly 'Experimental GT' gave rise to the Ferrari P series against which Ford ranged the GT40 Le Mans programme.

The mid-Sixties sports-racing car was therefore based upon contemporary Formula One car technology. However, its engine capacity was unlimited and it was required to have two seats, a full windscreen, token luggage accommodation, lights and a spare wheel. Thus, in essence a car such as the Ferrari P4 was a fully enclosed version of a Grand Prix machine, heavier but with a larger, hence more powerful, engine. The combination of slippery aerodynamics and a large displacement engine led to worryingly high speeds, particularly at Le Mans.

1968

In response the FIA's CSI sporting wing imposed a three-litre maximum capacity for 1968, albeit permitting 50-off homologated cars (such as the 4.5-litre Mark One version of the GT40) to run five litres while pulling a minimum of 800kg. rather than 650kg. This changed the face of sports car racing overnight: out went Ford's 7.0-litre Mark II and Mark IV models, Ferrari's 4.0-litre P4 and the 5.0-litre Chevrolet-Chaparral, the key players of 1967.

The Ford and Ferrari teams were due to withdraw in any case and the new regulations left Porsche's new 3.0-litre coupé to fight the old GT40. Porsche was committed to building its cars to be as light as possible and gained further assistance in 1969 by the abolition of the minimum weight limit for 3.0-litre 'Group 6' cars, together with the dropping of the requirements for a windscreen and token road equipment. In came the flyweight Porsche 'spyder'.

At the same time the Group 4 (soon to be renamed Group 5) homologation quantity was lowered from 50 to 25 units. That gave rise to Porsche's 5.0-litre 917 coupé, a pure prototype ballasted to 800kg. of which 25 examples were assembled at the start of the project. Ferrari replied in kind with the 512.

1972

Having blundered in its attempt to keep sports-racing cars to 3.0-litres, the CSI gave the homologated 5.0-litre category only until 1972, then sports car racing was reserved for the 3.0-litre machines. Regulations governing the now fashionable wings, tabs and suchlike followed Formula One practice, though cars devised for the World Championship for Makes tended to seek low drag above downforce. A typical runner of 1972 was the Ferrari 312PB: a two seater version of the marque's contemporary 3.0-litre Formula One machine with its wheels enclosed by a slippery spyder shell.

Ferrari and Matra slugged it out in '72 and '73 and then Ferrari resolved to concentrate upon Formula One leaving the French firm virtually unopposed. Sports car racing having fallen into decline, the CSI switched the World Championship for Makes to a new concept of 'Group 5' car – the silhouette racer. So long as the body resembled the general outline of a production car and the chassis set a production engine block in the right location, just about anything went.

The famous Porsche 935 quickly came to dominate Group 5 racing. Meanwhile, Group 6 continued with a lesser championship which initially Porsche and Renault contested with 2.1-litre turbo cars. In Formula One, 3.0-litres unblown had been equated to 1.5 litres supercharged but for sports car racing there had long been a more generous factor for forced induction, though prior to the mid-Seventies there had been no real interest in any form of supercharging.

1977

After 1976 Porsche and Renault confined their duel to Le Mans and the CSI championships both for Group 6 and for Group 5 cars failed to attract manufacturer interest. By the end of the decade, sports car racing had just about hit rock bottom and it was clear that something radical had to be done.

The Eighties

The answer was Group C and the World Endurance Championship. In essence, a Group C 'Sports-Prototype' was a fully enclosed racing car running to a minimum weight of 800kg. and with engine free but fuel consumption dictates to limit race day (if not qualifying) performance. In North America the IMSA organisation created its own form of Sports-Prototype, setting no limit on fuel consumption but equating various engine options via minimum weight stipulations.

Thus, the Sports-Prototype of the Eighties harked back to the fabulous sports-racing coupés of the Sixties – it was a direct descendent of the Ferrari P4, the Ford MkIV, the Porsche 917 and their ilk. A breed of uncompromised, fully-enclosed racing car that had been virtually extinct for a decade. This book analyses the 'born-again' mid-engined coupé of the Eighties; more details of Group C and GTP engine and chassis regulations being given in the text, as appropriate.

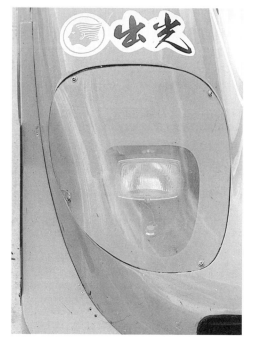

PART ONE

AERODYNAMIC EVOLUTION

Chapter One

Slippery Case

The story of the Sports Prototype since 1980 is the continuing history of the fully enclosed, mid-engined racing car. This is a breed of pure competition machine, every bit as specialized and uncompromised as the mid-engined Grand Prix car. Its main characteristic is its aerodynamics: with everything enclosed – wheels, cockpit and all the mechanicals – its lift and drag aspects are fundamentally different from those of the exposed wheel single-seater. It is also heavier and is traditionally used for endurance rather than sprint racing.

Prior to the era of mid-engines, there were few fully enclosed racing cars. GT cars yes, but pure racers with enclosed wheels tended to be open cockpit spyders: the Jaguar C- and D-Types, the Aston Martin DBR1, the Mercedes SLR300 and the Ferrari Testa Rossa, to name but a few of the many such which were classics of the Fifties. Those cars followed in the great tradition of the racing sportscars of the Twenties and Thirties, some of which were Grand Prix cars with mudguards and an extra seat. Of course, only a little earlier, Grand Prix cars themselves had been two-seaters.

The question of what constitutes a genuine racing sports car as opposed to a Grand Prix car or a Gran Turismo is not one to which this book addresses itself. This book is about a distinct breed of mid-engined racing car; whether it be called sports car, a Prototype, a Sports Prototype or even a Grand Touring

Prototype is irrelevant. It is clearly defined by FIA Group C and IMSA GTP regulations. Although it has two seats, its link with the past is with the tradition of Grand Prix racing rather than any form of production car competition. In the Thirties when the Vintage Grand Prix car gave way to the first of the moderns, the new breed of scientific racing machine was seen in both open wheel and fully enclosed guise.

The advanced Auto Union was even then a mid-engined machine. In fully enclosed track (AVUS) and record-breaking form it had a higher top speed but the enclosure of its wheels and cockpit brought some fundamental problems. Those problems of cooling, stability and sheer controllability emphasised the very different nature of the fully enclosed racing car to that of the traditional open wheeler. Its characteristics – not least its extra weight – presented a whole new avenue of development challenges.

Developing a special breed of fast circuit car was extremely costly and of marginal gain in an overall race programme. Consequently this intriguing avenue of development went little trodden for decades, and in the Fifties the designers generally insisted on keeping Grand Prix drivers in the open air.

Meanwhile sports car drivers were also exposed to the elements because that made for a lighter and cooler, less claustrophobic car. However, rule changes in the Sixties encouraged the new breed of mid-engined sports racing machine to be fully enclosed rather than a quasi-Grand Prix car with its wheels shrouded. Thus was opened the new avenue of development at which the exciting streamliners of the Thirties had hinted. It was an area of development that made a complete break from the long evolution of the racing car in terms of aerodynamics.

All racing cars are aerodynamic devices generating powerful forces as they travel through the air at high speed. Drag is the most obvious force, at least it was in the early Sixties when the two-seater, fully enclosed, mid-engined racing car was born. Drag pulls in the opposite direction to the thrust of a car, even a car running in a straight line through still air. All aerodynamic forces increase with the square of velocity, thus a representative drag force of 110 lb (50 kg) for a fully enclosed, mid-engined early Sixties Le Mans car travelling at 100 mph past the signalling pits equates to a drag force of 440 lbs (200 kg) for the same vehicle flat out at 200 mph on the seemingly endless Mulsanne straight.

Contemporary Grand Prix cars suffered a significantly higher level of drag for a given speed but rarely exceeded 150 mph. Nevertheless, they were built with a view to minimum drag as was evident in a slim, cigar-shaped fuselage which forced the driver to lie right back, his chin almost on his chest. Drag wastes power: clearly the reduction of drag is equivalent to obtaining more power and 1.5-litre Grand Prix cars did not have power to spare and needed any available aerodynamic gain.

The existence of the 3.5 mile (5.6 km) long Mulsanne straight focused the minds of unlimited capacity (power to spare) Le Mans car designers upon the challenge of drag reduction. In the early Sixties, when the fully enclosed, mid-engined racing car became established, the principles of drag reduction were well known. Drag arises since a car causes a disturbance in the air by travelling through it. The amount of drag produced relates to the amount of disturbance caused and in the case of any car there are a number of ways in which the amount of disturbance it creates for a given speed can be minimized.

The moving body travels within an invisible capsule of disturbed air. Assuming (as in the case of all cars with the possible exception of the Budweiser Rocket) the body is not travelling through the sound barrier, the air ahead receives warning of its arrival in time to move aside to make room for it. This reaction forms the nose of our imaginary capsule. Clearly, the disturbed air meeting the front of the body will try to compress. Although, unlike a liquid, gas is not incompressible, at the speeds we are dealing with the air can be considered incompressible.

Interestingly, since the air compresses very little, car aerodynamics can be tested in a water tunnel as an alternative to the wind tunnel. It is often enlightening to consider a car as if it were travelling through water rather than air. In trying to compress, the air in the front portion of our capsule is at high pressure and this contributes to the total drag force. It also means that the air tends naturally to follow the contours of the front of the body in a smooth flow. The flow of air can be assumed to be of low viscosity, as is that of water, and the low magnitude of viscous or frictional forces means that the behaviour of air in motion is similar to that of a perfect fluid.

Around 1791 Italian physicist G B Venturi observed that as a perfect fluid flow increases its velocity it is subject to a corresponding reduction in pressure. This phenomenon is consequently known as the venturi effect but earlier, in 1738, it had been explained by the Swiss mathematician and physicist Daniel Bernoulli, who applied the principle of energy conservation to moving fluids.

A moving fluid possesses kinetic energy as a consequence of its motion and potential energy because of its tendency to move under the influence of the Earth's gravitational field. At any point within the fluid, there exists a static pressure proportional to the height of the fluid above that given point: this is a measure of the potential energy of the fluid at that point. The kinetic energy of the fluid gives rise to a dynamic pressure which is a function of the flow rate – the velocity of the fluid.

Provided energy is neither removed nor added to the fluid stream, total energy will be conserved. This is the basis of the Bernoulli Equation. It follows that any change in kinetic energy as a consequence of increased velocity must be accompanied by a reduction in potential energy. The Bernoulli Equation shows that the sum of pressure of the fluid and the two types of energy is always constant, assuming a perfect fluid it should be added. In simple terms: a higher flow rate implies a lower pressure.

Air is not a perfect fluid but this so called venturi effect holds good for it and it explains why an aeroplane flies. The wings of the aeroplane are shaped so as to accelerate the airstream over the upper surface creating a pressure differential in relation to the lower surface where the airflow is at the speed of the body. Air at sea level has a pressure of 14.7 psi or 1.0 bar absolute. If this pressure is maintained below the body while a lower pressure is generated above, clearly there will be a tendency towards lift.

This application of the venturi effect can be experienced by trying to hold a piece of paper horizontal by the two corners nearest to oneself. Without any trickery, it will not happen: good old gravity ensures that the paper falls away. However, if you blow across the top of the paper, the acceleration of air over the curved surface will reduce pressure and the pressure differential can easily be enough to lift the sheet so that it is horizontal in defiance of gravity.

We find a flow of air of varying pressure within the capsule of our racing car. The path of individual particles of air through the capsule can be traced as streamlines. Against the surface of the body these streamlines do not move at all. Since air is viscous, it has a tendency to stick. It sticks to the surface of the body and this gives rise to shearing forces which retard the flow adjacent to the stationary surface layer. In fact, there is a steadily rising gradient of flow velocity from zero on the surface to full speed some distance away from it.

The zone of retarded air flow is known as the boundary layer. Within the boundary layer the flow can either be laminar or turbulent. Generally, the clinging stream at the front of the body gives rise to a laminar flow but this is not inevitable and the reasons for the regular transition from laminar to turbulent flow are not clear cut. The transition may be promoted by surface roughness or by velocity fluctuations within the flow caused by the contours of the body. The result of the all too familiar transition is an increase of what is known as skin friction drag. This is the component of total drag attributable to the shearing forces which retard the flow within the boundary layer.

Skin friction is only really significant in terms of overall drag when a body is well streamlined and is travelling at very high speed. Aircraft designers have found boundary layer turbulence promoted by the deposition of dead insects on a wing and rarely worry much about the suppression of skin friction where operational speeds are below 300 mph (as in the case of a racing car). In fact, sometimes turbulence is encouraged since it can help reduce so called form drag. Form drag is the drag caused by the shape and size of the body, the latter considered only in terms of its maximum cross-sectional area, or frontal area.

Form drag is the sum of the positive pressure at the front of the body which resists its motion and of a region of higher velocity negative pressure further back, which pulls against its motion. The latter is essentially the car's wake in which the air does not flow in smooth streamlines but forms vortices and eddies. A vortex is a fluid flow with a spiral motion, an eddy a flow with a circular motion.

Form drag can be significantly lessened through a reduction in the frontal area of a body but little can be done to reduce the pressure at the front. The pressurized air will follow almost any shape of nose but how the nose breaks the air is very significant it terms of form drag. It is easier to push than to pull air, thus what counts most overall is what happens to the progress of the boundary layer further back. However, what can be made to happen to it further back is heavily dependent upon what happens to it at the front.

By way of example, in 1989 the front wheel arches of the Nissan Group C car were increased in height and though this did not alter the frontal area, nor did it change the general shape of the car, it added drag. The change of form at the nose affected the airflow behind it which added to the strength of the wake pulling against the car's motion. The negative force of the wake is determined by the overall shape of the car. The key to reducing the strength of a wake is in keeping the boundary layer attached to the car for as long as possible, and this is where the tail shape is crucial. However, the tail has to operate within the flow conditions set by the nose.

In the free stream outside the boundary layer the static and the dynamic pressure of the air vary as it flows over a surface of changing contour. Bernoulli assures us that in a streamline flow the sum of these pressures remains constant. In the free stream, the flow is always able to proceed into regions of increased pressure at the expense of velocity. Thus, as the air flows over a surface of changing contour, the pressure and velocity of the air vary and the opposing pressure forces are balanced by the forces that result from the change in the momentum of the flow.

However, within the boundary layer the momentum of the air has been reduced in overcoming viscous forces and the remaining momentum may be insufficient to allow the flow to proceed into regions of increased pressure. When this condition exists boundary layer separation occurs. The boundary layer no longer continues to follow the contours of the surface of the body and it leaves the surface altogether. Beyond the point of separation, between the surface and the separated boundary layer, there exists a region of reversed, or upstream, flow. This reversed flow and the separated boundary layer subsequently coalesce to form the wake which absorbs energy, creating drag.

It is possible for the boundary layer to leave the surface of car body then reattach itself again a little later. For example, in the case of a Group C car, there is a tendency for air flowing over the roof to separate just behind the windscreen at the highest point of the body, then to reattach itself to the engine cover, or perhaps the rear wing. The initial separation over the driver's head creates a local low pressure area. A duct at this point will bleed high pressure air from the cockpit, encouraging a through flow of driver-cooling air.

In the case of a car without a rear wing, boundary layer separation at some point ahead of the rearmost part of its tail is almost inevitable; the aim is always to delay the final separation for as long as possible. Laminar flow is more prone to separation than turbulent flow, which is why the promotion of turbulent flow can help reduce drag. In the turbulent flow a mixing of the molecules of air gives rise to an exchange of momentum which produces a more even distribution of velocity and this dampens the tendency towards separation.

The contouring of the body in such a manner that the wake strength is reduced to a minimum is known as streamlining. In essence, the boundary layer air can withstand high acceleration of its velocity without separation but only low deceleration. Air is happy to flow from high to low pressure (as in the case of our cockpit roof air bleed) but finds the reverse almost literally an uphill struggle! As we have seen, it is when the air is asked to decelerate into a region of higher pressure that separation occurs. Since rapid deceleration of the flow promotes separation, the contouring of the body must make any deceleration gradual. This is the key to effective streamlining.

In general terms, the forward portion of any given body should be well rounded and the body should curve back gradually from the forward section to a tapering after section with the avoidance of sharp corners along the surface. In this respect the teardrop shape is ideal. Early wind tunnel work by German airship maker Zeppelin demonstrated that the teardrop shape offers the lowest drag of all practical three-dimensional forms in free air, lower than that of a sphere or a hemisphere.

Comparison of the 'draginess' of a given form can be made via a non-dimensional drag co-efficient, the Cd,

(Cw in German terminology, Cx in French), and this is based on wind tunnel measurement. A flat plate in free air registers a standard Cd of 1.17, a hemisphere of 0.41, a sphere of 0.15, while a teardrop shape registers only 0.046. These figures, of course, assume a perfectly smooth surface and are for the pure form of given proportions. However, practical applications of the pure teardrop shape were found to be effective in the world of aviation, and in the automotive world.

It is worth noting that the flat plate can have virtually only pressure drag: the oncoming air makes room for it and only licks the edges of the plate. On the other hand, if the plate is turned through 90° so that it is lying in the plane of the streamlines, it has only skin friction drag. Further, it should be noted that streamlining an object – as in the step from sphere to teardrop – tends to imply an increase in the area licked by the airstream.

The total surface licked by the air is known as the wetted area. Increasing the wetted area in the interest of streamlining unfortunately increases skin friction. In turn skin friction is becoming more significant in terms of total drag since form drag is being reduced. However, assuming a car has smooth bodywork, little can be done to reduce skin friction. Further, the skin friction of the body of a well streamlined car is far less significant than the combination of skin friction and form drag that arises from the internal cooling flows.

Cooling drag plays a major role in the overall drag of a well streamlined racing car. Efficient cooling flow management is essential. Typically, the process of streamlining a car body makes the car more prone to overheating since vital parts become shrouded. Further, when a car is well streamlined it becomes more prone to directional instability and overcoming this is another major challenge of drag reduction.

When an air stream is head on to a car, as when the car is proceeding straight ahead in still air, the aerodynamic forces act only in a vertical plane as lift and drag. The air flow splits symmetrically in the horizontal plane, hence no side forces result. However, air is rarely still, while in corners a racing car does not travel precisely in the direction in which it is pointing. The angle between the direction of motion and the direction of the air flow is known as the yaw angle and the introduction of any degree of yaw angle makes the airflow asymmetric, and side forces are generated.

By way of example, a car travelling at 60 mph through a 90° cross wind of 10 mph is being subject to an airflow with a yaw angle of approximately 9°. This exposes the side of the vehicle, or its so called keel surfaces, to the air flow and thus affects the drag co-efficient and the stability of the vehicle, the latter possibly to an alarming degree when high speeds and low drag are involved. A high drag car gains stability through pulling its powerful if unwanted wake, which acts as an invisible drogue: a low drag car is far more susceptible to crosswinds.

The pressure created by the resultant side forces acts through the centre of pressure, as do the other aerodynamic forces. As aeroplane passengers are aware, in total there are six components of the aerodynamic force that can act on any moving body, including vertical (lift), horizontal, lateral and roll inputs. The location of the centre of pressure is crucial in terms of stability. It can be at a point some way in front of the car, but for stability it needs to be behind the centre of gravity – otherwise the car will try to turn itself around under the influence of side forces.

As speed increases, the question of lift also has to be considered. A well streamlined car body assumes a longitudinal cross-section not dissimilar to that of an aircraft wing. Consequently, it has an inherent tendency towards lift and lift reducing wheel adhesion thus makes the car more difficult to control. Lift and drag are really the same force: drag is the portion which acts against the forward motion of a body while lift acts to try and raise the body in the air. If the lift force is greater than the weight of the body, the body will rise off the ground. Of course, the amount of force generated relates to the speed at which the body is travelling. It also depends on how the air is manipulated by the body.

Clearly, any acceleration of the airflow relative to the body will induce low pressure. Low pressure above, higher pressure below implies lift. As we have seen, air tends to separate from the rear of a car body and it creates a low pressure wake which generally starts over the tail. That induces lift. So does air packing under the nose of a car.

If our aforementioned experimental piece of paper is swept through the air, held firmly front and back at a forward-tilted angle it will experience a lifting force. Try it! This is the effect of air trying to compress against its lower surface. That ramming effect is exploited by an aerofoil which is a far more sophisticated means of creating lift than our sheet of paper. An aerofoil such as an aircraft wing exploits this high pressure underneath, as well as its carefully created low pressure above.

An aerofoil has to be so designed that it presents the air with a top surface route to which the boundary layer can stay attached. Of course, in exploiting the venturi effect, the top surface contributes more to lift than the bottom surface. Above a substitute flat plate or our sheet of paper is also low pressure but this is in the form of a separated airflow which causes a vast amount of drag to be produced for a given amount of lift.

The flat plate depends upon its angle of attack to create lift, needing high pressure which retards the motion of the body to which it is attached. Further, the separated air above it pulls against the motion of the body. An aerofoil section is effectively a streamlined alternative. It should be noted that, contrary to popular belief, an aerofoil section does not create a vacuum on its top surface, nor even what could be considered a partial vacuum. It merely exploits small pressure variations and thus a good deal of wing surface is required to lift an aeroplane off the ground.

The ratio of lift to drag is what interests the designer of an aircraft wing and this varies with the angle of attack. The total amount of lift generated also

varies. A typical example would be a lift:drag ratio of 24:1 at a 4° angle, falling to 12:1 at 15°, at which angle this representative aerofoil produces its maximum lift. At 20° our aerofoil stalls, the ratio of lift to drag falls to 3:1 and we might as well be using an angled flat plate since the air above has separated.

The sudden vast increase in drag in this stalling situation retards the speed of the aeroplane to which we have attached a pair of our hypothetical wings and this in turn clearly reduces the amount of lift available to support the machine. If we cannot recover the situation quickly our aeroplane will fall out of the sky.

In creating lift, by whatever means, momentum is imparted to the air and this momentum is not recovered and appears as drag. Another way of looking at this so called induced drag is to consider that the lift force cannot be quite perpendicular to the direction of the airflow since it is generated through deflection of the airflow downwards. Thus, the direction of lift is slightly backwards and so constitutes drag.

The drag co-efficient of a body recognises all three types of drag: skin friction drag, form drag and induced drag. An aerofoil has very little impact upon the drag co-efficient in itself, creating insignificant form drag if well designed. However, its impact on drag will be significant if it is used to create a high degree of lift. To complicate the matter, induced drag does not increase with the square of speed but relates to the speed relative to the lift generated. Logically, induced drag is only really significant in automotive terms where an attempt is made to exploit lift.

No such attempt was made by mid-engined racing car designers in the early Sixties. Unwanted lift was a by-product of early Sixties fully enclosed, mid-engined cars but its magnitude was slight, hence the induced drag was slight. However, during the Sixties the concept of harnessing negative lift became widely accepted and this significantly influenced the development of the fully enclosed, mid-engined racing car, as we shall see.

Chapter Two

Beetles and Hunchback Spyders

The first fully enclosed, mid-engined racing car seen at Le Mans was a 1953 Porsche special derived from the fledgling marque's road going Beetle-based sports car. The road car retained the Beetle chassis with its engine behind the rear axle: the Le Mans special had a bespoke frame and the powertrain turned through 180° so that it was ahead of the rear axle for improved weight distribution. This engine position echoed that of the Auto Union Grand Prix car of the Thirties which, like the Beetle, had been designed by Professor Ferdinand Porsche, father of Ferry and Louise Porsche who founded the family marque.

Both the Beetle and the Auto Union were teardrop-shaped, wind cheating cars of the Zeppelin school of aerodynamics. An early exponent of the teardrop shape in the automotive world was Dr Edmund Rumpler. In 1921, after a long spell working in aircraft and airship design, Rumpler produced a low drag road car shaped as half a teardrop, seeking greater speed from a given power output and better fuel economy for a given speed. Rumpler's car had roomy four-seater accommodation and its engine ahead of its rear axle to allow the tail to taper appropriately without excessive overhang. In free air, the body shape of this so called *Tropfen-Auto* or Teardrop Car was later found to offer the remarkably low drag co-efficient of Cd = 0.28.

Rumpler's associate Hellmuth Hirth later went to work for the powerful Benz company where he persuaded his colleagues to exploit the *Tropfen-Auto* concept. By way of publicity for this avenue of development, Benz produced a Grand Prix car with its fuselage shaped like a teardrop and dubbed the Benz *Tropfenwagen*. This open wheeler was first seen at Monza in the 1923 European Grand Prix.

Built under patents held by Rumpler, the *Tropfenwagen* had its 2-litre six cylinder in-line engine mounted ahead of the rear axle – it was the first ever mid-engined Grand Prix car – and was clothed in a streamline body that assumed an effective teardrop shape with the driver housed in a bullet nose and with a long pointed tail aft of him. Its streamlining even extended to having a crescent-shaped radiator straddling the engine cover. Further, it was crab-tracked, its exposed narrow front wheels set 6 in (152.4 mm) further apart than its exposed narrow rear wheels to echo the planform of the fuselage.

The *Tropfenwagen* gave a good account of itself at Monza but Benz was running into trouble and its subsequent enforced amalgamation with Daimler ended the teardrop programme. However, Professor Porsche continued to champion the concept with his 1934 Auto Union P-Wagen Grand Prix car, of which the smooth, torpedo-shaped fuselage had the amazingly low drag co-efficient

Doctor Edmund Rumpler's so-called Tropfenwagen of 1921 was streamlined on the teardrop principle yet offered roomy four-seater accommodation. It was later found to have a drag co-efficient of only Cd = 0.28.

of Cd = 0.057 in free air: in practice the passage of air between it and the wheels added considerably to drag, the car as a whole registering a drag co-efficient of Cd = 0.61.

Porsche's contemporary Volkswagen Beetle had a rear engine for logistical reasons but also enjoyed a suitable interpretation of the Rumpler teardrop philosophy. This helped ensure good fuel consumption. Meanwhile, the Auto Union Grand Prix car was mid-engined not only for teardrop considerations, but also since the unusual engine position offered a lower seating position for the

Ferdinand Porsche's Auto Union V16 Grand Prix car of 1934 followed Rumpler's teardrop philosophy and its fuselage alone had a drag co-efficient of a mere Cd = 0.057, the car as a whole registering Cd = 0.61.

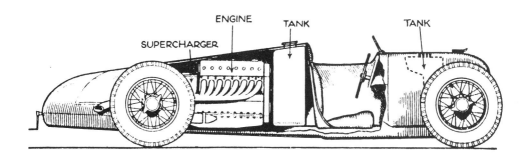

driver hence less frontal area, a lighter transmission package and better weight distribution.

With the adventurous *P-Wagen* Porsche was able to keep both the fuel and engine within the wheelbase rather than having the heavy fuel load outrigged behind the rear axle where it significantly affected weight distribution as it lightened. Further, grouping the major masses – driver, fuel and engine – within the wheelbase offered a lower moment of polar inertia, hence improved manoeuvrability.

In 1935 Porsche produced a semi-enclosed version of the Auto Union Grand Prix car, initially to attack speed records. It had a canopy to properly fair-in the cockpit and cowlings over the front and rear suspension linkages, these extending behind the front wheels and to enclose the rear wheels. Initially the car had been tried fully enclosed but hiding the front wheels made it undriveable, primarily since it hindered steering and springing movements. In its semi-enclosed, slightly higher drag but controllable form, the so-called saloon version of the Auto Union had a frontal area 25 per cent greater than that of the regular Grand Prix car for a drag co-efficient of Cd = 0.395 and an overall drag reduction of the order of 25 per cent.

The saloon was equipped with a 4.95-litre V16 engine offering in the region of 370 bhp and it tried for 200 mph on a section of Italian autostrada, clocking 199.92 mph after the nose radiator inlet had been almost completely blanked off, this ploy adding around 2.5 mph. Two years later Porsche produced a manageable fully enclosed body looking for even higher speeds. This followed wind tunnel work using 50 per cent scale models in an aircraft manufacturer's facility and it implied completely new clothing rather than adding additional fairings to the existing single seater fuselage.

The new shape was basically that of half a teardrop – a tortoise shell with a bubble on top to enclose the cockpit. It increased the frontal area by 45 percent compared to that of the open wheeler but the drag co-efficient dipped just below Cd = 0.30. This, a second attempt to produce the first ever fully enclosed, mid-engine racing car, was run on the ultra-high-speed Avus track. Alas, there were tyre and brake temperature problems, while the drivers soon rejected the bubble. Further, a lack of stability at high speed made the device somewhat unnerving to drive.

Daimler-Benz produced a similar shaped streamliner from its regular front-engined Grand Prix car but nose lift at high speed made the device downright dangerous, forcing a redesign. Early the following year, in January 1938, Auto Union and Daimler-Benz ran revised, fully enclosed streamliners on a stretch of Autobahn near Frankfurt. Porsche was no longer connected with Auto Union, the revisions being the work of Professor Eberan von Eberhorst.

Auto Union and Daimler-Benz were looking to improve upon 251.41 mph set by Bernd Rosemeyer in the Auto Union tortoise car (resplendent with bubble) on the autobahn the previous October. At that stage the Land Speed Record had only been 301.13 mph – a month later it was raised to 312.60 mph – just over 500 km/h. Having seen 400 km/h (250 mph), the German manufacturers wanted 450 km/h (279 mph) on home soil from a modified Grand Prix car. All the time the aerodynamic forces were climbing with the square of the speed.

In the face of instability caused by lateral forces or a lifting force at either end of the car, the obvious response is to build in understeer and, where possible, to provide a high moment of polar inertia – the dumb-bell effect – to dampen any tendency of the car to deviate from the chosen path. The Auto Union was based on a car with a tendency towards oversteer and a low moment of polar inertia.

For his fully enclosed, mid-engined record car, Eberhorst claimed a drag co-efficient as low as Cd = 0.22, fitting transverse skirts under the car to discourage air from flowing beneath the body. Eberhorst felt that the usual underbody flow could only increase drag since the body was in close proximity to the ground and his wind tunnel tests proved him right. So called ground effect shear was inducing flow separation. Diverting the flow to the sides of the car did nothing for reduction of pressure drag but overall there was an improvement in form drag.

Auto Union's fully enclosed, mid-engined record seeker ran a special ice, rather than water, cooled 6.33-litre version of the familiar V16 engine rated 545 bhp. Bernd Rosemeyer took it to 267.1 mph then crashed, the car apparently hit by a strong crosswind channelled down a clearing in woods that brought a sideroad to the autoroute. The Auto Union's slippery shape made it extremely susceptible to crosswinds. Rosemeyer was killed and the day of the large capacity, fully enclosed, mid-engined racing car was over, at least for the time being.

As a regular road racing car, the Auto Union had been notoriously tricky to drive. This was widely assumed to be due to its unusual mid-engine location, in particular to the fact that due to the length of the engine the driver sat well forward, with his feet between the front wheels. In fact, the difficulty of control was more to do with a combination of an unsatisfactory swing axle rear suspension and the low moment of polar inertia. It was the swing axle which encouraged the car to oversteer and the low moment of polar inertia did nothing to dampen the tendency of the tail to break away. With high power, it broke away all too quickly, calling for lightning reactions to drive the car on the limit.

In 1938 Auto Union produced a revised car with a de Dion rear suspension. This was far more satisfactory but it was too late to overcome the prejudice that had grown against the mid-engine layout and almost all Fifties Grand Prix and sports racing cars had a front engine location. However, as we have seen, the mid-

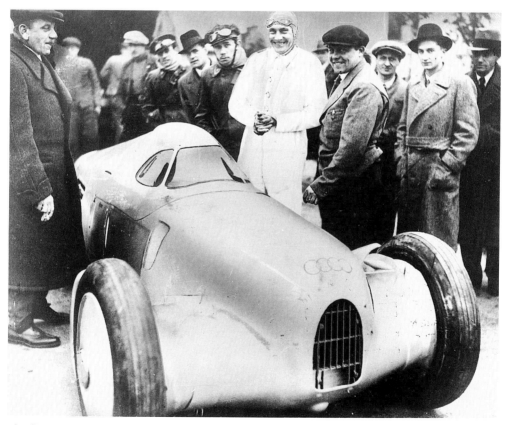

The first ever mid-engined racing car to have an enclosed cockpit was this 200 mph saloon version of the Auto Union V16, used for record breaking in 1935. Designer Ferdinand Porsche and driver Hans Stuck pose with the car.

engine concept and the Rumpler philosophy were carried to Le Mans by Professor Porsche's son and daughter.

Although the Porsche teardrop coupé of 1953 had a VW Beetle-derived engine displacing only 1500 cc and tuned to produce 78 bhp ahead of its rear axle, its slippery shape gave it an impressive top speed of 124 mph on the Mulsanne straight. The car's superstructure was detachable so that it could be run as an open cockpit spyder with aero screen rather than windscreen, the tail still falling away in this guise but the teardrop shape less pronounced. There was a consequent saving in frontal area and weight.

However, although it had a higher frontal area, the coupé's lower drag co-efficient was sufficient to endow it with less overall drag and thus a higher top speed. Although the coupé was almost unbearably noisy on Le Mans' endless Mulsanne straight, it offered a top speed advantage that was judged more important than a quiet life for its driver!

As we have noted, the existence of the seemingly endless Mulsanne straight made wind cheating of vital importance at Le Mans. Further, low drag helped fuel economy while ensuring the best possible straight line speed. That was important not only at Le Mans: whatever the nature of the circuit, unnecessary drag wasted fuel and wasted horsepower. However, increased weight also cost performance, so away from Le Mans the spyder option was often the logical choice.

For 1954 Porsche developed a limited production version of its 1500 cc sports racer for sale to customers interested in competition. In the finalization of the design of the so-called Typ 550, Porsche wind tunnel tested alternative coupé and spyder bodies in scale model form. The basic teardrop coupé as seen at Le Mans was found to have a drag co-efficient of $Cd = 0.23$ whereas the spyder version had a drag co-efficient of $Cd = 0.29$ with an aero screen for the driver and a lid over the passenger accommodation. In

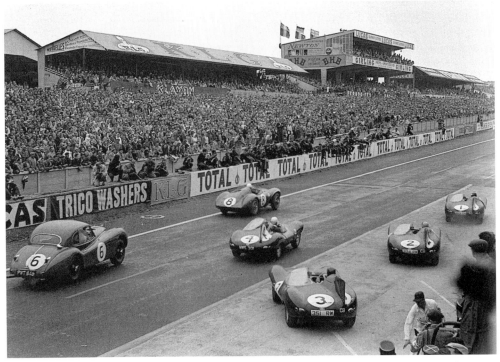

The start of the 1956 Le Mans race. Jaguar D-types 1, 2, 3 and 4 chase an Aston Martin and a Jaguar coupé, quicker off the mark. Note the characteristic D-type tail fin intended to provide lateral stability.

this form, the frontal area of the spyder was only 85 per cent of that of the coupé and Porsche quoted comparative overall drag factors as 23.2 for the coupé and 24.7 for the lighter spyder.

Interestingly, Porsche also evaluated the potential for an open body retaining a full windscreen but saving weight compared to a coupé and reducing frontal area slightly since the coupé's roof was domed. With the regular spyder-type rear deck the drag co-efficient was a lot worse, at Cd = 0.37. However, Porsche then tried raising the rear deck to windscreen height to give something of the effect of a proper teardrop body. This reduced the drag co-efficient to Cd = 0.31. The frontal area was still 95 per cent of that of the coupé and the overall comparative drag factor was 29.5.

The so-called Hunchback with open roof and matching high rear deck went into production but for serious racing Porsche developed the spyder option and used this as the basis of its 1954 factory Le Mans cars. Whereas the model had been measured as having a drag co-efficient of Cd = 0.29, in the Stuttgart Technical Institute's large wind tunnel an actual car was measured as having a drag co-efficient of Cd = 0.435. The difference was largely due to the effect of cooling air flows. With Porsche's own 1500 cc four-cam engine producing 125 bhp the spyder was capable of something in the region of 135-140 mph on the Mulsanne.

Others seeking low drag at Le Mans in the early to mid-Fifties included Jaguar and Bristol. With more powerful engines they had a higher top speed potential and thus faced a greater threat from directional instability. This, of course, was the problem that had been faced by the pre-war German streamliners. The D-Type Jaguar was good for around 170 mph.

In 1954 Daimler-Benz produced a similarly fast Grand Prix challenger with fully enclosed wheels but this low drag clothing had to be quickly abandoned as it made the car difficult to drive. In *The Grand Prix Car* L J K Setright has suggested that the body made the car more susceptible to side forces and that this was the root of the increasing

understeer with speed that upset handling.

Also in 1954, Jaguar and Bristol appeared at Le Mans with low drag bodies sporting lateral fins, primarily for straight line stability. The intention was to move the centre of pressure rearwards, behind the centre of gravity. Thus, the effect of the fins was that of putting feathers on an arrow. In the case of the 2.0 litre coupé designed by the car division of the Bristol Aircraft Company, twin fins were employed and air flowing over the windscreen was channelled across the roof so as to run down the sloping fairing between the fins. Bristol claimed that the fins were actually found to enhance fast cornering. Thus, it appears that the Bristol 450 Coupé benefited from lateral forces where the Mercedes W196 probably suffered.

Fins were commonly employed in the Fifties but little, if any, attention was paid to the promotion of negative lift prior to the early Sixties. One exception had been a Daimler-Benz Land Speed Record car designed by Porsche after the Auto Union V16. Targeted at 400 mph, this mid-engined device was fitted with short, stubby aircraft wings mounted upside down to check lift and to keep its tyres firmly on the ground for good traction. Alas, before the adventurous car could show its paces the war intervened.

In 1956 a somewhat tatty customer Porsche Typ 550 spyder turned up at the Nürburgring with a large aerofoil over its cockpit. The car was entered by Michael May – a young engineering graduate – and his cousin Pierre May. Michael May had an idea that was simple, effective and years ahead of its time. It was to harness the power of negative lift to load his car's tyres. Not just for improved traction – that wasn't his problem given 1500 cc – but for an all round improvement in grip. May saw that in theory loading a car's tyres so that they are pressed harder to the track surface increases adhesion and thus the car can corner faster and can brake within a shorter distance as well as being able to accelerate with less tendency towards wheelspin.

Making a car heavier increases the loading on its tyres but that is no way to

The first racing car to run with a wing was Michael May's privately entered Porsche spyder. This is how it arrived at the 1956 Nürburgring and Monza sports car internationals. It was declined a race.

enhance cornering power since, in effect, the additional mass multiplies the centrifugal force trying to make the car fly off into the bushes. Its unwanted inertia also makes acceleration slower and increases braking distances. On the contrary, lighter is faster. However, May saw no reason why aerodynamic downforce – negative lift – should not be employed to load the tyres without increasing the inertia weight of the machine.

May took an appropriate profile for his inverted wing from a table of NACA aerofoil sections and made the area of the wing as large as he dared, taking it to the full width of the car body. It was mounted on pylons over the cockpit to act through the centre of gravity, thereby not disturbing the handling characteristics of the car. To create maximum downforce the aerofoil had, of course, to be run at an angle of attack.

This added to the frontal area of the car and hence to total drag; while as the generation of any amount of lift creates drag, the angled maximum lift position was also the highest drag position.

To minimise drag on the straight, where downforce was unwelcome (except when braking or perhaps under hard acceleration) May arranged to be able to adjust the angle of his wing. The wing was mounted so that it ran flat until the driver actuated a cable control which tipped it 17° from the horizontal.

May calculated that his aerofoil would generate the car's own weight in downforce at a speed of only 93 mph. He first tested the wing on local roads and a daunting corner that was usually taken at 70 mph became a 100 mph corner without taking the crazy-looking spyder close to its limits! From Zurich the cousins took the car to the Ring for the 1000 km (620 ml) race where puzzled scrutineers passed the device as raceworthy. May took the car out for the practice behind Juan Fangio's Ferrari and Jean Behra's Maserati. It was wet and he had never been around the 14 ml mountain circuit in his life so he was hoping that the aces would show him the way.

A novice driver in a tiny Porsche spyder hoping to keep up with Fangio and Behra in pouring rain on his first ever lap of the circuit? Surely young Michael was somewhat optimistic as he pulled out onto the challenging Nürburgring! He must have felt that way himself, but to his astonishment he found he could not only keep up with Fangio and Behra, he was able to pass them. He ended up with a lap time just behind the best of the Italian cars and way ahead of the rest of his class.

The Porsche factory team cars did not sprout similar aerofoils overnight. Instead, the May cousins received a visit from the organizers accompanied by the Porsche Team Manager. It was suggested that the wing blocked the view of other drivers and that the car should be run without it. Like all entrants, May's participation was effectively at the discretion of the organizers and it was withdrawn. It is worth noting that the President of the organizing club was himself a former Porsche Team Manager. However, it has to be understood that the Le Mans disaster was fresh in the mind. The organizers of the following Monza 1000 km (620 ml) race rejected the wing on the grounds that it presented a scythe-like danger to spectators.

That, for the time being, was the end of the concept of harnessing downforce. The sports racing cars of the late Fifties were mainly front-engined spyders such as the D-Type, designed for low drag and experiencing only a small degree of lift, which tended to be positive rather than negative. Indeed, sports racing car constructors found positive lift to be a real danger at the front and at the rear of a light spyder, just as Daimler-Benz

In the face of the high-windscreen ruling Maserati produced this version of its Birdcage spyder to run in the 1961 Le Mans race. Note how the rear deck matches the height reached by the raked windscreen.

had found it a real danger on a heavier car at higher speed in 1937.

Testing at Monza in 1961 Richie Ginther found the rear end of his new mid-engined Ferrari V6 spyder going light at speed, making the car a handful to drive through the fast, sweeping Curva Grande after the pits. Ginther suggested a vertical strip of aluminium be fitted at the end of the rear deck to well up the airflow, thus creating a local high pressure area. In theory this would counteract the tail lift – and in practice it worked. In fact, the spoiler created pressure over the entire car.

The spoiler became a characteristic of early Sixties Ferrari sports and GT racing cars. At this time it became mandatory for all racing sportscars to have a high and full width windscreen. Thus the frontal area of the spyders increased massively and with it the drag produced. Reminiscent of the Hunchback version of the Porsche 550, Maserati produced a Le Mans version of its classic Birdcage spyder

with a high rear deck and a matching raked screen, which of necessity reached forward across much of the bonnet.

By 1961 the mid-engined Grand Prix car was well established, following Cooper's pioneering efforts with the underpowered 2.5-litre Coventry Climax in line four engine. The mid-engined Cooper benefited from reduced frontal area and reduced weight and a low polar moment of inertia, making it more agile. Cooper had been quickly followed by Lotus and with the switch to a 1.5-litre formula, all other serious teams followed the path of low weight and low frontal area for low drag.

Employing the same technology, Cooper had produced a 2.5-litre sports car and this spyder-bodied device was seen at Le Mans in 1961, together with a mid-engined version of the 2.89-litre four cylinder Birdcage Maserati and a 2.46-litre Ferrari V6 spyder. These were the first over 2.0-litre mid-engined cars seen at Le Mans and none of them lasted

The Ferrari 250 P the first mid-engined car to win Le Mans, which it did in 1963. There was nothing to match the open roof Maranello sports racer in that year's running of the 24-hour classic.

the race, though the so-called Ferrari 246SP – based on the marque's contemporary spaceframe Formula One car – ran strongly with the leading V12 Testa Rossas before its demise.

Essentially a sprint machine, the Cooper was not seen again in 1962 while Maserati returned to a front engined configuration following disappointing results with its rebuilt model. However, the Ferrari V6 was back and it was accompanied by a 2.65-litre V8 engined sister model. The V6 once again impressed with its speed while the V8 was significant in so far as it was the final step towards putting the V12 engine behind the driver. Ferrari had gained a lower frontal area, a reduction in weight, a lower centre of gravity and a lower moment of polar inertia with its switch to a mid-engined V6 sports racer. However, there was a fear that the V12 engine would push the driver too far forward: shades of the popular misconception over the Auto Union's

seating position.

Alas, Maserati was falling from contention due to financial problems but in 1963 arch-rival Ferrari took the plunge and led the inevitable move into really large capacity mid-engined sports racing cars with the 250P. Ferrari had at last gained sufficient confidence in the mid-engine layout to put its longer and heavier V12 behind the driver.

In truth, without Maserati opposition, there was nothing to match the 250P at Le Mans in 1963. This open-bodied sports racer was the first mid-engined car intended to challenge seriously for outright victory at Le Mans. Meanwhile a 2.5-litre fully enclosed, mid-engined coupé, the Coventry Climax-Tojeiro had run without success in 1962 and this year a larger capacity fully enclosed, mid-engined car, the 4.3-litre V8 Ford-Lola was to be found lurking in the field. The Sports Prototype – the fully enclosed, mid-engined racing car as we know it today – had been hatched.

The first fully enclosed, mid-engined racing car of large engine displacement was this 4.3-litre V8 Ford-Lola GT of 1963. It was the first of a new generation of Sports Prototype racing car.

Chapter Three

Flying on the Ground

The open-cockpit Le Mans-winning Ferrari 250P of 1963 was traditional in its body shape, clearly derived from the marque's earlier spyders. Ferrari shunned the Hunchback route. Behind its mandatory windscreen the 250P's cockpit was open and its rear deck was a flat surface at wheel arch height, in usual spyder style. It carried a spoiler, but this was no longer in the direct airstream, thanks to the high windscreen.

At this stage Michael May was to be found working at Maranello as a consultant employed to help develop fuel injection. He advised on development of the 250P's so-called aerodynamic anti-roll bar. This was a wide roll hoop at the back of the open cockpit matching windscreen height and carefully shaped to deflect air down towards the spoiler. Although it echoed the May Porsche's wing, the then Technical Director at Ferrari, Mauro Forghieri, emphasized to the author that its primary role was as a feed to the spoiler. The spoiler in turn was a device intended to counter lift in the interest of stability, rather than to create significant downforce.

Forghieri explained that Ferrari was careful to mitigate positive lift – particularly at the rear – by means of the spoiler so as to keep the car driveable. Other than that, it was concerned to minimize drag. As we have seen, lift spoils drag. Whether positive or negative, any magnitude of lift brings an unavoidable drag penalty. May's be-

winged spyder had been intended to trade that loss for enhanced adhesion: it was not an exchange to which Ferrari or others gave serious consideration at this time of low centrifugal acceleration.

Indeed, tyre advances had only just led to cornering forces in the order of 1.0 G. It was a widely held view that a co-efficient of friction of unity could not physically be exceeded, consequently a car could not corner at a force exceeding 1.0 G without sliding into the bushes. Although at this time tyre improvements were starting to challenge the force of gravity, few suspected that aerodynamic downforce could help unlock cornering forces that would allow a racing car to defy gravity as blatantly as a motorcyclist on a Wall of Death.

At this stage Ferrari did a certain amount of wind tunnel testing, the main aim of the programme being to reduce drag. None of the early Sixties racing car manufacturers made any attempt to harness a significant amount of downforce: low drag was the universal creed. Forghieri told the author that Ferrari wind tunnel tests revealed some downforce, but that the magnitude of this was invariably slight and was very sensitive to pitch. For example, as a car lifted its nose under acceleration negative lift at the front wheels would be reduced, sometimes to the extent that it became zero or even positive lift.

Few constructors other than Ferrari had access to wind tunnel testing. By and large both productionized Gran Turismo racers and one-off sports racers were streamlined according to art and intuition rather than science. The shapes adopted were those which looked right. Typical of this approach was the design of the aforementioned 2.5-litre Coventry Climax-Tojeiro of 1962. This machine had Cooper Formula One transmission and a racing car-style spaceframe chassis clothed in a pretty shell which was reminiscent of one of the commissioning

Écurie Écosse team's D Types carrying a hard top.

The interesting Tojeiro was followed by a coupé constructed by a Grand Prix manufacturer and featuring the very latest in Formula One technology, the monocoque chassis. This was the 1963 Ford-Lola Mk.6 GT. The Lola was equipped with a 4.3-litre Ford Fairlane V8 Indy engine and had Formula One-style running gear on its advanced monocoque tub. All the mechanicals

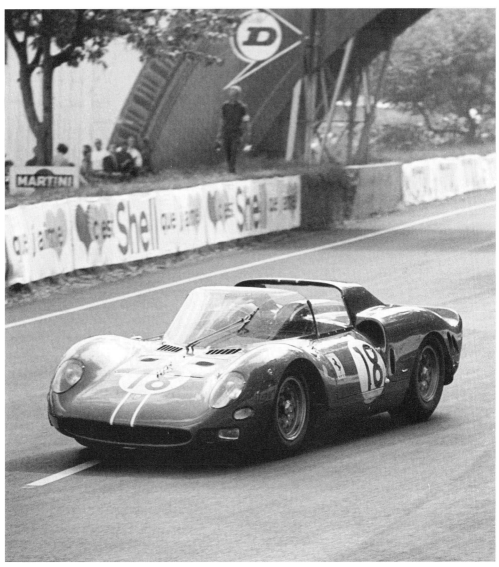

The Ferrari P Series cars of the early Sixties featured a clever aerodynamic anti-roll bar, shown here to good effect on a 1965 P2. The bar was shaped to deflect air towards the tail spoiler.

The Lola GT was unveiled at the 1963 Racing Car Show in London. The entire fibreglass nose and tail sections lifted off for easy access to the mechanicals. The body shape was styling rather than scientific.

were clothed in an attractive non-structural fibreglass body, of which the lines were not dissimilar to those of the Tojeiro.

The body of the Lola echoed the Porsche coupés of the Fifties and ended just behind the rear wheels, since extending the sloping tail far beyond the wheels (to the limit of permitted rear overhang) had a marginal effect on drag (separation of the air was an increasing tendency towards the rear eventually being inevitable) and added weight where it was unwanted. Thus, behind a full-width gently raked windscreen the Lola's roof blended into a gently sloping rear shroud that ended in the cut-off, or Kamm tail (which did not carry a spoiler). The entire tail shroud was quickly detachable for ease of access, as was the streamlined nose with its forward-set radiator inlet and perspex headlight fairings.

The lower flanks of the body were formed by the outer walls of the monocoque which curved inward in conventional sports car style. The lower lip of the nose also curved inwards, the philosophy of the day being to shape the car's underbelly to cut through the air just as a boat hull cuts through water. Air is a fluid, after all. Overall, the Ford-Lola was a fashionable mid-engined Gran Turismo in appearance (it did not look out of place alongside an E-Type Jaguar roadster, for example), if pure racing car under the skin.

1963 found Ford of Detroit working on a design study for a Le Mans car with a mid-engine and a fully enclosed coupé body. Ford designers started with a mid-engined roadster version of the production Mustang and ended up with a shape not dissimilar to that of the Lola GT. Again, the car had a spoiler-less Kamm tail. Ford, like Ferrari, could afford wind tunnel testing. Wind tunnel tests of models of the projected Le Mans car revealed drag of around 500 lb (226.8 kg) at a simulated 200 mph, traded for front axle lift of a similar magnitude and rear axle lift one third that of the front.

In conventional fashion, the Ford nose shape resembled the prow of a barge, air encouraged to flow underneath where the underbody was, as usual, closed, at least ahead of the engine bay. Lowering the bonnet line and fitting a bib spoiler under the radiator air intake while ducting the heated air out through the top of the nose proved a beneficial modification. It marginally reduced drag, while cutting front axle lift by almost 50 per cent, albeit at the cost of significantly increased lift at the rear. The top exit for the radiator air not only generated a download but also improved cooling.

The reduction in drag was probably the effect of the revised nose discouraging air from flowing under the car. It was generally assumed that the air had to be split as if by a bullet for minimum drag: stopping air flowing under the car was a major attack on conventional wisdom as represented by the E Type Jaguar school of streamlining. Of course, back before the war Eberhorst had demonstrated the benefit of a reduced underbody airflow with his Auto Union record car.

Not only was drag-inducing ground effect shear lessened, the lower nose clearly reduced the ramming, wedging effect of air under the nose, thereby reducing front axle lift. On the other hand, in lessening the underbody airflow, the bib spoiler could well have been enhancing the unwanted aircraft wing effect of the body, hence increased lift at the rear. However, the magnitude of positive lift Ford ended up with was considered manageable, the drag was a low as Ford had dared hope for.

At Le Mans in 1963 the Lola had been under-geared and had not managed to exceed 150 mph on the Mulsanne straight. With a similar engine Ford was now looking for 200 mph. However, at the Le Mans practice in April 1964 the new car proved unstable at speeds in excess of 100 mph. Some instability had been detectable on the Lola, though it had not been clear if this was an aerodynamic fault or a suspension development problem. When instability occurred more vividly on the new GT40, Ford's key engineer took the view that it was a suspension set-up fault and toyed with rear suspension adjustments.

To no avail. The prototype crashed heavily at the Mulsanne kink, its driver lucky to escape with his life. The second prototype was then taken to the British

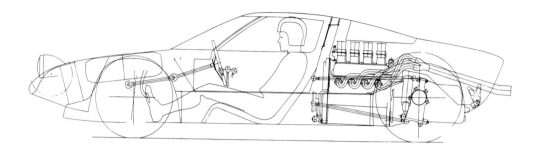

Drawing of the Ford GT40 in its original guise reveals the high nose prow designed to cut through the air as a ship cuts through water. Ford later found that air packed under it causing unwanted lift.

MIRA testing ground where the test drivers sensed the tail of the car lift and adopt a corkscrew-like motion at high speed, the effect that of an arrow without feathers. The problem, hence its solution, was aerodynamic. A 3 in (76 mm) high rear deck spoiler made the car stable to the extent that it could be driven at 170 mph with hands off the steering wheel.

Subsequent investigation in the full sized MIRA wind tunnel showed the basic design creating 312 lbs (142 kg) lift at the rear wheels at 200 mph – far more than the Ford's model tests had suggested. With the spoiler increased in height to 4.5 in (114.3 mm) negative lift was apparent, to the extent of 131.8 lb (59.9 kg) and for no increase in drag. This was hard to understand, since logically the spoiler should have created both lift and drag.

It was found that a tail spoiler does not automatically increase drag since by pressurizing the boundary layer air it helped it stay attached, reducing unwanted lift and drag. Ford found a taller, 6 in (152 mm) spoiler created 191.6 lb (87.1 kg) downforce but drag had then started to rise. The 4.5 in

(114 mm) spoiler was standardized and with it the drag co-efficient was apparently in the region of Cd = 0.35. Having almost 400 bhp on tap, Ford's high frontal area coupé proved capable of reaching 200 mph on the Mulsanne.

It was a speed close to that reached by the semi-enclosed Auto Union of 1935, which had a similar amount of power and a comparable amount of drag. Of course, the Auto Union had run in carefully controlled conditions in a straight line – it had not been asked to negotiate the Mulsanne kink.

Ford won Le Mans with a 7.0-litre version of the so-called GT40 in 1966, then returned with an even faster car, the Mk IV. This scored over its GT40-based Mk II stablemate in terms of lower drag, thanks primarily to a narrower superstructure. Regulations no longer demanded a full-width windscreen and Ford took advantage of this to significantly reduce frontal area.

The windscreen was now more raked and slotted between the front wheel arches while the cabin fitted between wheel arch height sponsons running the length of the wheelbase. The prototype of the Mk IV – the so-called J Car of

1966 – had a high tail but the 1967 derivative had a conventional rear end sloping down to a tail spoiler at rear wheel arch height. Significantly, though, the Mk IV had a low nose and slab rather than inward-curved sides to help dissuade air from flowing to the underbody.

As we have noted, traditional streamlined sportscar noses were designed to cut through the air as the prow of a ship cuts through water, hopefully thereby minimizing drag. The concept of discouraging the air from flowing under the hull had been generally assumed wrong, leading to an enhancement of the aircraft wing effect and thereby creating additional unwanted lift. However, the American engineers found that in fact discouraging air markedly reduced lift by mitigating the surprisingly significant lifting effect caused by air packing under the nose. At the same time, of course, it reduced drag.

Wind tunnel tests by Ford had found the Mk II producing 336 lb (153 kg) drag at 120 mph for a front axle lift of 143 lb (65 kg) and a rear axle negative lift of 79 lb (36 kg). In contrast, at 120 mph the Mk IV produced a drag of only 246.4 lb (112 kg) for a front axle lift of 55 lb (25 kg) and a rear axle lift of 39.6 lb (18 kg) these lift figures insignificant

After early dramas Ford found that a 4.5 in (11.4 mm) tail spoiler provided much needed straightline stability while at the same time actually reducing drag. It is evident on this MK II, the 1966 Le Mans winner.

The start of the 1966 Le Mans race shows V12 Ferraris mixing it with the V8 Fords and a lone Chaparral (car No. 9). Note coupé and spyder Ferraris and the rear air flap on Ferrari No. 18, a private entry.

The MkIV version of the Ford GT40 was immediately evident from the narrower width of its superstructure. Reduced frontal area increased top speed and in 1967 the car ran the Mulsanne at over 210 mph.

Two views of the car that brought the wing back to European sportscar races, the Chaparral 2F of 1967. Like that employed by Michael May back in 1956, the Chaparral wing ran flat on the straight for reduced drag.

given a car weight in excess of 2200 lb (1000 kg). At 220 mph – the target Mulsanne speed – drag was 831.6 lb (378 kg) with front and rear axle lifts of 189 lb (86 kg) and 132 lb (60 kg) respectively. In the event, the Mk IV ran the Mulsanne at a 213.1 mph best compared to a best of 206.2 mph for the Mk II with an identical 500 bhp, 7.0-litre engine. In spite of its lack of downforce, following some aerodynamic trimming, the drivers reported that Ford had achieved hands-off stability for the Mk IV on the Mulsanne, even in a crosswind.

For sheer speed, Ford's major opponent in 1967 was the Chevrolet- Chaparral. This was a radical car descended from a conventional early Sixties spyder. Over the years 1963-5 the Chaparral spyder first acquired a nose air dam to rid the original tendency for its front end to lift at speed, then this was replaced by an entirely new, cleaner nose profile that did the job without the same sensitivity to pitch. In the meantime, a rear spoiler had sprouted to keep the tail as firmly checked as the front end.

Further spyder developments included tabs on the front wings ahead of the wheel arches and hot-air ducting through the top of the nose section, GT40-style. In 1965 louvres were set into the top of each front wheel arch to bleed off the pressure caused by wheel rotation. However, the bibs and louvres disappeared when the spyder body was fitted with a hardtop – forming a conventional coupé shape – for 1966 International endurance races.

Meanwhile, back home the 1966 2E Can Am Chaparral re-invented the wing. Where May had placed a large wing over the cockpit of his spyder to act through the centre of gravity, Hall set his wing higher up and over the tail, to act directly through the rear suspension uprights. To overcome the problem of the additional drag created by the wing, Hall arranged for a hydraulic tipping system, whereby pressure on a foot pedal would trim the wing to its minimum drag, minimum downforce position. Thus the driver would keep his foot on the wing pedal on the straight, releasing it under braking for additional drag as well as its downthrust.

The Chaparral 2E did not run away

with the 1966 Can Am Championship but it proved the viability of the new aerodynamic device, which many contemporary observers saw as a means of aiding braking and stability; overlooking its key role as a means of enhancing grip. For 1967 Chaparral produced an endurance racing coupé fitted with the wing – the 2F. For maximum tyre-loading effect the Chaparral wing (a simple aerofoil section, without lateral fences to stop the migration of air around the ends of the wing) was again mounted directly to the rear uprights and set high above the body in undisturbed air. Also following the 2E, to minimize drag on the straight, the driver was able to control the wing's angle of attack.

Since the Chaparral aerofoil was mounted on the wheel side of the springs, the body did not feel the downforce it generated. Like Ford with the Mk IV, Chaparral discouraged air from flowing under its body, having a low set nose intake and slab-sided sponsons. In fact, the rear of the high (rather than sloping) tailed but spoilerless body generated a small amount of lift while the front created downforce. Consequently, as speed increased the entire body pitched forward and this had the effect of reinforcing the creation of downforce at the front axle. At 150 mph the downforce was sufficient to fully compress the front springs.

One way to avoid locking the front suspension solid would have been to fit a spoiler to the rear of the body but Jim Hall had a more elegant solution which left the rear deck airflow unchecked: a trap door in the floor of the nose. This was spring loaded and was designed to open at 140 mph to bleed air into the underbody region, thus creating nose lift. It was effective, and induced progressive understeer.

Although the 2F did not totally overshadow its contemporaries, it collected a number of lap records and won some races. It was a car in advance of its time, one that was only just starting to scratch the potential of aerofoil-generated downforce. The fact that its front suspension could not take the downforce generated by the body showed that its chassis technology was

Mauro Forghieri adjusts the wing of the 1968 Formula One Ferrari. This season Forghieri introduced the wing to Grand Prix racing at Francorchamps and was immediately followed by Jack Brabham.

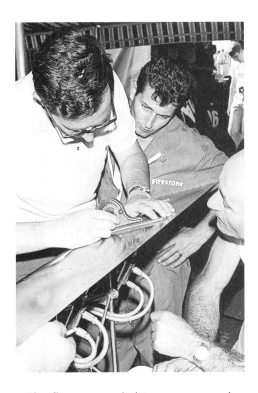

not yet ready for its aerodynamics.

Given tyre developments at this time, cornering forces were reaching 1.3 g without aerodynamic aid. With the Chaparral aerofoil the potential was far higher than that, yet even 1.3 g was venturing far into the unknown. The Chaparral was a bold step towards an even further distant region and the team had to proceed with caution. A straightforward example: at Francorchamps Chaparral won pole but in race day rain had to watch others disappear as it cautiously trod a treacherously wet surface for the first time ever using a wing.

In 1968 wings sprouted on Formula One cars, the trend led by Ferrari. Ferrari had pulled out of endurance racing for this season but towards the end of the year produced a Can Am car with a centrally located wing. Mauro Forghieri had similarly mounted his pioneering Formula One aerofoil over the cockpit, following the May concept of putting downforce through the centre of gravity in the interest of good handling. The Can Am car followed this reasoning and thus its wing echoed the aerodynamic anti-roll bar that Forghieri had continued to exploit through to 1967. Forghieri told the author that, in leading the Formula One wing revolution he was influenced by the aerodynamic anti-roll bar and by the Chaparral.

Indeed, for a single-seater the central wing was a substitute for the aerodynamic anti-roll bar, Forghieri reasoned. To minimize drag on the straight, the Ferrari Formula One wing was activated by a complex hydraulic system which responded to pressure on the brake pedal, and to gear selection with the driver having an override button. The wing section and its operation was copied directly for the Can Am car, but in its sports car application the wing was even more elaborate, incorporating automatic air braking flaps. There were two small flaps on the wing and a third was fitted on the nose.

The flaps responded to pressure on the brake pedal and the nose flap was perforated, its perforations inducing additional drag-creating turbulence. Apparently it was copied directly from a French Caravelle aircraft. The net result of the braking flaps was found to be lurid pitch changes which destabilized the car but the big wing improved lap times by 15 per cent in Forghieri's estimation. However, when Ferrari returned to endurance racing in 1969 with a scaled down 3.0-litre version of the Can Am spyder, the so-called 312P spyder was surprising for its absence of a wing.

Ironically, 1969 was the season in which the Formula One constructors really started to get the maximum work out of wings. Prior to a mid-season ban on remote mounted aerofoils, downforce of up to 440 lb (200 kg) at 125 mph, rising to over 770 lb (350 kg) – half the weight of the car itself – at a theoretical 190 mph was experienced. This complemented a further increase in the width of the flat crown tyres now in use, grip rising dramatically. However, some cars suffered suspension failure as a

The Porsche 908 of 1968 was the first large displacement sports racing car from the German manufacturer. It had a slippery shape with rear fins for lateral stability when conditions dictated, as here at Monza.

consequence of the massive download exploited.

Of course, the downforce created by a wing was at the expense of additional drag and this cost fuel consumption and top speed. Forghieri explained to the author: "Endurance racing is a compromise between performance, reliability, fuel consumption and driveability. Lower cornering loads are less stressful. Fuel consumption was a very important consideration, particularly since refuelling had to be through small diameter pipes without pressure. Top speed was also very significant with so much traffic around in the races".

Likewise the 312P's key rivals of 1969 – the Porsche 908 and the Chevrolet-Lola T70 – did not sport wings, although nose tabs and prominent rear spoilers were generally employed in those days. For the sinuous Brands Hatch circuit, Ferrari fitted the 312P with two pairs of nose tabs and a lip across the nose radiator air outlet, although there was still no sign of a wing. While the

recent dropping of the requirement for a proper windscreen had made a low frontal area spyder the logical choice for most circuits, Ferrari nonetheless produced a coupé version of the 312P specifically for Le Mans.

While the spyder body was now eligible for one-off Group 6 Sports Prototypes, it was not eligible for Group 4 25-off homologated sportscars. The latter were essentially productionized Sports Prototypes such as the T70 which had to carry more weight but could displace 5.0 litres rather than the 3.0 litres allowed for Group 6. First seen in 1967, the T70 Mk III Coupé was a rebodied version of Lola's Can Am spyder with a striking body that cut right across conventional wisdom. It was generally accepted that a coupé body should slope down from the cabin roof to a rear spoiler at wheel arch height. This approach plus a streamlined, domed windscreen led to the characteristic whale-shaped superstructure of the Ford Mk IV and its kind.

The Lola T70 MkIII coupé had an uncharacteristically high tail. In 1967-8 it was generally accepted that the tail should slope downwards following the teardrop pattern. Lola rejected that notion.

As we have seen, this shape, in following teardrop philosophy, minimized drag. The key was in the shape of the whale's dorsum: its progressively reducing sectional area encouraged the boundary layer to stay attached to the body, thus minimizing the size of the wake. However, in minimizing drag this led to instability which became an increasing problem as speed rose. Lola had found inherently greater stability from its Can Am spyder than was enjoyed by contemporary coupés. The flat tail of the spyder was crucial in this respect and it was echoed by the striking new tail of the T70 coupé.

Like the Ford Mk IV, the T70 had a narrow superstructure, but behind the cabin roof the engine cover did not slope in established coupé fashion. It was horizontal and the rear spoiler was thus at cabin roof height. In effect, the T70 Coupé had a spyder-type rear deck. The T70's high tail put consideration of lift ahead of drag. It had been evident that the mid-Sixties Ford and Ferrari coupés had required a lot of rear spoiler area to maintain stability at high speed, this observation going back to Ford's experience with the original GT40 shape.

Straight out of the box, the T70 Coupé worked very well in sweeping curves. Its unique body shape endowed it with sufficient downforce front and rear for good grip and handling and excellent all round driveability. Good aerodynamics plus a Can Am proven chassis allowed the T70 Coupé to use its tyres well. That much was evident in the wet at Francorchamps on its début: Paul Hawkins was closing on that master of the circuit and master of the wet, Jacky Ickx, when he handed over to his slower co-driver.

Hawkins, who had driven contemporary Ford and Ferrari prototypes, later told *Autosport*: ''I didn't have much time in practice to get the car set up properly, but it certainly went well in the race. What a wonderful car to drive! It went exactly where you wanted it to, and you could slide it confidently at 140-50 mph in the wet. It didn't seem to be affected by side winds or other things that affect most cars, like uneven road surfaces or bumps in the middle of corners.''

The Lola T70 Mk.IIIB homologated for 1969 Group 4 had a reshaped nose. In essence, the nose reached further forward so that the radiator intake was lower set. Its bottom lip then became virtually a horizontal splitter, cleanly dividing the oncoming air and encouraging the air to flow over the top surface of the nose rather than underneath. Of course, the discouragement of the airflow to the underbody could be taken further through a slab-sided body, as had been employed by the Ford Mk IV and the Chaparral in 1967 but for the Lola this would have required a new chassis.

The Mk IIIB nose created significantly more downforce than the older conventional nose on its upper surface. Increased downforce at the front of the car was matched by a more prominent rear spoiler which was significantly wider. The Mk IIIB's low droop nose was a complete success and the high speed cornering of the car was again superb: it was the envy of Porsche which introduced its first really powerful coupé in 1969.

Chapter Four

Enter Porsche

The first of a new generation of Porsche coupés produced under the technical direction of Professor Porsche's grandson Ferdinand Piech had been the 2.0-litre Carrera 6 of 1966. This had a coupé body with a state-of-the-art, narrow windscreen, whale-shaped superstructure; the well raked windscreen reaching well between the front wheel arches. The nose prow was low and there was no radiator intake, the engine primarily air cooled. Overall, the Carrera 6 was streamlined on the traditional teardrop principle and it had a Kamm tail carrying an 3 in (80 mm) high spoiler.

Porsche later published some enlightening figures for the aerodynamic performance of the Carrera 6 through Paul Frère's book *Racing Porsches* (PSL, 1973). During the season 20 per cent models of the car were tested in the wind tunnel of the Technical High School, Stuttgart. In its standard form the Carrera 6 registered a similar drag co-efficient to that of the contemporary GT40: Cd = 0.346; it experienced slight lift over the front axle and more pronounced negative lift at the rear.

Porsche tried the model with nose tabs and achieved slight downforce at the front while reducing the downforce at the rear for a drag co-efficient of Cd = 0.35. It then tried a nose spoiler as an alternative to the tabs and this reduced nose lift without going so far as to produce negative lift, while at the rear downforce was again reduced, but to a

lesser degree than had been the case with the tabs. The co-efficient was now Cd = 0.342.

In addition, tests were carried out to minimize the drag co- efficient, regardless of any consideration of lift. Removing the rear spoiler increased drag: clearly its removal allowed earlier breakaway of the airflow over the tail. However, by retaining the spoiler, fitting wheel rim discs, taping all body joints and blanking off all air inlets and outlets the drag co-efficient was reduced to Cd = 0.308.

Porsche track-tested the front tabs and found that front wheel adhesion was enhanced, at the cost of rear wheel adhesion. This was due to the decreased downforce at the rear, reinforced by the fact of the strong downforce at the front pitching the car forwards, lifting its tail.

Later tests carried out on a full-sized car in the same wind tunnel at a more representative wind speed generally confirmed the earlier findings except for the supposed effect of the front tabs of inducing downforce over both axles. It was found that the pitching of the car around the front wheel axis removed all rear downforce, causing a lift over the rear axle of 110 lb (50 kg) for 198 lb (90 kg) downforce at the front axle. Further, the static angle of incidence (degree of pitch) was found to be highly significant. For example, a rearward-pitched angle of just 0.35°, although raising the nose of the car only a tiny

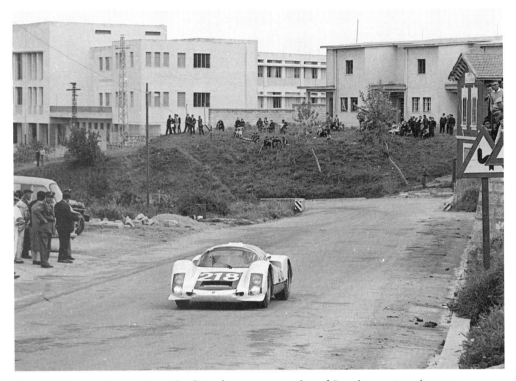

The 1966 Porsche Carrera 6 was the first of a new generation of Porsche sports racing cars produced under the direction of Ferdinand Piech. Note front tabs to counter nose lift on this Targa Florio runner.

amount was sufficient to transform the 198 lb (90 kg) downforce at the front into 140.8 lb (64 kg) lift.

Porsche continued to race the Carrera 6 with the front tabs, since the degree of lift induced at the rear was only equal to around 15 per cent of the total weight carried by the rear wheels. Further, the raked body stance promoted by this configuration was considered important since it ensured that driven over a Nürburgring-type *yump* with the front suspension fully extended, the car would not be induced to point its nose skyward.

For Le Mans, mindful of the Mulsanne, Porsche produced a long tail or Langheck version of the Carrera 6, extending the converging tail to the maximum permitted overhang length. This of course added weight, and overhung weight at that which made the car less manoeuvrable but without a spoiler it was good for a drag co-efficient of Cd = 0.326 which provided a top speed increase in the region of 10 mph.

Although in 1966 low drag was everything, Porsche tried adding prominent flaps to the nose and tail of its 2.0-litre Carrera 6 to generate a significant amount of downforce. Although these were found to enhance cornering ability, it was at a cost in terms of slower acceleration and inferior speed which the marque felt it could not justify. Porsche did not race its experimental flap car. To some extent, confined to 2.0 litres it simply did not have the power to make the added downforce work. However, it is doubtful if Porsche would have traded downforce for higher drag, given more power. At Zuffenhausen low drag was gospel.

In 1967 Porsche continued to run 2.0-litre, sometimes 2.2-litre, coupés derived from the Carrera 6: the *Typs* 910 and 907. Frontal area was further reduced and in general the bodyshape was tidied up with the progression from Carrera 6 to 910. However, the 910 had been designed without reference to wind

In view of the importance of low drag at Le Mans Porsche produced this long-tail version of the Carrera 6 for the 1966 24 hour race. The tail extension added outrigged weight but increased top speed by 10 mph.

tunnel tests and it was later found to have a marginally worse drag co-efficient than the Carrera 6, for which its lower frontal area compensated, providing the same overall level of drag. Porsche produced the 907 in the light of wind tunnel tests of the 910 and, avoiding the use of nose tabs, achieved a drag co-efficient of Cd = 0.27 together with a still lower frontal area.

In 1968 the 907 chassis was equipped with a new 3.0-litre engine to produce the *Typ* 908. This more powerful car – circa 350 bhp – appeared with nose tabs and with fixed flaps in place of the usual rear spoiler, one to the rear of each wheel arch and taller than the spoiler and set at an angle, which could be adjusted to vary the downforce obtained.

Porsche wind tunnel tested the 908 in race trim, recording a drag co-efficient of Cd = 0.422 with the front tabs at 18.5° from the horizontal, the rear flaps at 25°. There was then 11 lb (5 kg)

downforce at the front, 35 lb (16 kg) at the rear. Raising the flaps to 35° increased the downforce at the rear to 52.8 lb (24 kg) with no effect at the front but worsened the drag co-efficient to Cd = 0.448. Without the flaps the co-efficient was Cd = 0.382 (worse than the 907 primarily due to a higher cooling requirement) but there was 4.4 lb (2 kg) lift at the rear. In contrast, the front tabs hardly affected drag, while without them there was 15.4 lb (7 kg) lift at the front.

Porsche again produced a long tail for Le Mans. Predictably this reduced stability running in its pure form, without tabs and rear spoiler. It was tried at Francorchamps where the car was not stable enough to race. In response Porsche devised a clever arrangement of small vertical lateral fins, between which was suspended a tiny aerofoil section incorporating an articulated flap at either end. These flaps were connected to the rear suspension so as to rise and fall as the suspension

The Porsche 910 of 1967 was a more aerodynamic version of the Carrera 6 with reduced frontal area and a tidier shape. However, it was designed without reference to wind tunnel studies due to lack of design time.

moved through bump and droop. Tail squat with suspension bump was countered aerodynamically by a corresponding drop of the respective flap: tail lift in droop was countered by a rise of the flap. Since the flaps were worked independently of one another, together they countered roll.

Porsche wind tunnel tested its Le Mans long tailer with interesting results. With nose tabs and its tail appendage, the long-tail 908 recorded downforce of 11 lb (5 kg) at the front axle and (with the flaps at 6° 22 lb (10 kg) at the rear. Without the fins and tail assembly no downforce could be achieved at the nose. However, the assembly did not increase drag: the co-efficient was Cd = 0.345 with or without the tail appendage. Porsche's tests showed that the rear aerofoil assembly helped keep the flow across the tail attached, this effect countering its own drag.

The 908 coupé continued in service in 1969, alongside the 908/2 which was designed to take advantage of the new freedom for spyder-type bodywork, together with the abolition of a minimum weight limit. Initially the ultra-light, low frontal area spyder recorded a drag co-efficient of Cd = 0.70 and it was used at Sebring, Brands Hatch and the Targa Florio whereas the coupé was run at Daytona, Monza and Francorchamps. For the Nürburgring, Porsche produced a revised spyder body with lower drag but this was later found to have worrying lift characteristics which helped explain two accidents in practice.

A subsequent long tail version of the modified 908/2 was run at Le Mans, with front tabs and rear fins to aid stability. It proved as fast as the 908 coupés on the Mulsanne and quicker around the lap.

Quicker still was Porsche's new 5.0-litre challenger, the Group 4-homologated 917. This 550 bhp projectile – with a 100 plus bhp advantage over the 5.0-litre stock block-engined Chevrolet-Lola T70 – had first been seen at the Le Mans test weekend in April.

Just as the 908 had essentially been a 907 with a new, larger engine so the 917 was essentially a 908 with a new, larger engine. The two long-tail versions taken to the Le Mans test weekend ran the Mulsanne at almost 200 mph but weaved all over the Route Nationale, to the extent that full throttle could not be applied. Fitted with a short tail, the model weaved even more alarmingly.

Since in its early guise the 908 had been more stable through Francorchamp's sweeping bends in short-tail than in long-tail trim, the example race-débuted in the Spa 1000 kms

(620 ml) was in short-tail trim, with nose tabs and rear flaps, the latter articulated and responding to suspension movement as those already seen on the 908. Nevertheless, Porsche admitted that the new 917: ''was quite unstable and dangerous in the fast bends of Spa . . . and did not behave much better on the straight.''

Jo Siffert took pole from Paul Hawkins' 5.0-litre, 440 bhp T70 Coupé by a mere 0.6 sec, in spite of his massive power advantage – and elected to race a slower 908. For Le Mans the 917 was set up with a slight forward pitch – just half a degree – and this improved stability. Steeper front tabs and modification to the rear flap linkage for a higher average angle of attack also helped, allowing the powerful car to be run flat out on the Mulsanne.

Nevertheless, running an estimated

The 907 was a refined version of the 910 in the light of wind tunnel studies. Its shape set the pattern for subsequent 3.0-and 4.5-litre cars and was designed for low drag with no provision for downforce.

Porsche devised these articulated flaps for its 908 3.0-litre racer, the flap each side linked to the respective suspension so as to move down with droop and up with bump, thereby countering tail lift and squat.

215 mph – roughly the speed of the Mk IVs in 1967 – the car still required a lot of road and was a real handful through the kink. None of the hands-off stability of the big Fords. A lot lighter than the Ford Mk IV, though, the 917 accelerated faster and could brake later. Over the entire lap it was a little quicker (allowing for the installation of a chicane just before the pits). With a little more weight and a far lower power level the higher drag T70 could not compete with the 917 at Le Mans. However, at the Österreichring the 917's inferior aerodynamics let it be hounded mercilessly by Jo Bonnier's low budget T70 MkIIIB, in spite of what had grown to a 25 per cent power advantage following Porsche engine development work.

The sensation of the 1969 Geneva Motor Show was the 4.5-litre Porsche 917 coupé, which essentially retained the body of the 908 including characteristic tail flaps. The 917 was designed for low drag.

Lola T70 leads Porsche 917 at the Österreichring in 1969. The T70 had less power than the new Porsche but far more grip thanks to a higher downforce body shape. Porsche had subsequently to revise its tail.

At the Österreichring the 917 was again running in short-tail trim, with front tabs and the rear flaps, these now fixed thanks to a regulation change and set at a high angle. The drivers did not like the car, particularly the way it oversteered around the blind righthander at the top of the hill past the pits. It had taken some persuasion to get Porsche's star driver Jo Siffert to drive the winning car.

Much better handling was enjoyed by a Can Am spyder version of the 917 run at the same circuit in testing a couple of months later. The Can Am car ran alongside the coupé, the latter still in short-tail trim and with stiffer springs to reduce pitch changes. Nevertheless, the flaps had to be set vertical and the car handled nowhere near as well as the spyder.

The first step was fitting a nose with an air dam prow below the small radiator inlet: this brought immediate improvement and made it even more evident that rear downforce was missing. JWA had been invited along to the test since it had agreed to run the works Porsche team in 1970. JWA chief engineer John Horsman noted from the pattern of splattered gnats on the bodywork that the airstream appeared to be shooting right over the rear flaps. Horsman and his crew chief Ermanno Cuoghi came up with the idea of trying a high rear deck, one that reflected the lines of the Can Am spyder.

Right from the outset the 917 had been designed for low drag and that implied a whale-shaped superstructure. Porsche knew that its 5.0-litre 25-off challenger would be followed by a similar machine from Ferrari: that car would have state-of-the-art four-valve heads. Thus, it would run to a higher speed without significant loss of breathing or combustion efficiency and in so doing would take power beyond the air-cooled Porsche's reach. With that in mind, the 917 had been designed to keep right on the1760 lb (800 kg) minimum weight limit and to enjoy the minimum of drag.

To fit the T70-pattern high deck improvised by Cuoghi was a major challenge to Porsche philosophy. Yet, in the circumstances, it was the obvious fix to try . . . and it worked. With the higher downforce nose and the new tail, driver Kurt Ahrens reported: ''Very good, very stable. Good roadholding and good stability in the turns.''

The Technical Director of Porsche, Ferdinand Piech, later commented to the author: ''All Porsche coupés up to the Osterreichring had a tail with a rounded rear part. In the wind tunnel the aerodynamics were much better. But previous cars had too little power; with the 917 suddenly we had too much. Aerodynamic stability was suddenly a very important factor. We saw from this modification that . . . reducing top speed and gaining stability was the right way to go . . . ''

Low drag could not be everything. Porsche duly produced a refined high-tail body for the 917 that took its drag co-efficient from the original $Cd = 0.400$ in short-tail trim to $Cd = 0.464$. This was the basis of the good handling of the so called 917K (*Kurz* – or short) version which dominated sportscar racing in 1970, in spite of the opposition of a new 5.0-litre Ferrari, the 512S.

The Ferrari 512S was seen in coupé trim with a similar high tail to that of the 917K – again following the pattern set by the Lola T70 – and in semi-spyder trim. In other words it ran without a roof canopy and with a form of aerodynamic anti-roll bar guiding the air in the centre of the tail which added downforce, as did a larger rear spoiler area on either side of the central area, where the high deck was retained.

The so-called spyder version of the 512S saved weight and pleased some drivers who felt claustrophobic in a coupé. However, its performance was only marginally different from that of the coupé and in the rain it was a misery for the driver. More significant was an early switch from a traditional-style nose

The Porsche 917K of 1970 sported a high tail designed for downforce at the expense of increased drag. Porsche had learned that it had to sacrifice some straightline speed for stability in the corners.

Porsche 917K versus Ferrari 512S at Monza in 1970, both high-tailers. The latter is running in spyder trim without a cockpit roof and with a version of the aerodynamic anti-roll bar as seen on the P-series cars.

with an inward-swept lower lip to one with an air dam prow which provided additional downforce. It was modified to run with a splitter at Francorchamps: Forghieri told the author that this cut down the influence of pitch changes as the car took the high speed sweeps.

The lower drag nose re-appeared on a long-tail version of the coupé seen at the Le Mans test weekend, which was washed out. In consequence, Ferrari tried the car on a Fiat-owned section of autostrada, fitting a small spoiler and prominent fins to the tail for stability. Nevertheless, Ferrari sportscar engineer Giacomo Caliri later told the author that the 600 bhp car was ''at the limit of stability'' as it ran 215.5 mph. That did not compare well to the speed of the Ford Mk IV three years earlier, the Ford having less power at its disposal: around 515 bhp.

The 512S was tried with the air dam nose but this was not a success, too much downforce at the front relative to the rear, worsening rather than improving stability. Following the autostrada tests the so-called *Coda Lunga* (long tail) version of the 512S was run at Monza with small tabs on an original nose, and this was confirmed as a workable solution. However, some drivers preferred the alternative of an air dam nose and more spoiler area at the rear to balance it, this cutting Mulsanne speed but making the car easier to drive. The intended long-tail configuration was reckoned to be worth a 9.4 mph top speed advantage on the Mulsanne over the regular 512S coupé.

After Le Mans Ferrari revealed a new version of its regular coupé, the 512M which featured revised aerodynamics and less weight. Wind tunnel tests had convinced Forghieri that the 512S was wanting and the car was duly reworked by Caliri. The nose was revised to have a more pronounced wedge shape and a cleaner radiator air top exit, while slots were cut in the rear of each front wheel arch to relieve pressure within. The tail was also revised, the new form based on

Ferrari 512M a re-worked version of the 512S in the light of wind tunnel testing. Note the small aerofoils at the end of the tail replacing a conventional spoiler as Caliri waves the prototype out.

the spyder shape but with a closed roof and hence no aerodynamic anti-roll bar. However, a small adjustable aerofoil section was fitted in place of the spoilers, sitting clear of the deck.

The aerofoil ran the full width of the tail but across the centre section it virtually touched the deck, this portion thereby acting as a spoiler rather than as a wing. Following early tests, it was replaced by an actual spoiler, this arrangement providing more control over the aerodynamics. Adjusting the angle of attack of the aerofoil sections which remained either side of the spoiler altered rear end downforce, while adjusting the height of the spoiler shifted the centre of pressure, altering the car's balance (increased spoiler height moving the centre of pressure towards the rear). This was the effect of the spoiler effectively creating pressure over the entire car.

The 512M was a great success on its début at the Osterreichring, comfortably faster than the 917K, and it won the Kyalami season finale. Alas, Ferrari chose to exploit the 3.0-litre spyder route in 1971, mindful of the imminent demise of the 5.0-litre category. Customers were left to pitch the 512M against the 5.0-litre Porsches. One such customer was Roger Penske Racing. Penske and driver/engineer Mark Donohue further improved the 512M, reconstructing the side sponsons for proper slab sides and fitting a full-width rear wing of regular low-drag aircraft section which was mounted higher off the deck to make it more effective.

Giacomo Caliri remarked to the author that these modifications were the sort of development the factory had in mind, but had not been able to offer run-of-the-mill customers. The revised sponsons required a costly chassis rejig while the more effective wing made the car more tricky to balance, hence was less appropriate for the average privateer. Donohue was no average driver and the Penske 512M was faster than the 5.0-litre Porsches at Daytona, Sebring and

The Penske 512M seen at Le Mans in 1971. Note the slab-sided sponsons and the full-width tail aerofoil which is fully adjustable to trim rear-end downforce. It made the car somewhat more tricky to set up.

Watkins Glen. Another modified 512M was the Écurie Filipinetti car devised by Mike Parkes and Caliri. This likewise had slab sides and a full-width wing and in addition it had a lower frontal area thanks to a rebuilt, slimmed down superstructure. It was thus the ultimate development of the model.

Meanwhile the *Typ* 917 Porsche had undergone a great deal of aerodynamic development. Compared to the original short-tail 917, the high-deck 917K had its tail open above the engine. Development engineer Helmut Flegl explained to the author: ''Here the (overhead cooling fan) engine is sucking air down. We though maybe we could cut the middle of the tail out to let the driver see out of the back.'' Thus, a central channel ran back from a window at the rear of the cockpit.

The 917K was characterized by an air dam nose and a distinctive tail having a gently upswept ramp either side of the central channel. At the end of each ramp was a spoiler which was adjustable. Front wheel arch extractor vents were employed while widening the body to accommodate wider wheels and tyres added 10 per cent to the frontal area, which was thus comparable to that of the 512S/M. The first significant aerodynamic modification to the 917K was made by the JWA team which had taken over the running of the factory effort.

JWA set an alloy panel in the rear of the central channel of the tail to sweep it up to the height of the ramps each side. It then added a full-width spoiler for additional downforce. The penalty was a tiny amount of additional weight and a touch more drag. At Francorchamps where it was first run, the modified tail worked very well. JWA Technical Director John Horsman later told the author: ''From Stavelot to La Source the back end really stuck, the driver could keep his foot down in top . . .''

For Le Mans JWA further modified the tail, removing the upswept valley infill

JWA added an aerofoil to the tail of its 917K in time for the 1970 Le Mans race. This added a little more downforce for no drag penalty and was less sensitive to yaw angle than a conventional spoiler.

and full width spoiler and substituting a manually adjustable aerofoil at the end of the valley. The logic was that an aerofoil section – again a regular aircraft pattern wing – in free air produces a given amount of downforce for less drag than a spoiler. The aerofoil tail proved less sensitive to the yaw angle and permitted less spoiler effect at the end of the ramps. Sure enough, the net result was a little more downforce for no drag penalty. For Le Mans JWA preferred to concentrate upon this development rather than run a new *Langheck* – 917L – devised by the factory specifically for the French circuit.

Porsche was determined to find a significant reduction in drag in the light of the Mulsanne straight. True, much of the top speed gain might be lost to a better handling car over the rest of the circuit but the *Langheck* should consume less fuel, wasting less time in the pits and, if more tiring to drive through the corners, would be able to overtake more easily on the straight. Fuel consumption was the most significant consideration of all: ''*Langheck* development was always for fuel consumption'', Ferdinand Piech emphasised to the author.

The aim in the development of the 917L was to maintain the drag co-efficient of the 1969 car with enhanced stability in spite of the ban on movable aerodynamic devices. The initial version of the 917L tested in April 1970 had an extended version of the air dam type nose, this adding stability while cutting down on ground-effect shear. The tail followed the pattern of the 1969 *Langheck* but behind the engine it contained two transverse slots for engine and transmission ventilation and it had an upswept tip if not a spoiler. It also had prominent stabilizing fins.

As soon as Kurt Ahrens went out in the car on the test track it started to rain lightly. With the rain came gusts of wind

The 1970 Le Mans version of the 917 as developed by the factory but rejected by JWA. It was quicker on the Mulsanne than the 917K but was a real handful through the corners. It did save fuel, however.

down clearings in the wood through which Volkswagen's Wolfsburg high speed test track ran. Helmut Flegl commented: ''Having big fins, the wind upset the car more. With the wind and the fins the forces got so high that there wasn't enough friction on the damp track . . . the fins would normally have stabilized the car but the forces got too high and the car just broke loose''.

Shades of Rosemeyer's accident in 1938. Thankfully, Ahrens escaped from the wreck with his life. A little later Kauhsen wrecked a replacement when he aquaplaned at Wolfsburg, escaping without injury. Meanwhile, further wind tunnel tests were conducted in conjunction with the French SERA design office run by Charles Deutsch, well known for a succession of small capacity low drag Le Mans cars that had raced against the teardrop Porsches. The SERA organization was based at the fixed-floor Eiffel wind tunnel in Paris and Deutsch

was assisted by Robert Choulet.

Important results were a concave shape for the upper panel of the nose and another concave surface replacing the slots behind the engine, while smaller fins carried a full width aerofoil. Interestingly the base of the long tail was closed behind the engine and it was given a pronounced upsweep to meet the base of a narrow rear panel (carrying the rear lights). This followed the design of the original 917 and was an extension of the teardrop low-drag philosophy. However, with it Porsche came very close to the production of an underbody venturi generating a significant amount of downforce under the car.

Aerofoil adjustment provided an easy method of varying rear-end downforce. Stability was improved at the cost of a small drag penalty. The drag co-efficient was now Cd = 0.36 while the longer tail put 55 lb (25 kg) on the rear of the car. The top speed advantage was just over

12.5 mph and with 600 bhp that speed was in the region of 230 mph. Vic Elford put his example on pole. He told the author:

"Compared to the 1969 car it was chalk and cheese... it was more driveable and it was flat through the kink... you could place it accurately and it didn't zig-zag if the back started to come out. The short-tailed car braked better and was more manoeuvrable in traffic but at Le Mans you go past people on pure speed.

"At the start of the race Siffert (in the lead JWA 917K) and I cleared off. Each lap I gained 400 or 500 yards on the Mulsanne which he caught back, a little bit under braking, a little bit in speed through the corners, but he couldn't pass. I could keep him behind until we got back on the Mulsanne. It was a lot easier for me . . ."

Although the 1970 *Langhecks* hit trouble, one won the Index of Consumption. A standard (rather than JWA modified) 917K won the race. For 1971 the factory modified the standard short tail, the revised version having the valley filled in behind the engine and a slightly convex deck flanked by fins. Porsche wind tunnel tests suggested 20 per cent less downforce at the rear yet 20 per cent more at the front and an overall drag reduction of 15 per cent.

On track JWA found less drag and less downforce: an extra 300 rpm was at the cost of some stability. It retained its own modified tail. Content with the rear end bite of this at high speed, Horsman remarked that lack of front end downforce was a potential weakness. "If we had been pushed by Ferrari we might have redesigned the front end", he later told to the author. However, the factory *Kurz* tail proved useful at Monza and Le Mans, adding approximately 5 mph to the top speed.

Meanwhile Langheck development

The 917K was slightly reprofiled for 1971 with a concave rear deck flanked by lateral fins. Wind tunnel tests revealed slightly lower drag and 20 per cent less downforce at the rear with 20 per cent more at the front.

Front and rear shots of the 1971 long-tail Le Mans version of the 917. This version was far better handling than the 1970 streamliner and JWA used it for the race. Note the full-width aerofoil and wheel covers.

The so-called Pink-Pig Porsche's attempt to produce a compromise between the regular 917K and the long-tail Le Mans version. Strictly a one-off, it pointed the way to the coupés of the Eighties.

continued for Le Mans, a revised car appearing at the Test Weekend. This had a shorter nose which accentuated the concave form and featured lower arches, as also seen at the rear. Lack of suspension movement at Le Mans allowed the arches to be lowered but wider tyres called for wider bodywork, marginally increasing the frontal area. Nevertheless, in spite of that and the increased downforce at the front, overall drag was not increased. Further, the rear fins were no longer in the backwash from the cabin, keeping the car more stable when operating through a yaw angle.

There was again a full-width aerofoil while the rear wheels were partially faired in. Derek Bell drove the car for JWA and told the author it was stable even through the kink, but that driving it was like "having a caravan on the back". Nevertheless, touching 240 mph on the Mulsanne, it was very quick around the lap. It was far quicker than the modified 917K, though its fuel

consumption advantage was marginal.

The major disadvantage of the 917L was the extra weight outrigged at the back and in view of this Porsche had developed the shorter yet low drag 917/20: a *Langheck* without a caravan! Again developed in conjunction with SERA, this was a cross between long- and short-tail cars with a compromise drag co-efficient. It was notable for extra body width which was to provide wheel arch overhang, the aims of this being to reduce the interference between the flow along the sides of the car and the air whipped up by tyre rotation, and to ease the flow from the arch.

Of course, the drawback of the overhang was increased frontal area. The 917/20 carried a stubby version of the air dam nose developed for the 1971 *Langheck* with prominent louvres set into the wheel arches. The car was slab-sided (unlike the 917K) and the trailing edge of each wheel arch was carefully rounded to ease air from the arch. The tail left the engine exposed in conventional *Kurz* style but there was no valley behind, instead the deck was concave and was flanked by fins.

The 917/20 ran a fifth gear ratio between those of the *Kurz* and the *Langheck*. Driver Reinhold Joest told the author that the car was easy to drive: ''The long-tail cars were faster on the straight; I was faster in the curves. The *Langheck* oversteered more in the turns. I did not lose much on the straight by slipstreaming. The car was secure under braking whereas the *Langheck* was nervous. But with its width, it was difficult to enter the pits, needing much care!''

Although the unique car did not finish the race, Helmut Flegl remarked that it was a technical success: ''It showed how the aerodynamics of the *Kurz* could have been improved. It had speed between the *Langheck* and the *Kurz* – in 1972-3 we could have expected an 'in-between' car''. For his part, Ferdinand Piech confirmed the 917/20 was ''a future car – it had stability like the JWA-inspired *Kurz* tail but the drag co-efficient the way Porsche wanted it''.

Chapter Five

From Wings to Ground Effect

Serious development of the fully enclosed, mid-engined racing car broke off after the 1971 season following the demise of homologated sports cars. In 1972 the Porsche 917 and the Ferrari 512 were no longer accepted in World Championship racing. Instead 3.0-litre (later 2.1-litre turbocharged) one-off Group 6 prototypes ruled the roost and with no weight restriction and no demand for a windscreen the spyder body became standard wear, even at Le Mans. Its weight and frontal area advantages were overriding. The Mirage team run by John Horsman tried a long-tail coupé in testing for the 1973 Le Mans race but the experiment was not a success.

The years 1972-9 were spyder years, even at Le Mans. Sadly, during these years, aside from a short-lived battle of Renault and Porsche turbocars, sportscar racing fell seriously into decline. In response to this Le Mans introduced a so-called GTP class in 1976, admitting coupé-bodied prototypes with no restriction on engine but a fuel consumption limit. Two marques responded with new cars: Rondeau and WM. GTP called for equal size front and rear wheels, a proper windscreen, token luggage space and a higher minimum weight than Group 6 while the maximum fuel consumption was 350 litres per 620 miles (1000 km). Both Rondeau and WM were new French constructors and both envisaged using the Peugeot V6 engine

but to attract sponsorship Rondeau found it had to switch to the Cosworth DFV.

The Rondeau design was conventional enough. Essentially, thanks to small wheel diameters, the mandatory windscreen height and the use of a concave rear deck it was a spyder with a bubble over the cockpit and engine. Sponsons at wheel arch height ran into the concave deck that was much lower than the roof and was flanked by prominent fins. The central superstructure took the form of a whale-shaped bubble and the mandatory windscreen width ensured it was uncommonly wide over the cockpit. There was no nose radiator: the nose was concave behind a low air dam prow. The radiators were mid mounted with ducts set into the slab sides of the sponsons.

The Rondeau coupé was designed with the assistance of Robert Choulet at SERA who had not only worked with Porsche on the Langheck programme, but also later with Matra on its higher downforce 3.0-litre spyders. Following the more advanced versions of the 512M, the JWA 917K and the later low drag Porsches, the Rondeau soon made full use of the excellent lift:drag ratio of an aerofoil. A NACA section aircraft-type wing was slung between the lateral fins.

Given the use of an aerofoil section, it was imperative to keep it far enough off the rear deck to avoid interference

The years 1972-9 were spyder years, even at Le Mans. This is the Ferrari 312PB which dominated the 1972 Sports Car World Championship in the long-tail form in which it contested the 1973 Le Mans race.

between the airflow around it and the deck. If there was such interference, the aerofoil would not work any better than a large spoiler, to the detriment of lift and drag. Rondeau kept its wing in clean air off its low deck and to help balance it used a prominent front splitter. A splitter creates useful downforce, redirecting air trying to enter the underbody. Oncoming air dips down, pressing onto the upper surface of the splitter, then it is deflected over the nose.

Seventies race car engineers found that a splitter length of around 3 in (75 mm), provided maximum downforce: additional length did not supply any additional pressure. Running a splitter, a concave nose and a low-drag, aircraft-style rear wing as appropriate to Le Mans rather than a high-drag, high-downforce Formula One type rear wing, the Rondeau would have generated perhaps 550 lb (250 kg) downforce running 200 mph on the Mulsanne – around one-third its own weight. Three-quarters or more of that downforce would have been at the rear of the car and the lift:drag ratio would likely have been in the region of 1:1.

Towards the end of the decade Rondeau rolled out a lighter, otherwise unchanged Group 6 version of its Cosworth DFV coupé with the aim of seeking an outright win. A spyder body conversion had been considered but the team had found it had insufficient budget to implement this plan. Meanwhile, the even more tightly funded WM challenger – with characteristic narrow track to minimize frontal area and thus maximise speed on the Mulsanne – had gone the turbocharged route but lacked the resources to make such an ambitious challenge. However, the Rondeau bid had been gathering strength and the marque sensed its opportunity as the Porsche factory team followed the

The Le Mans GTP category brought a couple of French coupé designs to the 24 hour race in the late Seventies. This is the Peugeot-WM contender with its characteristic narrow, low frontal area body in 1979 guise.

Renault factory team into retirement at the end of the decade.

By 1980 the major factory teams had all abandoned sportscar racing, which was at a very low ebb. Having killed off the glorious Sixties coupés, the FIA had soon lost interest in the hugely expensive Formula One engined spyders but had failed to make a silhouette replacement work. Silhouette racing required the support of major manufacturers and too few had been interested. Further, it shut out the specialist constructor – the backbone of contemporary Grand Prix racing. The only interest in the mid-Seventies had been the battles between the Porsche and Renault turbocharged Group 6 spyders, which soon confined themselves to Le Mans.

By the late Seventies Formula Porsche 935 was established elsewhere, for the FIA World Championship of Makes and the growing North American IMSA Camel GT Championship, another playground of wealthy customer racers. This pleased no one, not even Porsche. The FIA's renamed sporting wing FISA and IMSA looked to the Le Mans GTP class for inspiration.

The GTP concept was appealing. It catered for fully enclosed, mid-engined racing cars built by specialist constructors and having a variety of possible engine solutions thanks to the consumption, rather than a displacement limit. The class allowed a major manufacturer to back a project that married his engine to a specialist chassis production and it allowed other specialists to look to proprietary racing engines, just as had the majority of teams in Seventies Formula One races.

FISA opted to create a new Group C class fashioned after Le Mans GTP with freedom of engine and a specific fuel allocation according to race distance. IMSA retained the GTP tag and the coupé concept but opted to avoid the potential for dreary economy runs by setting specific minimum weights to equalize different types of engine and different displacements. In other words, car weight was used as the basis of a handicapping system.

Significantly, IMSA was prepared to juggle its weight breaks in the interest of close racing between different types of engine at different phases of their development and it wanted to actively encourage the privateer. The FIA wanted to encourage the participation of major manufacturers and consequently an IMSA-style system would not have been appropriate given the ongoing manipulation of handicaps that it implied.

Another significant difference was that the FIA demanded 102 RON octane fuel, IMSA allowed the higher octane American racing fuel on which the relatively inexpensive American pushrod engine thrived. Engines such as the Chevrolet V8 were offered attractive weight breaks. The chassis regulations also differed between Group C and GTP but both sought to curb the potential for downforce. Since the fully enclosed, mid-engined racing car had last dominated the sportscar racing arena, motor racing had been swept by a new phenomenon – the underwing.

Previously, ground effect had always meant an unwanted drag-inducing shearing effect if air was not discouraged from squeezing between the moving underbody of a car and the stationary ground. However, in the late Seventies Formula One constructors found that the underbody flow could be smoothed and carefully managed to create a highly significant amount of low pressure. Ground effect now meant a careful sculpturing of the underside of the car to work in conjunction with the ground in the creation of downforce. The term underwing is somewhat misleading since such a sculptured underbody cannot create lift without the presence of the ground, unlike a conventional wing.

As we have seen, Formula One development for high downforce had commenced in 1968 with the appearance of Chaparral 2F-type wings located high in the air and feeding directly into the uprights. Regulation changes had soon restricted wings to non-moveable devices mounted low and attached to the bodywork. Consequently, standard NACA low-speed aeroplane sections were no longer appropriate and in the early Seventies the bespoke race car wing came into being. There were a wide variety of workable types but all recognized the special conditions in which the wing had to operate.

Clearly, there was a good feed for the front wings of a single-seater at any height. However, since these wings had to stay below wheel rim height, they worked in close proximity to the ground. Testing revealed no real problem with this, provided the section employed allowed for it and provided there was enough flow under the wing to permit proper air circulation. If the wing got too low, not only would the circulation be spoiled but air could wedge underneath it, creating lift.

Clearly, a narrow chisel nose offered the greatest possible wing span within the maximum permitted overall width but most Formula One designers opted for a wedge-shaped body with a relatively wide nose. The wedge fuselage was thought to produce useful downforce from the pressure on its upper surface. Some designers shunned nose wings for a sportscar-type nose partially fairing the front wheels, again looking for pressure on the upper surface. It was felt that this might also enhance the feed to the rear wing.

At the rear, the main challenge was to ensure a clean air feed for a wing which was logically mounted as far back and as high as was permitted. Of course, with aircraft sections inappropriate wing design was an art in itself. Wings were invariably equipped with lateral fences or endplates. Limited by maximum width constraints, the wings had to have a low aspect ratio – the ratio of width (span) to length (chord) – and were consequently of inherently low efficiency. However, endplates stopped the interaction of the upper and lower flows at the sides of the wing, markedly improving the lift:drag ratio.

The new, closely regulated wings were usually multi-element, having one or more flaps. Having a main element plus additional flap surface and sometimes a spoiler-like tab on the trailing edge of the top flap allowed a wing to produce far more downforce without stalling. The Rondeau Le Mans car had fins acting as endplates but only a simple single-element, low-drag wing. This followed the pattern of the earlier winged Le Mans coupés, and of contemporary Le Mans spyders. Bespoke slotted-flap race-car wings were appropriate elsewhere, universal in Formula One. Only at Le Mans was drag the overriding consideration.

The flap is a secondary aerofoil of shorter chord positioned towards the rear of the main element and at a steeper angle of attack, leaving a slot between it and the main element. The overall effect is that of a steeply cambered wing with an air bleed through to the underside where the surface starts to climb in earnest. This air bleed helps keep the high velocity boundary layer attached to the underside (which is, of course, equivalent to the topside of an aircraft wing).

Meanwhile, the additional tab – an L-section strip presenting a simple perpendicular lip and commonly called after instigator Dan Gurney – creates low pressure in its wake and this further helps delay separation of the boundary layer on the underside. With the combination of a couple of flaps and a Gurney it is possible to encourage air to stay attached even when the camber of the wing as a whole is so steep that the air ends up having to climb a cliff face.

The ultimate early Seventies high-downforce race-car wing was the so-called banana wing which presented a high leading edge, encouraging as much air as possible to go the short route over the top. It looked like a large builder's hod and kept the high-velocity air on the long switchback underside route attached via a combination of slotted flap and Gurney. It was long chord, hence of low aspect ratio and was run with deep endplates.

The banana wing was designed by one

Doctor Liebeck who patented it in conjunction with the McDonnell-Douglas Corporation. It was employed not only by the Formula One cars but also by the Can Am spyders of the early Seventies, the most powerful of which was the awesome Porsche 917/30 turbo. Porsche sought a high level of downforce for the first time ever from with this immensely powerful machine which sandwiched a large single-slotted flap Liebecker between two fins at the end of a long horizontal tail. The long tail shifted the wing back, providing a cantilever effect while helping put the wing in cleaner air.

Cantilevering a wing at the back of a car clearly provides leverage which increases the downforce applied at the rear axle. However, equally it creates a lifting moment at the front axle which has to be balanced by front-end downforce. It also affects the dynamic moment of polar inertia. For the front of its Can Am blockbuster, Porsche developed a shovel-type nose which was flanked by lateral fences and carried a prominent splitter. The shovel nose was a radical high-load derivative of the earlier concave nose. Running at up to 230 mph this 1100 bhp car was able to produce its own weight – around 2200 lb (1000 kg) – in downforce and it was measured as pulling 2.0 g on the Porsche skid pan.

The increase in downforce as Can Am, Formula One cars and the like got to grips with wings and sometimes shovel noses in the early Seventies, saw a move towards significantly stiffer springs and less wheel movement to avoid undesirable changes between low- and high-downforce wheel camber settings. Ferrari later went as far as evaluating a de Dion rear axle for its Formula One car, thereby keeping wide tyres flat on the track under all conditions. Another factor to consider was control of the nose to keep the front wings the optimum height above the track surface.

Through the mid-Seventies, Formula One development saw the evolution of a less radical replacement for the Liebeck wing with a lower leading edge and resembling a simple coal shovel. Typically with one slotted flap and a Gurney, it was often run in conjunction with deep endplates. By this stage some flat-bottom Formula One cars are thought to have experienced a degree of negative pressure in the underbody region. Clearly, any reduction of pressure underneath the car represented useful negative rather than unwanted positive lift. At that time less air was finding its way under the car and, given the right local conditions, the air that did (both from the front and from the sides) was logically accelerating into the pronounced low pressure region under the regulated height rear wing, rather than holding road speed until it mingled with the wake. In other words, assuming an appropriate tail form, the under car airflow was experiencing a spatial acceleration.

Spatial acceleration is a change of velocity in space as opposed to time – where velocity through a given space varies with time the acceleration is known as temporal. Spatial acceleration of air relative to the speed of the bodywork (as opposed to its wings) had previously only been significant on the top surface, where the so-called aircraft-wing effect it produced was unwelcome.

The underbody acceleration – if any – was less pronounced and was felt towards the rear of the car, where the air broke loose from the undertray on its rush towards the wing. Given low ground clearance and a low-set nose intake, the effect could be likened to that of blowing between two closely spaced, parallel sheets of cardboard, one sheet representing the undertray, the other the ground. The suction created by the rear wing and the natural wake caused the spatial acceleration of the air on the undertray relative to the ground, which in turn produced suction in the underbody region. This application of the venturi effect was not pronounced but could have been enough to nudge underbody pressure at the back of the car below the 14.7 psi of atmospheric pressure.

However, this much is guesswork with the benefit of hindsight. In truth, very little was known about underbody aerodynamics at that time. Certainly, nobody had done any pressure plotting under the car and wind tunnel work was mainly done via tufting. It was based on fixed-floor testing with stationary wheels. Ground effect still meant unwanted drag. In 1976 Imperial College in Kensington, London opened a rolling road tunnel to investigate the effect of aircraft wings flying in close proximity to the ground. It accepted 25 per cent car models and one of the first tested in this pioneering facility was the Cosworth-Shadow DN8 designed by Tony Southgate prior to his move to Lotus. ''Immediately the figures from the rolling road with the wheels revolving were different from those we had seen before'', Southgate recalls.

This, then, was a time of intense learning. It was over the period 1976-7 that ground effect got its new meaning. The DN8 had conventional wings and a flat bottom and, following the fashion of 1976, it was fitted with skirts along the side of its monocoque, these joined in a vee under the nose. Under certain conditions the skirts rubbed on the track and their general effect was to sweep the air aside, in snowplough fashion. Thus, the overall effect was not one of spatial acceleration of the underbody air, it was one of exclusion. The flow blockage allowed the forward migration of the naturally low pressure air at the back of the car into the skirt's exclusion zone. This was the principle of the so-called open tailed box. A box with the road forming its bottom and only its tail open will experience a pressure reduction within as it progresses along the track, forming the usual wake behind it. However, since the pressure reduction is due to the inward migration of the low pressure in the wake, the pressure reduction that can be achieved is limited to the pressure to be found in the wake. Nevertheless, aided by the local effect of a high-downforce wing's air circulation it was possible to achieve a significant pressure reduction behind a vee skirt, getting as much as half the downforce of the wing.

However, the following year Colin Chapman's R&D team of Peter Wright and Tony Rudd at Lotus went a step further with the Lotus 78 wing car. This car was the vital step towards the underwing. Its origins lay in a 1969 BRM devised by Wright using fixed-floor model testing. Southgate had joined

BRM that year and had been amazed to find the team with its own aerodynamicist: "at that stage BRM was very switched on". Wright's BRM wing car had stubby sidepods of aerofoil section and was designed to work in close proximity to the ground, just like a front wing.

BRM did not put the car on the track but the idea was realised via the 1970 Cosworth-March. Very, very low aspect ratio (hence very inefficient) aerofoils slung between the wheels achieved little. However, Wright and Rudd later found that fitting an endplate to the pod improved its effectiveness and that extending the endplate right to the ground produced a highly efficient side wing. The wing section was still designed to work in close proximity with the ground, of course, while a seal between its endplate and the ground was the key to optimum performance. That seal made a long-chord aerofoil of very low aspect ratio work surprisingly well.

The successful Lotus 78 wing car of 1977 led logically to the Lotus 79, the first underwing car. The essence of the Lotus 78 was the creation of low pressure underneath the car and it was found that an aerofoil section was not required to achieve that. Air circulation around

the sidepod was not necessary: this discovery was the breakthrough. In fitting the sealed endplate to their aerofoil section pod, Wright and Rudd had provided a channel for the air not dissimilar in form to a venturi tube as is used to accelerate air to provide a pressure drop in a carburettor. Consequently, it was only a short step to design a pod underside specifically as a type of venturi tube.

Indeed, it may well have been that the Lotus 78 was operating more as a venturi tube equipped car than as a wing car, hence the surprising effectiveness of its low aspect ratio pod sections. Certainly, the Lotus 79 was designed specifically to create low pressure in its underbody region without the benefit of any circulation around an aerofoil section. Interestingly, the concept of an underbody venturi was not a new idea, having been mooted as long ago as 1928, when the September issue of *The Automobile Engineer* carried a letter from R Prévost, President of the Technical Committee of the Air Club of Algeria with the accompanying drawings and the following notes proposing a new design of Land Speed Record car:

"Bearing in mind solely the side of

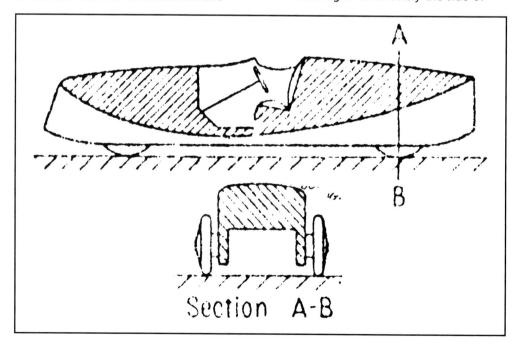

Section A-B

the question concerned with aerodynamics, I had endeavoured to find a form of keel offering minimum resistance to advance in the air while at the same time giving the machine the maximum stability and power of keeping on the track. In fact, I am convinced that by means of rational study of forms it would be possible with the tremendous speeds reached nowadays to utilise the flow of air around the keel, and also below it, to avoid the car's tendency to rise (to become unstuck as we say in aviation).

The keel in question resembles in outward shape through in rather rounded fashion, the silhouette of a rectangular parallelepiped. The underneath is nothing more than a venturi tube, to be divided longitudinally by a plane, which in ideal circumstances should be the ground. In fact, this division is made a little above the ground, for it is impossible not to leave a certain space, although as small as possible, between the ground and the lateral bows of the keel.

In a word, I have endeavoured to allow the currents of air to flow with the minimum loss of pressure while at the same time utilising the depression resulting from this flow to increase adhesion to the ground.''

The venturi tube so familiar from its carburettor application is a device invented by American engineer Clemens Herschel in 1886 specifically to measure the flow of water. Herschel used the venturi effect to measure a given flow rate through altering the pressure of the fluid flow in a controlled manner. His venturi tube consisted of an inward-tapering mouth section, a narrow throat and an outward-tapering diffuser section.

We have seen that by constricting the area through which any fluid flows a spatial acceleration is achieved, hence the pressure drop. A fluid flow speeds up through a restriction in direct proportion to the reduction in cross-sectional area. Herschel recognized that by comparing the pressure of the flow through known two cross-sectional areas its velocity can be accurately determined. He also recognized that ideally the pressure

should be restored without loss of energy. While a simple convergent – divergent tube accelerates a flow without loss of energy, the subsequent deceleration of the fluid may lead to a loss of mechanical energy: the venturi tube diffuser is shaped to avoid this. In the case of a pipe containing a simple convergent-divergent channel, the fluid accelerating into the throat will tend to flow full, ensuring good results from the Herschel pressure comparison.

However, if the divergent section is a mirror image of the convergent section then the flow exiting the throat will tend to separate from its boundaries forming a central core of moving fluid surrounded by a dead fluid region. The dead fluid region is filled with eddying fluid which is constantly feeding on the energy of the jet. Further down the pipe these two regions become indistinguishable and conditions are once again reasonably uniform across the section.

The energy which is carried into the eddying motions is lost in the mechanical sense, being finally converted into heat. In a proper venturi tube the divergence beyond the throat is made gradual enough to negate the tendency of the fluid to separate from the boundaries and form eddies. A venturi should have a diffuser designed to reduce the velocity of a fluid exiting its throat in an appropriately controlled manner, avoiding loss of mechanical energy. It was such a venturi tube that Prévost proposed to employ.

The efficient venturi tube's diffuser design will suit the mouth and throat design to ensure the appropriate degree of expansion. Successful operation will depend on its shape, and upon its having a well behaved flow at its entrance. The venturi tube is, as we have noted, used to achieve suction in a carburettor air passage. Here there must be no overall pressure loss – an engine needs all the air pressure it can get to produce maximum power.

Prévost's suggestion of an underbody venturi tube was tried by Chaparral creator Jim Hall but it didn't work since the wedging effect of high pressure air entering the wide mouth of the quasi tube created excessive lift at the front axle. That was in the Sixties and Hall turned instead to air exclusion, creating the famous Chaparral vacuum cleaner Can Am car which employed fans to suck air out of an underbody region which was carefully sealed to the track. It was extremely effective and was quickly banned. In 1978 Brabham tried the same thing in Formula One to combat the new Lotus underwing: again the ultra-effective fan car concept was quickly outlawed.

Lotus had meanwhile adapted Prévost's general concept to suit the race car situation. The venturi tube is used to achieve a local pressure drop in a piped-flow rather than a free-air situation. Nevertheless, the Lotus research team found that the venturi principle could be similarly applied to manage a car's underbody airflow so as to achieve a highly effective pressure drop. In essence, Lotus simply provided a channel having a small-volume mouth and a large-volume diffuser with a long throat in between. As the car moved through the air, the diffuser at the back of it constantly filled with air arriving at high speed through the throat. It did so due to the suction effect of the pressure to be found behind the diffuser.

Had the wedge-shaped diffuser not been filled from ahead with air, had its throat been blocked off, it would have acted as a form of open-tailed box into which the low pressure from the wake would have migrated. Allowing it to communicate with the higher pressure air at the front of the car through a throat of small cross-sectional area provided much more downforce. A carefully controlled spatial acceleration of a throughflow provided a much greater pressure reduction than is possible via exclusion and migration.

As we have observed, the Lotus 79's underwing was not a form of aerofoil. An aerofoil is active on upper and lower surfaces and its operation can be seen in terms of the local circulation of air around it. Further, it needs a high aspect ratio for high efficiency. An underwing has only one active surface but works only in conjunction with the ground. An earlier flat-bottom Formula One car towed through the air fast enough would create its own weight in

downforce and thus turned upside down would fly. A car with an underwing generating the same amount of downforce could not fly but could run upside down on the ceiling!

Aspect ratio does not come into the underwing equation since it is not really a wing at all. On the contrary, the sheer surface area available under the car provides the potential to achieve a great deal of downforce, irrespective of the relationship between the width and the length of the car's plan area. Once Lotus moved from pod aerofoil to venturi tunnel, it was possible to activate more of the underside of the car. Twin tunnels ran from close behind the front wheels to the rear wing, divided by the fuselage, the base of which was active to a lesser degree.

The underwing made a large surface area active, much larger than the surface area of any conventional aerofoil that could be mounted within the prevailing regulations. The underwing surface area made active in the case of the Lotus 79 was in the region of 3000 sq in. To obtain the 750 lb (340 kg) downforce experienced by a contemporary Formula One car at around 160 mph it was necessary to reduce the pressure over that area by an average of only 0.25 psi. It was found that the average pressure reduction it was possible to achieve over the large active area was far higher than that.

Given that was the case and the fact that the modest pressure reduction implied a clean flow of underbody air between the pod side seals, carefully avoiding separation of the boundary layer, the downforce was won at a very low drag penalty. With the underwing the rear wing became more important as a means of creating suction in the diffuser than as a wing in its own right. As a wing it produced downforce at a higher drag penalty than the underwing.

Overall, therefore, it was more efficient to run a simple single element wing as a tunnel extractor than it was to run a conventional high-drag race-car wing. The lack of drag for a given level of downforce was the major breakthrough of the underwing. Southgate notes that the Shadow DN8 produced 750 lb (341 kg) of downforce at the expense of high drag whereas the first Shadow underwing car straightaway produced around 1100 lb (500 kg) for hardly any drag at all. That level of downforce at the car's 160 mph maximum speed was only just scraping the surface.

To produce a lot of downforce from the underwing with low drag it was necessary to provide a generous diffuser volume and to keep it running full. Given the free-air situation and the pressure conditions around the car, it was not necessary to provide a mouth of matching volume to keep the diffuser full. In filling the diffuser, air from ahead of the channel accelerated through the mouth and held high speed through the throat and there the most significant pressure drop was felt. Of course, there was also low pressure in the diffuser, the air losing speed there only gradually.

Activated by the base pressure created by the wing and the natural wake behind it, the diffuser is the lungs of an underwing, drawing the air in through the mouth and throat. We suggested earlier that a flat-bottom car with a full-length undertray can be seen as having a crude substitute for the diffuser in the strong low pressure area under its rear wing. Logically, the throat is then its undertray, the mouth the lower lip of its nose. However, in practice it is likely that it will be found that the throat is really just the back of the undertray where the air breaks loose. Unless the undertray is very carefully raked, everything ahead of that point will tend to form part of the mouth. Further, the separation of air at the undertray exit will create a lot of drag: without a carefully shaped diffuser section the lift:drag ratio will be very poor.

The aim of the new Lotus underwing was to accelerate the airflow to as high a speed as possible and to hold it there for as long as possible, then to progressively decelerate it back to road speed with the minimum loss of energy while maintaining uniformity of flow. This recognises that the overall objectives are, of course, high downforce with low drag. As we have noted, the pressure drop is not very impressive as a meter reading at any given point but with plenty of active area, it only takes a small average drop below 14.7 psi to

provide a lot of downforce. Of course, as with the operation of an aerofoil, it is all a question of pressure balance rather than the attainment of a vacuum or even partial vacuum.

The underwing's carefully shaped diffuser minimises drag and ensures that the throat area forms a considerable proportion of the underbody. As we have noted, the flow through a venturi speeds up in direct proportion to the reduction in cross-sectional area. Since the underwing is operating in free air rather than managing a piped flow and since the diffuser is acting as its lungs, the effective reduction in cross-sectional area between mouth and throat is defined by the size of the diffuser rather than the size of the mouth itself. In other words, the degree of expansion of the air in the diffuser rather than the physical dimensions of the mouth determines the effective contraction of air into the throat, hence the maximum airspeed that will be obtained.

The jet of air leaving the throat has to be progressively decelerated back towards road speed through the diffuser. As we have seen the rate of expansion of a diffuser is critical to avoid separation and loss of energy. Clearly, the rate of expansion of the diffuser is as important as is its volume. The diffuser pulls in air to fill its own volume, converting the kinetic energy – that arising through motion – created in the throat back into pressure energy. It has to slow the air without provoking separation of the boundary layer. If there is no separation and the diffuser runs full then the pressure drop in the throat – and the overall downforce – will be maximized and drag will be minimized.

It is worth noting that a diffuser is, of course, a three-dimensional entity as, indeed, is the entire underwing which might not have a funnel type mouth. Provided there is the possibility of a smooth inward flow, there exists the basis for the venturi effect. Thus, the mouth might take the form of a horizontal splitter. It all depends on the philosophy of the overall aerodynamic package in question. That in turn relates to the regulations within which it has to be designed.

Clearly, the ground clearance at the

mouth has to be taken into account, as does interference with the airflow at the side of the car unless some form of lateral sealing is employed. Further, as we have seen, although a larger volume diffuser can pull air faster than a smaller volume diffuser, if the rate of expansion of the diffuser is too great separation will be the unhappy result. Of course, a long diffuser implies a relatively short throat, so the air will not be held at high speed for so long.

The overall length of the available tunnel area comes into the equation. A very short diffuser working in conjunction with the local effect of a rear wing and a correspondingly long throat might create a lot of downforce but at a high drag penalty. Both the early separation of air and the sheer length of the throat would provoke drag. More throat area implies more downforce and more drag. With the additional burden of early separation, the lift:drag ratio of this short diffuser option would be likely to be unacceptable.

To work efficiently an underwing clearly needs an extensive diffuser section and thus there is a practical limit to the length of the throat area and, to make room for the diffuser, the throat area must be positioned well forward of the rear of the car. Whatever the length of its diffuser, it is worth noting that an efficient underwing will create negative pressure most keenly towards the centre of the car, in the throat of the venturi. An echo of the May and Forghieri wings producing downforce at the centre of gravity.

It is important to remember that the underwing is only part of the total aerodynamic package: its mouth functions in conjunction with the nose of the car (in particular the front wings and the front wheels in the case of a single seater) while its diffuser works with the rear wing. In turn the mouth works in conjunction with the diffuser, and so on. Everything is inter-related. An underwing will work without a rear wing since there is still low rather than high pressure behind the car in the form of the normal wake. However, the local effect of a wing is that of a powerful force pulling air from the underwing. How much wing

is employed will be a compromise which recognizes that an effective underwing produces downforce at a lower drag penalty than any external aerofoil.

Lotus' pioneering work led quickly to the ultra-high downforce Formula One cars of 1979-80 which were equipped with sliding skirt sealed underwings. The typical sealed underwing started just behind the front wheels where the influence of pitch was less than at the nose and employed all of the planform area of a sidepod-equipped chassis aft of that point, with tunnels taking the width of the car aside from that accounted for by the base of the monocoque, the block of the engine and the transmission case. Monocoque sides tapered to keep the base as narrow as possible while engines with a narrow vee angle were favoured (Alfa Romeo moved from 180 to 90° vee) and some teams produced bespoke narrow transmissions.

Skirts were fitted one either side of the car between the front and rear wheels, thus sealing only the throat area. The underwing tunnels snaked inwards to clear the rear wheels making sliding skirt sealing of the diffuser somewhat impractical. Similarly, there was little to be gained by sealing off the twin channels from the fuselage base, which was active to a lesser degree since it interacted with the tunnels.

In side elevation, the sliding skirt sealed underwing form found to work best was headed by a mouth that resembled the leading edge of an inverted aerofoil, its upper surface forming the base of a channel which fed sidepod-mounted coolers. The curvature of the mouth blended gently into the throat area close behind and this in turn blended into the diffuser section which swept up through the S-bend as the tunnel cleared the rear wheel. Careful design of the rear suspension kept the respective spring/damper unit and most linkages clear of the rising diffuser, though nothing could be done about the lower wishbone and the driveshaft. The twin diffusers exited under the rear wing.

Given efficient sealing via sliding skirts and effective underwing design, this form of Formula One ground effect car could pull well over 3.0 G. It could generate its own weight in downforce at a far lower speed than a flat-bottom car equipped with big wings. For fast circuit work, front wings were redundant while the rear wing became an extractor-cum-trim tab. The location of the throat kept the centre of pressure well forward while the sheer level downforce which could be generated by the sliding-skirt-equipped underwing was highly impressive.

Indeed, the skirted-underwing cars of this period were prone to porpoising – a combination of pitching and bounding of the chassis. This was caused by the suction developed in the throat pulling the underwing down to the extent that it choked. The underwing did not actually have to hit the ground for it to choke: squeezing the boundary layer to a certain extent was enough. As soon as it choked, the underbody suction was lost and the nose popped up again, followed by the tail, only for the process to repeat. The main solution was in rock-hard suspension, virtually eliminating bump and droop.

Sliding skirts were banned for 1981 but it was still possible to provide a seal by lowering the chassis at speed or simply by allowing the pods to sag under load. A more subtle, if less effective way to form some sort of seal is to set a horizontal lip at the base of the pod flank – or perhaps a lip carefully shaped to create a swirling effect that takes air away from the side of the car. It is also worth noting that air in the wake of the front tyres tends to be at low pressure. Further, increasing the volume of air flowing through the throat makes it less sensitive to interference from the side.

By this stage it had been found that diffuser action could be enhanced by discharging the exhaust into the upsweep, at its base. This followed the principle of using the efflux from jet engines to keep the boundary layer attached to an aircraft wing by encouraging turbulence in the layer.

All this new technology was applied to Formula One rather than enclosed wheel cars: the spyder bodied Sports Prototypes in action at the start of the new decade were invariably traditional flat-bottom designs. Although it was possible to exploit ground-effect underwings to achieve an unprecedented level of

downforce, this approach was perhaps inappropriate to Sports Prototype racing given considerations of stress in particular. However, in theory a Sports Prototype designer could look to the underwing to supply the sort of downforce that was achievable with wings at a fraction of the drag.

Running an extremely high drag wing package it was theoretically possible to generate enough downforce to run an 1760 lb (800 kg) Prototype upside down on the ceiling at 200 mph, perhaps less. Equipped with an efficient underwing the same car could achieve the same feat for far less drag and would thus burn less fuel. Of course, given a long enough ceiling and enough power, the machine would go on accelerating to a higher and higher top speed, all the time generating more downforce. If the ceiling was 3.5 miles long then, as we have seen, the top speed potential would be well over 200 mph.

Yet on the Mulsanne straight downforce was unwanted. At Le Mans, as elsewhere, it was all a compromise but with the low drag implied by ground-effect, an underwing would always potentially be a better compromise than a flat bottom and wings. However, the ground-effect package had to be right. It needed to be rolling-road wind-tunnel tested, while the underwing form could not be easily changed once it was on the car. It was easier to adjust or change a wing than an underwing.

In the framing of the regulations for the new generation of fully enclosed, mid-engined racing cars, both FISA and IMSA agreed that flexible skirts should not be permitted and FISA went a step further with a mandatory flat-bottom area of 39.4 in (1000 mm) x 31.5 in (800 mm) to further reduce the scope for underwing design. Other significant differences between Group C and GTP were a feet-behind-the-front-wheel-axis ruling for GTP while Group C demanded central fuel accommodation. Fuel-free GTP permitted 120 litre tanks, Group C cars were restricted to 100 litres and to a standard minimum weight of 1760 lb (800 kg).

Both sanctioning bodies imposed dimensional criteria, including provision for a proper windscreen and maximum overall length and limited front and rear overhang. For example, Group C called for a maximum overall width of 78.7 in (2000 mm) and maximum overall length of 189 in (4800 mm) with front plus rear overhang kept within 80 per cent of the wheelbase dimension. GTP regulations demanded that front and rear wheels be the same size and banned gullwing doors.

Both Group C and GTP were scheduled for implementation in 1981. In 1980 the Camel GT Championship was, as usual, contested only by quasi-production machinery – primarily the silhouette Porsche 935. Meanwhile, World Championship for Makes races were open to Seventies-style production based cars and Group 6 spyders with Le Mans as usual also running its Le Mans GTP coupés. The World Championship was contested primarily by Porsche and Lancia Group 5 (silhouette) cars with various Group 6 spyders adding variety.

Le Mans 1980 lacked its usual Porsche factory team Group 6 2.1-litre turbocharged spyders but one such was lent to Reinhold Joest. However, the Classic was won by a 3.0-litre Cosworth-Rondeau driven by its constructor. The Peugeot-WM 2.7-litre V6 turbo was the only other fully enclosed Sports Prototype, this strictly GTP model likewise seen only at Le Mans. Running fastest on the Mulsanne, the WM notched a fourth place finish. Meanwhile, Rondeau's splendid victory lifted the curtain on a new era of the fully enclosed, mid-engined racing car with a flourish.

Chapter Six

Stuttgart to Southampton (via London, Paris, Turin and Michigan)

The new era of the fully enclosed, mid-engined racing car got underway at a damp, overcast Silverstone circuit on February 6 1981 with March Engineering rolling out the first IMSA GTP contender. The 3.5-litre BMW straight six engined car was striking with a lobster claw nose, concealed rear wheels and a catamaran tail. Underneath were unskirted Formula One-type tunnels which ended in vast diffuser funnels erupting to deck height. A full width rear wing spanned the twin diffuser exits, held off the horizontal deck by prominent lateral fins. The deck was at wheel arch height, the sponsons were high and slab sided and the superstructure was whale-shaped in conventional fashion.

The skirt ban was reflected in a narrow horizontal lip at the bottom of each sponson's slab side. The rear wing was staggered back relative to the tunnel exits, emphasizing its special relationship with the underwing. Unlike the deck, the rear arches extended the full length of the car, producing the distinctive twin boom tail treatment. The catamaran effect was consistent with an IMSA ruling that a wing could not extend outside the plan area of the coachwork while the lobster claw nose was purely dictated by aerodynamic considerations.

The car had a top-vented front radiator, the upright matrix set in the centre of the nose as usual. In plan, the middle portion of the nose was cutaway ahead of it and a low set aerofoil-like device was held by the claw-like parts that remained. Although it looked like an aerofoil, this was in fact a form of splitter dividing the air between a flow to the underwing and a flow to the radiator. Its lower surface was thus the mouth of the underwing – echoing Formula One pod-tunnel design – while its raked rather than horizontal top surface acted as an air flap and guide. Both this device and the simple, single element rear wing were designed to enhance the operation of the unskirted underwing.

The mouth's feed was divided under the nose between twin channels, one running either side of the cockpit back into the engine bay diffuser sections. The portion of the nose remaining above the radiator ahead of its of top vent was formed as a further front aerofoil section. The dramatic looking car was quickly dubbed *The Batmobile*! Neither it nor the GTP Chevrolet-Lola T600 unveiled a few weeks later were Group C legal since their wide Formula One style diffuser throats left a central flat-bottom area (forming the cockpit floor) that was smaller than that required by FISA. Further, fuel was carried in the side sponsons.

The sponsons were integral with the monocoque in both cases, and had contoured undersides forming much of the throat of the underwing. Both cars were based on conventional aluminium tubs with running gear as per established

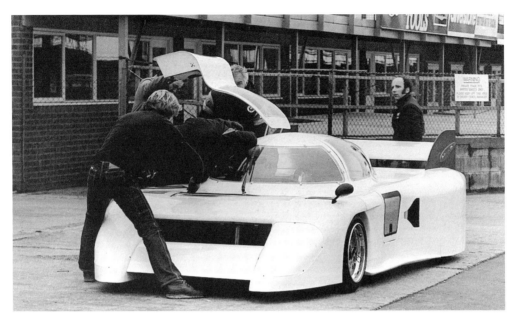

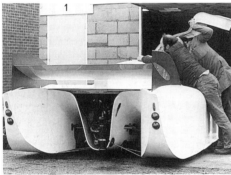

The new era opens at a damp Silverstone circuit on 6 February 1981 as March Engineering rolls out the first ground-effect car to the new IMSA GTP regulations. It was quickly dubbed The Batmobile.

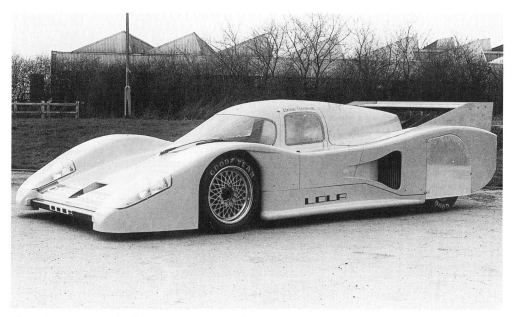

The Lola T600 ground-effect GTP car was unveiled shortly after the March challenger, at the manufacturer's Huntingdon base. This sleeker car was likewise based on an aerodynamic study by Max Sardou.

racing practice, the rear suspension designed to clear the diffuser upsweeps. Both chassis carried a stock block engine semi-stressed (Lola employing a three-quarter length monocoque) while the T600 customer car was designed to accept a variety of vee or in-line configuration engines. Like the March production, its aerodynamics had been developed from initial studies carried out in conjunction with Max Sardou.

Sardou had worked with Robert Choulet at the SERA fixed floor Eiffel wind tunnel, which had, of course, been involved in the design of the 917 Langhecks, the 917/20 and the Rondeau coupé. Still using the Eiffel facility, Sardou was employed as a consultant by both BMW – which commissioned the March design – and Lola. While BMW engineer Raine Bratenstein gave Robin Herd's March Engineering concern a Sardou shape to work within, Lola did more of its own subsequent investigations, using the rolling road wind tunnel at Imperial College to test 25 per cent models. Rolling road investigation was, of course, essential for serious ground effect study, though the scale of the model and its accuracy and the airspeed at which it was tested were very important considerations.

Imperial College – used at this time by John Barnard to develop the McLaren MP4 chassis – was still one of the few available rolling road facilities. The Lola T600 study was supervised by Eric Broadley with Andrew Thorby as project engineer. The T600 remained less faithful to the Sardou concept than the BMW imposed March design. The Lola was equipped with side radiators – situated alongside the engine bay and fed via a NACA duct in the respective flank – and had a far cleaner nose than the March. The leading edge of the nose was formed by an adjustable length splitter-type device.

This was again no simple splitter plate, but a thicker version presenting a curved face to the air and with an underside that extended back beneath the nose forming the mouth of the underwing. This echoed the March approach and the rest of the Lola followed the general March pattern right down to sponson lips, enclosed rear wheels and a catamaran tail. Both cars were based on the same philosophy, which was a logical interpretation of contemporary Formula One underwing design. However, detail design varied significantly and it was detail design which was crucial to underwing performance.

Both cars were in the USA in late March and first appeared at Road Atlanta in April, the BMW-March on the track, the Chevrolet-Lola on a stand. A week later the 5.7-litre V8 propelled Lola made a winning début at Laguna Seca. Brian Redman went on to take a total of five wins from nine starts, never finishing lower than second. In contrast, the 3.5-litre straight six BMW car lacked power. It could run to a lighter weight but the permitted minimum was hard to achieve while the old saying 'there is no substitute for cubic inches' rang true. The March handled well and had plenty of grip but no grunt. It was converted to take an in-line four 2.0-litre turbo, without success.

Redman did not totally overshadow IMSA's ruling 935 class. Qualifying boost gave the Porsches a 50 per cent power advantage and on race day Redman had to pick them off one by one as they dropped back to a prudent charge pressure. That pressure was still worth at least 20 per cent more power than Redman's Small Block Chevrolet could muster (around 570 bhp) but the Lola scored on grip, handling and manoeuvrability. With its engine hung out behind the rear axle, and a production silhouette flat-bottom body the 935 could not compete in the chassis stakes. From the outset Redman found the uncompromised T600 ''truly excellent in all major areas''.

Meanwhile, a 3.3-litre Cosworth DFV-propelled version of the T600 introduced the new breed of fully enclosed ground-effect car to Europe. For this final season prior to the introduction of Group C, Group 6 cars could run any displacement and there were not yet any fuel restrictions. The GTP-legal T600 ran as a 1975-legal Sports Prototype with a small hole cut in its roof! It contested rounds of the new World Endurance Championship which offered Makes and Drivers titles, the latter contested over more races. All races featured a mixed

The Lola T600 has conventional front suspension but at the rear the spring-damper units were set partially within the wheel wells to clear the big diffuser tunnels running either side of the transaxle.

bag of machinery, primarily silhouette cars and spyders.

Débuted at Monza, the T600 was regularly quick and won at Enna and Brands Hatch. At Silverstone it was leading strongly at half distance, then a fuel pick up problem stranded it out on the circuit. Another disappointment was Le Mans where speed on the Mulsanne fell well short of expectations. Lola had registered a Cd of 0.34 in Le Mans trim (with the minimum of wing and splitter downforce) but the 500 bhp car would not pull its projected top speed of 210 mph plus. It reached 195 mph in qualifying, 185 mph in the race and was not competitive with Porsche's 620 bhp 935-engined turbo-spyder which had conventional flat-bottom aerodynamics and ran at over 220 mph.

Le Mans also saw a rush-finished Porsche-Lola T600 fail to qualify. This 935-engined machine had a heavily compromised underwing thanks to the pancake configuration of its engine. It did not get a chance to show its pace in France due to development hassles and though intended subsequently for IMSA it was effectively shut out by a regulation change and went straight into a museum.

Other coupés at Le Mans in 1981 were familiar Rondeau and WM models, the Rondeau team taking second and third overall to the Porsche factory team. Porsche was back with its familiar (anti-Renault) 936 spyder carrying a larger, 2.65-litre flat six (boxer-type) fan-cooled turbo engine from the 935 programme. It featured four valve water-cooled heads and Bosch mechanical injection and was intended for the marque's 1982 Group C

car. It proved its durability with an easy win.

The Porsche 917K was also back at Le Mans: the Kremer brothers had collected parts for their own museum piece and saw a chance to race a classic following the lifting of the Group 6 displacement limit. Porsche welcomed the idea as refresher course in coupé aerodynamics: the car was given slab sides and a full-width single-element rear wing. It also had a new spaceframe, suspension modifications to suit modern tyres and a factory-prepared engine. But the project ran late: trouble in practice and the race ensued. The car was seen again at Brands Hatch, where it led, only to retire.

Brands Hatch was also notable for the début of the Cosworth-Ford C100 coupé intended for Group C and fitted with same 3.3-litre engine as the Lola. This car was based on a project initiated by Alain de Cadenet with Len Bailey as designer and it was run from Ford Cologne. On pole, the C100 led but its gearbox failed. It was significant for the return of Ford to endurance racing. For 1982 the World Endurance Championship shaped up as Porsche versus Ford and Lancia, with Ford represented by a variety of Cosworth engined cars including the C100 – revised to incorporate an underwing – a new T610 Group C version of the T600 and a new ground-effect car from Rondeau.

In 1982 the World Endurance Championship continued to admit silhouette cars and 2.0-litre Group 6

The Ford C100 in original prototype form, as penned by Len Bailey who had worked alongside Eric Broadly on the Ford GT40 project. The C100 Group C car first appeared towards the end of the 1981 season.

Enter the first ground-effect Porsche, the crushingly successful 956 turbocar. Three examples were entered for the 1982 Le Mans 24 hour race and three came home filling first, second and third positions.

spyders but only Group B (modified production) and Group C cars could score points for the Makes Championship, which was run over five rounds. However, with three extra rounds, the Championship for Drivers was open to all-comers. All cars were fuel restricted with a maximum tank size of 100 litres and a maximum of five stops in a six hour or 620 ml (1000 km) race, 25 in a 24 hour race.

With 600 litres available per 620 ml (1000 km) compared to 350 litres under Seventies Le Mans GTP regulations it was evident that an awful lot more power could be run than the initial 520 bhp offered by the new 3.9-litre DFL version of the Cosworth V8 which Ford had sponsored. Cosworth instigated a turbocharging programme in the light of the surprisingly generous fuel allowance, the fruits of which would not be seen before 1983. Meanwhile, Lancia aimed for the Drivers title with a new 1.4-litre turbocharged spyder that used Group 6 regulations to exploit low weight, low frontal area and an uncompromised skirted ground-effect underwing. While Cosworth-Ford and Ferrari-Lancia worked towards 1983 Group C turbocars, the 620 bhp, 2.65-litre, four valve Porsche 956 turbocar was the class of the field.

The brand new Porsche Group C car made its début at Silverstone where it had to soft-pedal to run six hours on a fast circuit and the cheeky little Lancia went further on 600 litres in the time available (clocking up over 682 ml (1100 km). Porsche then convincingly won Le Mans, getting three cars home one – two – three as the Lancias died early and a fleet of Cosworth-propelled rivals crumbled. With a substantial power advantage, Porsche had the legs of any Cosworth rival. Flat out, the Cosworth cars couldn't burn all the available fuel. They could hope to save a fuel stop but a gain of two minutes simply wasn't enough. Porsche went on to win the Francorchamps Makes finale, for three maximum scores from three races.

Meanwhile Rondeau had spread its wings this year and had won the season opener at Monza and had taken maximum points behind Lancia at the 'Ring, again in the absence of Porsche. Its new Sardou-sculptured (hence Eiffel school) 4 Series ground-effect car with swooping bodywork and big diffusers was a disappointment, only running Silverstone due to shortage of time to sort its aerodynamics: lack of cooling and excessive downforce were the key

bugbears. However, Rondeau's familiar flat-bottom 3 Series coupé took points on every outing including Le Mans where the factory concentrated on the 3.9-litre DFL and an engine vibration problem ended most of its hopes. Overall, Rondeau amassed more points than Porsche. In spite of that, Porsche claimed the points for a Group B class winner at the 'Ring and was duly acclaimed Makes Champion.

Rondeau was not the only Cosworth team affected by vibration-related failures at Le Mans: the DFL problem similarly cost the chances of two Ford

Lola lost direction in 1982 with the aerodynamic development of its T610 Group C version of the T600. This is how it ran at Le Mans with a low-set rear wing and a stubby nose. Behind is the Kremer Special.

C100s, two GS Tuning Sauber SHS/C6s, a GRID and and two T610s. The problem was cured in time for Francorchamps. Earlier, revised and run by Zakspeed, the C100 had set fastest lap at the 'Ring only to retire when leading after four hours. The Lola T610 was no more successful, while smaller engined Cosworth cars which failed to impress included a Cougar C01, a URD C81 and a de Cadenet converted from a Group 6 Lola spyder.

The T610 proved faster on the Mulsanne than the T600, running shallower diffusers and a lower set wing. It ran 218.7 mph, second fastest overall behind one factory 956. With the mandatory central fuel tank it was much revised and externally the aerodynamic package was very different with a new nose, tail and underwing, all of which underwent constant revision through the season. The nose essentially followed the March lobster pattern, though there was still no radiator, merely a rounded snout behind the central aerofoil which took a number of guises.

Meanwhile, the rear wing (outrigged from a shorter tail) and diffuser package were similarly changed from race to race as the project lost direction. For the late season Brands Hatch race drastic measures were employed to pick up downforce on the relatively slow Kent track. A vast full width shovel-type wing was set in front of the snout (attached to the hidden lobster claws) and the rear wing was set higher, to act as more than a tunnel extractor. For 1983 Lola planned a new design to accept the turbocharged Cosworth engine and Ford likewise planned to replace the C600.

The Southgate-designed replacement for the C100 was typical of the state of the art in Cosworth-engined ground-effect Group C designs at this time. Southgate had experience of contemporary Formula One cars, of wind tunnel Prototype research and of working with the C100 in 1982. It was his modified car that had taken pole at the 'Ring and had led for four hours.

Top side of the 956 in original prototype guise the NACA ducts in the doors were quickly replaced by larger square-shaped openings in the interest of enhanced cooling. Note underwing intake notch in the nose.

Southgate meanwhile had enjoyed the chance to do a good deal of wind tunnel testing, following Lola into the Imperial College facility.

Southgate favoured a wedge-shaped nose which dictated the Lola approach of side-mounted radiators. The mid-location of the coolers was good for weight distribution and beneficially shortened the plumbing system but was less efficient than the nose from the point of view of cooling. Southgate told the author that cutting NACA ducts in the flanks of the car ''is not perfect, but does the job'', the air then being ducted out through the rear deck with the floor of the exit tunnel formed by the front of the wheel arch.

Southgate went for a straightforward, conventional body shape with a slim whale-shaped superstructure and a deck at rear arch height. The wedge nose was headed by a simple splitter, adjustable for length (a longer splitter providing more front end downforce). The underwing's tunnels started directly behind the front wheels and in plan ran down either side of the mandatory flat-bottom area, then took the inevitable S-shaped route between the rear wheels and the engine. Southgate's research showed that airspeed lost through the first half of the S was regained through

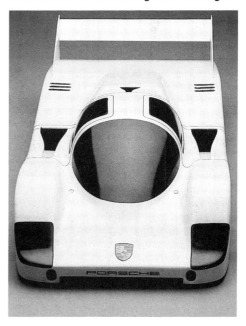

the second half, thus the effect was that of a straight-walled diffuser.

The throat blended into the diffuser section as the tunnel reached beyond the mandatory flat area and Southgate developed a complex multi-tier tunnel arrangement to blend air from the flat bottom area into the diffuser section. A remote wing mounted on a central post rather than lateral fins sat just off the deck, only its leading edge overlapping and with enough clearance for a proper lower surface flow. The clean, smooth deck helped ensure the simple, single element wing (with small end plates) functioned properly.

Southgate's wind tunnel work revealed that the wing allowed a steeper diffuser exit profile: set up so that it created 300 lb (136.1 kg) downforce in its own right it helped air extraction to the extent that an extra 600 lb (272.7 kg) downforce was generated by the underwing. The aerodynamic split was then in the region of 30 – 70: more on the front would have been preferred but that would have called for a big front wing making the car harder to drive and spoiling the overall airflow. A rearward aerodynamic bias was an inherent characteristic of mid-engined coupés, leading to understeer. Ground effect did not immediately overcome the problem.

In total Southgate found around 4000 lb (1814.4 kg) downforce (twice the car's own weight) at 200 mph for 1200 lb (544.3 kg) drag, a lift:drag ratio of 3.3:1. His car could (in theory!) run upside down on the ceiling at a speed in the region of 140 mph.

At the other end of the downforce scale in 1982 was the old-fashioned flat bottom Aston Martin-Nimrod which was directly descended from the Lola T70. Nimrod Automobiles had, with Eric Broadley's help, come up with a very solid car to run the stock block Aston Martin 5.3-litre V8. In its strength lay its main drawback – a weight in excess of 2200 lb (1000 kg). It also lacked power (the quoted 580 bhp was optimistic) and downforce. The example fielded by Nimrod suffered endless engine failures but another run on behalf of Viscount Downe ran the same engine all season and trundled to some useful placings, giving Aston Martin third in the 1982

Makes Championship.

The Nimrod chassis employed a derivative of the T70 tub with a square rather than the classic U-shaped cross-section. This promoted greater chassis rigidity as well as providing slab sides. The Nimrod also had more contemporary nose with a prominent splitter which, in conjunction with a smooth (flat) undertray, was found to reduce drag as well as to provide useful front end downforce. The Nimrod borrowed the T70 windscreen but had a lower deck since it carried a substantial rear wing. As standard the full width wing was single element with small endplates. The claimed drag co-efficient was Cd = 0.38 while there was more drag than negative lift (but precious little of either by Eighties standards).

The Ray Mallock run Downe car was modified away from the specification of the works machine through the season. The model had been designed with Le Mans as top priority and Mallock understandably found it "woefully short of downforce". For its first race at Silverstone he duly modified the wing to slotted flap specification and added more splitter and a lip across the front of the nose radiator's top surface exit. This lip offered useful downforce for little drag and helped draw air from the radiator, assisting cooling. With these modifications and running 6500 rpm compared to 7200 rpm for the works car, the Downe machine lost 15 – 20 mph on the Mulsanne. However, it was just as quick as its sister around the lap, thanks to superior grip.

Interestingly, since it was heavy and lacked downforce compared to a ground-effect car it was hard on its brakes and the Downe team had to change cracked discs on a couple of occasions. Nevertheless, their car made it to the finish in seventh place, in spite of an engine malady. At the other end of the spectrum was the fabulous one – two – three finish for the Porsche 956: the car of the year.

The 956 was Porsche's first monocoque racing car, and its first ground-effect car. Its aerodynamics were developed by a team led by Norbert Singer using 20 per cent scale models in Porsche's own fixed-floor wind tunnel. Unlike contemporary

Wind tunnel model of the 956 reveals the car's underwing in original guise. Between the front wheels is an indent or so-called bubble, immediately behind is the flat bottom area ahead of the diffuser.

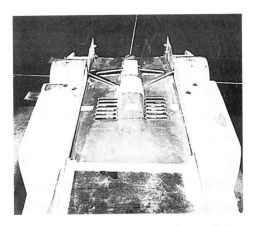

British designers, Singer did not produce a straightforward interpretation of contemporary Formula One underwings. The configuration of the Porsche boxer engine barred that route: its breadth left precious little room for conventional diffuser upsweeps. Instead, Singer devised a clever single central underwing that ran right under the engine, which was tilted to make room for its diffuser upsweep.

The 956 underwing took the form of a central channel which ran the entire width of the car and exceeded the mandatory 39.4 in (1000 mm) flat-bottom width. Thus, the regulation 31.5 in (800 mm) long flat area between the wheels formed its throat. The channel all but filled the available width between the wheels and there was a step in the monocoque floor to offer more depth than that provided by ground clearance alone. Further, the base of the central fuel tank was curved upward to accommodate the start of the diffuser upsweep, right behind the mandatory flat area. The engine was poised above the gently rising diffuser but the transmission unavoidably encroached into the central channel, as did the lower wishbones. A blister on the upsweep faired in the gearbox.

Since the upsweep was gentle ahead of the rear wheel axis it ran under the driveshafts but it was necessary to set engine ventilation slots into the diffuser. Thus, the fan-cooled unit blew air down into the underwing and clearly this was not in the interest of maximum downforce. The underwing was headed by a notch in the base of a nose air dam prow which funnelled air into the central channel. Between the front wheels the channel deepened temporarily, forming a so-called bubble. Apparently the bubble was a popular concept in German circles – it was suggested to Southgate while he was doing some work on the C100 in the Ford Cologne wind tunnel.

The central underwing concept assisted the problem of sealing, since the channel

was flanked by an expanse of essentially inactive undertray between the wheels. The 956 kept its nose free of radiator inlets, mounting radiators and turbo aftercoolers in a central location. The cooler feed was taken through the horizontal section of the door and hot air was exhausted through the top of the tail, over the rear wheel arch. The clean nose was concave above the air dam into which the underwing funnel was recessed. The central superstructure had a conventional form, blending into a clean deck at the usual wheel arch height and carrying a prominent long-chord single-element rear wing via lateral fins.

Right from the outset there was a choice of long or short tail, each with its own nose undertray (the long-tailer losing the bubble) and diffuser profile. The higher-downforce short-tail car had its wing higher set and partly outrigged to draw air through a steeper, higher and shorter diffuser and with the outrig it shared the same overall length as the Langheck. Its higher downforce made it heavier to steer, while the drivers understandably found the Langheck more prone to slide.

With its compromised underwing, even in Kurz trim the 956 could not match the aerodynamic performance of the best of the Cosworth/Ford cars. On the Porsche skid pan the 956 pulled 2.5 g while its lift:drag ratio was in the region of 2.5:1 and its aerodynamic split was around 20 – 80. Although it could not match the downforce of the British twin-tunnel cars, the 956 did not suffer a lot less load at slow to medium speed. Further, with its power advantage it could run more downforce in the corners while still matching rivals for top speed – as was evident at Le Mans. Indeed, Porsche's first ground-effect coupé was not far off the speed of its 1981 flat-bottom spyder running the same engine in spite of its higher frontal area and it lapped fractionally quicker on race tyres than the spyder had managed on sticky Q-tyres.

Aside from the Cosworth/Ford and Aston Martin cars, other Prototypes overshadowed by the 956 included the Peugeot-WM and the Chevrolet- March. WM ran a full Makes season but its familiar machine proved fragile as (predictably) did two 5.7-litre Chevrolet-March 82Gs – customer cars derived from the BMW-March chassis – seen only at Le Mans. The pushrod Small Block Chevrolet could not survive on the mandatory Five Star fuel, needing a high-octane American racing brew for longevity.

Porsche entrants Reinhold Joest and Kremer ran specials equipped with 935 engines and the Joest car – a converted 936 spyder – ran high up at Le Mans until it retired late in the day. There was nothing to match the Porsche 956 at Le Mans but the Joest special came closest! Meanwhile, in North America John Paul Junior won the 1982 Camel GT Championship using both a Porsche 935 and a Chevrolet-Lola T600. The T600 took five wins again, one in Paul's hands, the others via the Interscope team. The Porsche 935 won the rest of the races, aside from one win for a new Ford USA-entered silhouette Mustang based on the Group 5 Zakspeed Capri.

In GTP the Chevrolet V8 engine was used by Lola, March and Rondeau (3 Series) privateers while the March 82G was also seen with a 3.5-litre BMW straight-six engine, this time without factory backing. The 82G chassis was a brand new design drawing on the lessons of the BMW car and again heavily involving Max Sardou. The aerodynamic package retained the overall form of the 1981 car but the new machine was lower and slimmer for a smaller frontal area while work with 25 per cent models in the Southampton University rolling road tunnel had helped detail design. Revision to the diffusers kept them under the

driveshafts while the rear wheels were now exposed for practical considerations.

The Small Block-82G started the season strongly with pole at Daytona and a second place finish at Sebring but thereafter the March year was barren. Towards the end of the Camel trail the unsuccessful Cosworth- GRID appeared in the USA, while adding further variety, the exciting Jaguar XJR-5 made its début with third place at Road America. The XJR-5 was a purpose built Group C/GTP coupé produced by Bob Tullius' Group 44 team with the support of the American Jaguar importer and propelled by the 5.3-litre V12 from the team's Trans Am XJS.

The Group 44 car was the work of freelance designer Lee Dykstra and had been specifically designed for long-term Le Mans potential. Dykstra had previously designed the CAC-1 and CAC-2 Can Am spyders, the latter a Formula One inspired sliding-skirt ground-effect machine that found much success in 1981. A roofed CRC-2 was the starting point for the XJR-5 but Dykstra specifically incorporated the Group C mandatory flat-bottom area given the team's Le Mans intent. Dykstra did a lot of work in the University of Michigan's fixed-floor wind tunnel using highly detailed 25 per cent models. He came up with a very clean design from air dam prow to remote rear wing, the wing central post mounted above twin booms for GTP conformity. The car had a March/Lola type underwing with the tunnels skirting the mandatory Group C flat-bottom area.

In 1983 the XJR-5 had a very strong IMSA season, its primary obstacle en route to the Camel title a Porsche-March 83G campaigned by Al Holbert. There was little in the way of strong push rod representation in 1983, though various privateers wheeled out Chevrolet-Lolas, others Chevrolet-Marches. Holbert started the season in a 935, won Miami in a new Chevrolet-March 83G (a refined version of the 1982 car), then switched back to a 935 to finish third at Sebring. He missed Road Atlanta where Tullius gave the XJR-5 its début victory but was back to take a second and then a first with Small Block power before switching to Porsche motivation.

Wind tunnel model of the Jaguar XJR-5 and the real thing in its 1983 guise. The car was designed by Lee Dykstra as a dual-purpose IMSA and Le Mans challenger, thus had a Group C flat bottom area.

The Porsche-March project had the full backing of Stuttgart. To suit IMSA regulations the car ran a single turbo, two valve, 3.2-litre engine, good for 670 bhp. This was installed at an angle, as per the less potent but more sophisticated engine in the 956, to assist the diffuser upsweep. The conversion work was carried out by Adrian Newey who spent four days at Southampton and got the best figures March had ever seen for a sportscar. Working with the University Department from which he had recently graduated, Newey achieved what was described as a Formula One level of downforce in spite of the restriction of the pancake engine. The Porsche car's diffuser tunnels were less pronounced while the lobster claw nose was shortened by 15 in (380 mm) and the rear wing was shifted back a comparable distance.

The German-engined March retained the excellent chassis performance of Small Block propelled 82/83Gs and had the power to outrun the field. The 600 bhp Jaguar – which likewise pulled 1980 lb (900 kg) – was its closest challenger. A private attempt to produce a Porsche-Lola was not a success and the 935 was still the mainstay of the field. Ford moved into the GTP ranks with a unique front engined Prototype propelled by a 1.7-litre, later 2.1-litre turbo engine. This intriguing device with hi-tech chassis and full ground effect underwing arrived too late to upset the establishment, but won first time out and was running strongly in the Daytona finale when it retired. At that same race there was an impressive new challenge from a factory backed turbo-charged Buick-March which augured well for General Motors' chances in 1984.

Earlier, Al Holbert won first time out in the Porsche-March at Charlotte then won at Brainerd, Sears Point and Portland. Though the XJR-5 came back to win

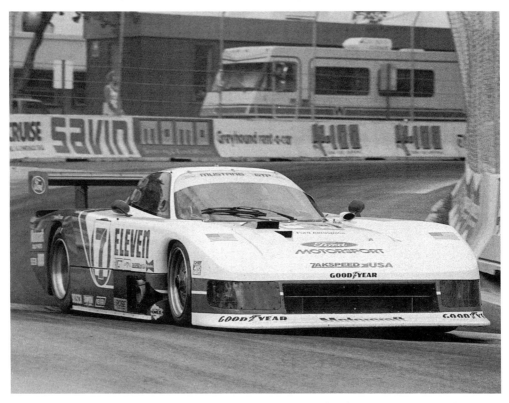

Ford produced this unique front engined ground-effect GTP car for the 1983 season, the old-fashioned engine location keeping the rear of the vehicle clear for the diffuser upsweep. A novel approach, indeed.

In 1983 Porsche sold customer versions of its World Endurance Championship-winning 956 design. This version (chassis 106) was run by the British-based Richard Lloyd Racing GTi Engineering team.

Mosport, Holbert finished third, thereby clinching the Camel crown. Thereafter the Jaguar won at Pocono and Holbert took the season's finale. Holbert had also taken time out to win Le Mans in a factory Porsche 956.

The 956 was again the class of the World Endurance Championship field in 1983, which was now restricted to Groups C and B (with a C Junior sub-division running to 1540 lb (700 kg) with 55 litre tanks). There were no longer any six hour races: everything aside from Le Mans was over 620 ml (1000 km). Alas, Ford had pulled the plug on the Southgate design and the turbo Cosworth, thereby leaving Porsche threatened only by Lancia. Lancia simply did not get its act together in its first season with an all new Group C car. However, Porsche ensured some competition for its factory team by selling no less than 11 customer examples of the 956.

Joest took a surprise win at Monza first time out with a 956 and later in the season the Fitzpatrick team won in the wet at Brands Hatch, having blanked off the underwing engine air vent for additional downforce since cooling was less critical in the conditions. Elsewhere the factory team was in charge and the customers grumbled at having to run a lower compression ratio and mechanical injection rather than the latest Bosch engine management system.

Lancia had an engine management system on its Ferrari V8 turbo engined car which copied Porsche's 2.65-litre displacement and had a conventional, Cosworth car-style underwing developed in Pininfarina's Turin fixed-floor tunnel. The underwing was headed by an aerofoil- like splitter, shades of the March approach. The team lacked development time but won the Imola Drivers Championship race in the absence of the Porsche factory. A customer LC2 sold to the Scuderia Mirabella beat the pair of works entries at Francorchamps. The old LC1s had been converted to Group C team by the Sivama team but lacked power, as did the Joest and Kremer Porsche specials that came out again, along with a Porsche-URD (seen only once).

The Interloper the BMW-Sauber was the only non-Porsche in the top ten at Le Mans in 1983. The Swiss-constructed 3.5-litre atmo car lacked power but proved it had sheer staying power over 24 hours.

Interestingly, Kremer's flat-bottom Special had been designed with a dorsal fin running from the firewall bulkhead to the rear wing in the interest of high speed stability. The car was tried without it on the Mulsanne and felt more stable, less twitchy. Overall, experimentation and variety was the spice of the big crowd behind the strong Porsche fleet which filled nine of the top ten places at Le Mans.

The interloper – in ninth place – was a new Sauber, this C7 model propelled by the underpowered 3.5-litre BMW straight-six. This car had an underwing that was a cross between that of a 956 and that of a Cosworth car, having a Porsche-type funnel intake and a bubble between the front wheels, then conventional twin tunnels. Another BMW project was Walter Brun's 3.2-litre turbo engined Sehcar which crashed at the 'Ring on its sole outing. For Le Mans Brun tried a Porsche engine instead but didn't make the start and bought a 956.

Meanwhile, Rondeau soldiered on with the DFL, bringing out three of the Series 4 ground-effect cars at Le Mans. Serious porpoising on the Mulsanne ruined the effort. Porpoising was hitherto unknown in Prototype racing due to the lack of skirts but the Rondeau had a highly effective underwing and the Mulsanne was an exceptional, ultra-high speed run. The bumps of the *Route Nationale* were not compatible with the hard springs needed to combat the porpoising generated by the 482's excessive downforce and in any case all three cars suffered engine failure. The unhappy event left the over-stretched team's very future in jeopardy.

Of course, plenty of hopefuls made up the numbers using 3 Series Rondeau and other Cosworth cars from 1982 while Zakspeed tried a Capri turbo engine in a C100, though this project was seen only at Francorchamps. To the Cosworth ranks were added two new names, those of Cheetah and Dome. Cheetah was a Swiss manufacturer, Dome Japanese and a couple of other Dome variants were seen on home ground at Fuji with 2.1-litre Toyota four cylinder engines. Nissan had a similar configuration engine in a March 83G and in a new prototype from the Le

For 1983 Ray Mallock was able to extensively modify the Nimrod Aston Martin, creating the Aston Martin Downe. This retained a flat bottom but had more downforce and a better lift-drag ratio than the original.

Mans Company, these cars likewise seen only on home soil.

This year Chevrolet was represented by a late season car from Tiga while the Peugeot-WM was out again at Le Mans. In the absence of Nimrod Automobiles, the Mallock run Aston Martin-Nimrod was joined by a new Aston Martin chassis, the EMKA. This Len Bailey design carried full-length tunnels, split at the nose by an unusual protruding beak. By this stage ground-effect underwings were commonplace among the hopefuls chasing the 956s but Mallock showed that a careful flat-bottom design could still go well at Le Mans.

For 1983, Mallock was able to lighten the Nimrod and reshape it and was even able to narrow the body very slightly. A 25 per cent scale model was evaluated in the MIRA fixed floor tunnel, Mallock having the benefit of the figures for Nimrod's original model in the same tunnel. A great deal of attention was paid to nose detailing and the sides of the splitter, immediately ahead of each front wheel, were led into an under-arch diffuser. Thus, air accelerated more vigorously under the splitter and diffused into the wheel arch, a region of air circulation with alternate high and low pressures around the tyre. It was found that setting a vertical air exit slot into the car's flank just behind the wheel arch helped draw air through the venturi.

The overall nose shape was subtly reprofiled and the tail was lengthened with Le Mans the priority and only the budget for one rear body option. However, fast and slow circuit settings were identified. For Le Mans a single element wing was mounted high and since it was then in relatively undisturbed air it could be flattened off. It was run in conjunction with a low tail spoiler. Elsewhere, the wing was run at an angle of attack that gave significantly more downforce but this had a cantilever effect, pitching the entire car so that the nose lifted. In response the wing position was lowered. However, the spoiler height could be raised since this was found to increase pressure over the entire car.

Another interesting detail was a rear wheel arch infill so that the arch ceiling was as close as possible to the tyre. A tyre acts as an air pump: reducing the volume of air whipped around by tyre rotation reduced drag. The net result was a drag co-efficient equal to that of the original car with three times the downforce, the lift:drag ratio rising to 2:1. At Le Mans speed rose to 214 mph thanks to a more efficient engine air intake and over the lap no less than 11 seconds were gained. The underpowered one-off Aston Martin-Downe, now at 2090 lb (950 kg) still wasn't a 956-beater but it had strong points gathering potential. Alas, an oil line broke.

Early in 1984 the Mallock machine was taken to Daytona where it matched XJR-5 race pace. It had less power than the Jaguar but less drag and, according to Mallock: ''seemed better balanced, able to go through the corners more consistently''. Its wheel bearings broke under the strain imposed by the banking but its performance against the Coventry-backed contender inspired Aston Martin owner Peter Livanos to support an 1984 European campaign. This was to employ a turbo-charged version of the V8 but, sadly, reliability proved elusive and two regular versions of the 1983 Downe car turned up at Le Mans.

Mallock at least had the luxury of a spare engine and could thus pull the full 7200 rpm in qualifying and together with Q-tyres he gained another two sec, outrunning the Group 44 Jaguars by over two sec. Alas, both team entries were knocked out by a nasty accident at the kink. Meanwhile, the highly trumpeted return of Jaguar to Le Mans saw the two Group 44 cars retire from mid- field. In the absence of the factory Porsche team – boycotting the event in protest at threatened rule changes – the event was customer Porsche versus Lancia. Porsche won.

Lancia ended up with only pole positions to show for its 1984 campaign with the LC2: Porsche won everything that year. This was in spite of the fact that the Group C minimum weight had been raised to 1870 lb (850 kg) which suited Lancia more than Porsche. The Porsche factory team generally won with Joest winning Le Mans and the Canon and Brun teams various Drivers Championship races, likewise in its absence. With this level of Stuttgart

In 1984 Richard Lloyd Racing devised the concept of a nose wing to give the 956 some bite at the front. It was an idea quickly copied by other teams for slow circuits, including Le Mans winner Joest Racing.

domination the World Endurance Championship had gone stale.

In 1983 the various Porsche customer teams had concentrated on getting to grips with the newly available 956. In 1984 some teams started their own technical experimentation to try to combat the factory advantage. This went as far as a replacement honeycomb monocoque devised by Richard Lloyd's GTi Engineering team but equally significant were the aerodynamic modifications made by Lloyd and others. The most obvious was a nose wing fitted first by GTi Engineering for the Brands Hatch race and quickly copied by most other privateers. This gave extra bite at the front, so short of downforce in standard trim. However, it was at the cost of affecting the entire airflow over the car, in particular reducing the effectiveness of the rear wing.

More subtle modifications made to the GTi car under the guidance of Nigel Stroud were typical of the overall aerodynamic development of the top privateer cars. Stroud designed a replacement underwing for GTi without the budget for wind tunnel testing. It took up slack, keeping the diffuser section as tight as possible to the powertrain and it offered additional tunnel width and depth. The area under the sponsons flanking the standard central channel was now treated as further throat area. There was modification of the bubble to encourage flow to the sponson undertrays while the revised undertrays were carefully blended into a wider, two-tier diffuser which gained in depth either side of the powertrain. The additional depth provided extra clearance above the lower wishbones.

That clearance was very significant, for it was thought that the proximity of the standard upsweep to the wishbones might have been causing the tunnel to choke. A clear problem area was the engine air outlet into the diffuser. This Stroud blocked off, replacing it by vertical slots running either side of the transaxle which bled the engine air into a higher portion of the diffuser, and

These photographs show how Richard Lloyd Racing modified the underwing of its Porsche 956 (chassis 106). The major modification is to the diffuser section which is wider and deeper and has no engine vent.

In 1984 Jaguar returned to Le Mans as a major challenger for the first time since the Fifties. Alas, the Group 44 GTP car did not adapt readily to Group C and the event was again dominated by Porsche.

exhausted it in such a way as to blend it harmoniously with the tunnel flow. This was not found to adversely affect engine cooling.

The revised underbody was complemented by a new rear wing, which was two element with a shorter chord main element plus a slotted flap. Stroud explained: ''The standard 'barn door' rear wing does not allow the driver much feel. The flapped wing moved the centre of pressure of the wing back and was less pitch sensitive''. With his wing and underwing package and the extra nose wing, Stroud reckoned to have achieved an aerodynamic split in the region of 38-62, far from the 20-80 of the original 956.

This season the only new Group C1 projects were a Porsche-Grid, an Aston Martin powered Cheetah and a turbocharged Mazda-March 84G, while significant revamps were confined to the Cosworth-Cougar, the Nissan-Le Mans Cougar and the Peugeot-WM. The Cheetah and March/Mazda efforts were intriguing but did not worry Porsche in the slightest.

IMSA was more inspiring for the technical observer with Chevrolet- March beating Jaguar and a new GTP version of the 956, the Porsche 962. The prototype 962 ran well on its Daytona début but customer cars were late arriving and soon showed that the option of a 2.8-litre engine pulling 1870 lb (850 kg) rather than 1980 lb (900 kg) wasn't strong enough. A 3.2-litre engine was needed to get the model up to speed and half the season had then been lost. Meanwhile, Jaguar hadn't been able to replace its 6.0-litre engine to find sufficient power to deal with the surprisingly fleet Chevrolet-March of Champion Randy Lanier.

Group 44 Jaguar had a poor season interrupted by the Le Mans escapade. Worse was the season of the front engined Mustang, while the turbo Chevrolet engine intended to put new life into the T600 simply didn't materialise. Like the Ford, the 3.4-litre Buick-March V6 turbo proved fast but fragile while a Buick-Argo, a Cosworth-Argo and a Cosworth-Alba all lacked power. However, an even less powerful Mazda-Argo picked up an impressive number of points finishes. BMW and Chevrolet Saubers were also seen in action (the former the ex-Le Mans 1983 car), though without success.

Thus, the Champion GTP car of 1984 was still a close derivative of the first

ever GTP car, that BMW-March of 1981. The 84G chassis which March developed from Holbert's 1983 Porsche car was seen in Porsche, Buick and Chevrolet guises with the good old Small Block pushrod engine of 1955 vintage delivering the goods, just as it had for Redman's Lola in 1981. It took the late arrival of the 3.2-litre Porsche turbo to end the Small Block's glory days. Meanwhile, the Pegasus Racing Buick turbo March was seen at Le Mans where its GTP legal horsepower made it the second fastest car on the Mulsanne at 222 mph, but reliable it was not. In contrast, the ex-Holbert Porsche-March won the 24 hours of Daytona.

By the end of 1984 Porsche had firm grip on Prototype racing on both sides of the Atlantic.

The stock block V8 Chevrolet-March 84G was the surprise winner of the 1984 IMSA Camel GT Championship. This car was directly descended from the BMW-March that opened the GTP era back in February of 1981.

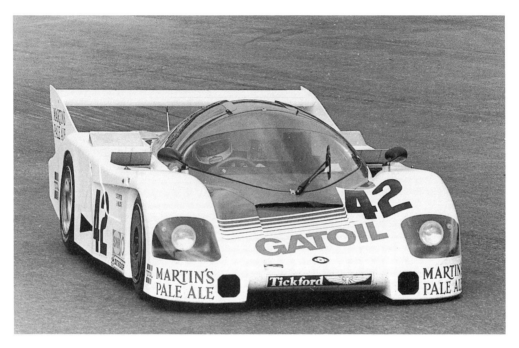

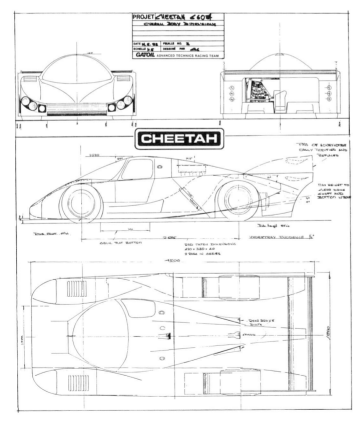

The Aston Martin Cheetah was the first Group C car to have an advanced composite monocoque. As the photograph and plans reveal, Chuck Graemiger's machine had a Porsche 956-inspired underwing.

Chapter Seven

Southgate Revolution

As we have seen, there were only three WEC and IMSA title-winning Group C and GTP Sports Prototypes over the period 1981-4: the Porsche 956, the Lola T600 and the March G series. In truth, these cars had only two other real rivals: the Lancia LC2 for the German Group C conqueror and the Jaguar XJR-5 for the British GTP machines (which also eventually met the might of Porsche).

All five models were designed during the era of full ground effect (if unskirted) Formula One cars and were full-length tunnel cars. And only the two British chassis were designed with reference to rolling-road wind-tunnel testing; Lola using Imperial College, Kensington, March, Southampton University's Wolfson Unit.

Of course, there should have been a sixth force in the form of the Cosworth-Ford turbo Group C car designed by Tony Southgate with reference to studies at Imperial College. Instead, Southgate found himself designing a Ford rally car and brooding over Prototype design. However, in October 1984 he was given the go-ahead to do a significant amount of fresh work at Imperial College. By Christmas he knew the general aerodynamic configuration of Tom Walkinshaw's new TWR Jaguar Group C car. It was not a full-length tunnel car. It had a new style of underwing which set the pattern for the rest of the decade on both sides of the Atlantic.

Southgate had found that full-length

tunnels made the C100 difficult to balance aerodynamically. In the wind tunnel he found that making the tunnels increasingly shallower in the throat area made for increasing downforce. Like all major steps in race car engineering, this one was simple yet effective. Southgate opted to use the entire expanse of the car's nose, cockpit and sponson undertray area as a uniformly flat surface ahead of two big engine bay diffuser tunnels.

Southgate had discovered that the suction developed in a Prototype's diffuser section was sufficiently strong to pull in air from the sides of the car. Air that had previously been assumed to have been flowing parallel to the flanks of the car was in fact being drawn inwards, turning through 45° to sweep under the sponsons towards the area of lowest pressure which was located immediately ahead of the diffuser. Since in the absence of lateral skirts it was impossible to stop this influx of air, it was logical to provide for it.

Conventional wisdom had it that the only effective feed for an underwing was from the nose. However, Southgate had discovered that in the absence of lateral seals the entire concept of a venturi tube style throughflow was wrong. Again, it is worthwhile to think of our example of blowing between two parallel sheets of cardboard. But instead of blowing, suck: the effect is the same while it becomes clear that the air comes rushing in from the sides as well as the front. The air from the sides is, of course, just as useful as that from the front: it all helps stick the two sheets together due to its high speed.

Southgate planned for a feed from the nose and from the sides, which clearly made any form of tunnel ahead of the diffuser inappropriate. What was appropriate was attention to the way in which the air entered at the nose and at the sides. Southgate opted for a nose splitter and pronounced lateral lips – horizontal side skirts – these lips extending the splitter area along the sides of the car. This confused the air rushing down the flanks of the car, forcing it to regroup before it joined the air at ground level which was being drawn into the underwing against its natural direction of flow.

Interestingly, since the feed from the sides was as important as that from the nose, scraping the nose on the track did not starve the underwing. However, the aim was not necessarily to run extremely low but was to ensure the right degree of throughflow. In practice, given the width of a Prototype nose, it was a case of running as low as was feasible and this implied designing the front end to rub and survive.

The new look tunnels started in the midst of the flat bottom area (roughly at the back of the central fuel tank) with an angled join and rose progressively forming conventional wedge-shaped diffusers, one either side of the powertrain. As usual a remote rear wing helped pull the air through the underwing. The pressure in the wake of a Prototype running without a wing was still enough to activate the new-style underwing but the wing could roughly double the amount of downforce it was possible to achieve.

Of course, Southgate's approach led to a greater flat-bottom area than was mandatory for Group C. He found that the pressure over the entire undersurface was no greater than zero (14.7 psi) and for the most part was negative. It was negative over something like two-thirds of the underbody, this representing a plan area of at least 5000 sq in. Since the average drop at 180 mph was in the region of 1.0 psi a total downforce of

5000 lb (2268 kg) was comfortably attainable at top speed.

It is worth noting that the air did not accelerate into the underwing, but was drawn in at road speed. Once under the car it speeded up on its rush into the tunnel entrances and the highest speed was registered at the entrance. Thereafter, as usual, the air was progressively slowed back down to road speed, prior to mingling with the wake. Although the lowest pressure of all was registered where the air funnelled into the diffuser tunnels, the overall centre of pressure was forward of that point.

With careful design of the entire aerodynamic package it could be well forward, giving an aerodynamic split of up to 50-50 without the use of a nose wing. The key to the location of the centre of pressure within the flat bottom area was the use of the rear wing. In general terms, lowering the wing increased the degree extraction hence the amount of suction under the car which moved the centre of pressure forward.

The side skirts that were central to Southgate's new pattern underwing could not have been fitted to the standard Porsche 956 since its body was the maximum permitted 78.7 in (2000 mm) width. Southgate kept his new XJR-6 chassis 39.4 in (100 mm) narrower which offered the added benefit of reduced frontal area, though its track was slightly compromised. For maximum effect, the skirts were carried right to the back of the car, across rear wheel sealing plates. Those plates, helping seal the entire planform area of the car, were worth 10 per cent of aerodynamic performance, according to Southgate.

Under the nose horizontal wheel sealing plates extended the XJR-6 underwing plan area as closely as possible to the front wheels (leaving just enough room for steering movement). Its tunnels commenced close behind the mandatory extent of flat-bottom area and their entrances formed much of the span of the rear bulkhead either side of an engine recess.

The inner tunnel walls hugged the drivetrain while the outer walls curved inwards to avoid the rear wheels.

The Tony Southgate-designed TWR Jaguar XJR-6 arrived at Mosport Park in 1985 and immediately challenged the Porsche domination of Group C. The car enjoyed superior aerodynamics to those of the 956.

Although the tunnels narrowed in plan, their growth in height was made to compensate: the three-dimensional form of each diffuser was all-important and this increased evenly in terms of cross-sectional area. Outside the tunnel plan area, the gap between the tunnel wall and the outer edge of the bodywork was carefully sealed. Further, the wheel arches were brought as closely as possible to the front and rear tyres.

Aside from aerodynamic considerations, the design of the new Jaguar-sponsored XJR-6 was dominated by the sheer length and weight and the high centre of gravity of the Coventry V12 engine. Southgate sought a better chassis layout than enjoyed by Group 44 and this led him to a nose radiator. Thus, only one major air inlet was required and this was logically set over the splitter. The inlet was formed in a forward panel that concealed the near horizontal radiator. This concave panel linked the front wheel arches while behind it the hot air exhausted over a sloping scuttle that

blended into the windscreen.

Naturally, the windscreen was as low and as narrow as was permitted while the usual whale-shape superstructure blended into a flat rear deck flanked by rear wheel arch bulges. Big 19 in (482.6 mm) rear wheels were employed since the spring/damper units were set within the rim to clear the tunnels and the bulges needed to accommodate these wheels added to drag. Naturally, the deck was designed to feed air smoothly to the rear wing, which was mounted higher and slightly overlapping the un-spoiled trailing edge of the deck. The narrow central post-supported, endplate-equipped wing had a slotted flap and, of course, the deck/wing/tunnel spatial relationship was crucial.

The downforce generated by the XJR-6 took Dunlop into a region unexplored by its regular Porsche 956 customers. The car came out for the first time at Mosport Park with a lip across the front of its radiator air exit and its chassis package not yet fully matching its aerodynamic potential. TWR's number one car headed the race for ten laps, then tracked the works Porsches until a wheel bearing broke. The sister car finished third. At the subsequent Francorchamps and Brands Hatch races the team played with, respectively, nose tabs and a nose wing, while Southgate shortened the tail and brought the wing forward to match.

It was all a question of getting the aerodynamic balance right while coping with the chassis balance problem posed by an unwieldy engine. At the same time the engine was undergoing race development (it was not the same as the V12 run by Group 44). It was too late in the season to hope for victory for such a new challenger but steadily the chassis was being dialled into the aerodynamic potential and, at the Malaysian finale, second place was secured. Meanwhile, Porsche had mopped up another World Endurance Championship, the major surprise of the season being the defeat of the factory team at Le Mans by Reinhold Joest and GTi Engineering, both running standard long tail bodywork.

This year the fuel ration was down to 2210 litres at Le Mans, 510 litres elsewhere. For the first time since 1983 the Porsche factory team built itself new cars and these had to conform with a ruling that any Group C car built after the end of 1984 had to have its pedals behind the front wheel axis. Thus, Porsche had to produce a Group C version of the 962 IMSA chassis at the cost of poorer turn-in due to the combination of a longer wheelbase, the rearward centre of gravity shift implied by additional length in the cockpit area and the excessively rearward-biased aerodynamic split of the basic 956 package. In response Porsche switched to taller, slightly narrower tyres for a wider and deeper diffuser section. The factory cars shunned the popular nose wing but had followed the Stroud-style underwing modifications.

The factory team won every race it contested, aside from Le Mans, Monza and Francorchamps, Monza going to a Kremer car that happened to be the leader when a tree fell on the circuit.

The 962C version of Porsche's super-successful Group C car was outwardly unchanged from the 956. However, the car had a longer chassis to keep the driver's feet behind the front wheel axis.

The Ferrari-Lancia LC2 was often rapid in qualifying but rarely lasted a race. Note the tail fins channelling the airflow to the rear wing. The car was designed using fixed-floor wind tunnel testing.

Francorchamps was also lost in exceptional circumstances, Lancia winning its first major Group C race in the wake of an accident that cost the life of 956 driver Stefan Bellof. Lancia's LC2 was often on pole and often led races but rarely finished strongly.

The only WEC race that the Porsche factory team did not contest was the Fuji event from which all the European teams withdrew in the face of a flooded track. It was won by a locally run March 85G equipped with a factory-supplied 3.0-litre Nissan V6 turbo engine. March conversion work to allow its G series cars to run in Group C involved putting a flat plate of mandatory size under the monocoque, reducing the tunnel plan area but not filling the tunnel space above. Thus, the scope for downforce was reduced but there was the minimum of interruption to the airflow between the standard nose and the standard diffuser.

Another March seen in the 1985 WEC races was a converted Porsche-powered 84G GTP car, the conversion extending to replacing the IMSA two-valve engine with a 956 unit. Porsche encouraged this project to help add variety to the WEC grid. It arrived mid-season and there was some fuss about the underbody conversion, until the Japanese race at which it and the Nissan 84Gs were finally confirmed as Group C legal.

Another Porsche 956 powered special was the latest Cougar C12 which had a narrow-track low-drag body. Working with Marcel Hubert who had been responsible for the Renault turbo spyders, Cougar devised an underwing which produced the downforce of his previous flat-bottom Le Mans car with less drag and he ran the Mulsanne at 231 mph, the fastest speed recorded since 1978.

The Chevrolet-Tiga was converted to 3.9-litre DFL specification but was no more successful in this guise and there were no other new C1 projects, aside from a Mercedes V8 turbo engined Sauber C8 which did not race. Derived from the C7, the C8 design somersaulted at the brow after the Mulsanne kink and there its one 1985 outing ended. Le Mans saw the return of the Jaguar XJR-5 and of the 1983 Aston Martin- EMKA. Converted to flat-bottom specification, the performance of the EMKA embarrassed Group 44. Neither Group 44 nor EMKA could run with the Porsches but the Aston Martin car won the British engine class after an overnight battle.

The EMKA was an interesting project. Fixed-floor wind tunnel tests suggested that the original underwing hardly worked at all, although, perhaps due to its lack of downforce, the car had a good drag co-efficient at Cd = 0.384. The underwing was discarded, leaving the engine bay floor and tail open to the benefit of engine cooling while saving weight. The car was then fitted with a splitter and its rear wing was set higher in the airstream, no longer called upon to work in conjunction with a diffuser. In this fashion, with less air running under the car thanks to the splitter and the wing running flat, the co-efficient of drag was Cd = 0.371. Further, the centre of pressure had moved forward providing a 40-60 aerodynamic split rather than a 25-75 split.

However, while the downforce was now greater than with the underwing it was still a meagre 213.4 lb (97 kg) at 150 mph. This could be increased dramatically to 1584 lb (720 kg) with a deeper wing at a suitable angle of attack but the costs were a drag co-efficient of

The Buick-March 85G unleashed tremendous horsepower. The heart of the car was the GM V6 turbo engine seen also at Indianapolis. In twin turbo GTP guise it could produce a four-figure power output.

Zakspeed aluminium in-line four 2.1-litre turbo engine slotted into the Ford Probe chassis, designed to replace the front-engined Mustang GTP car. Note cooler door channels, ducting air from the nose.

Cd = 0.451 and a centre of pressure that had slipped back for a 20-80 split, promoting understeer. Nevertheless, the low drag option provided sufficient downforce for Le Mans where the car ran so well with its original, inefficient engine air intake replaced by a funnel type. A further modification was a blanking-off of the deck hot air outlets for the mid-mounted radiators, the air then finding its own way out through the better ventilated engine bay.

The EMKA figures – from the same MIRA tunnel as used by Ray Mallock – show how flexible is the aerodynamic package which does not employ an underwing. However, since a properly designed underwing produces a given level of downforce at a lower drag penalty, even at Le Mans it is the optimum solution, provided it is tailored to the special needs of the circuit. If an underwing creates excessive drag through inappropriately high downforce there is little that can be done to alter the situation short of leaving it off. Similarly, if it does not work then it is just extra weight and extra heat in the engine bay.

The XJR-5 had a carefully tailored Le Mans underwing. Alas, a number of factors handicapped the XJR-5 in France, not least lack of Le Mans experience and lack of Group C experience. The 1985 fuel cut did not help either. The XJR-5 had been developed to run on unlimited higher octane fuel and to pull a higher weight than the Group C minimum 1870 lb (850 kg) while confined to 6.0 litres. The Group 44 engine was not the right basis for a 956-beater and although its chassis had been developed with a view to Le Mans, Lee Dykstra had done little rolling road testing. However, he had gained access to the rolling road facility owned by the Williams Grand Prix team and by 1985 had conducted over 500 wind tunnel runs in total, including some in the full-sized Lockheed facility in the USA.

Back home, on high octane juice the Jaguar now ran 670 bhp and a full IMSA season but could not match the performance of the Porsche 962, nor that of the Buick-March. Those cars were stronger under the 1985

With its very clean lines, Zakspeed PR claimed extremely high aerodynamic efficiency for the Ford Probe. Air for the coolers and the turbos was collected by the low-set nose intake.

weight/displacement balance. The Buick car was sometimes fast, sometimes badly off balance in the chassis department and was fragile. Its 85G-type chassis had a revised nose with a venturi shape incorporated into the lower surface of the aerofoil-like splitter. The splitter was made adjustable, as was a revised nose top panel ahead of the radiator. A narrower gearbox allowed wider diffuser tunnels.

With chassis development hassles and lack of durability bugging the Buick challenge, the 962 won 16 of the 17 1985 IMSA races. Only at Road Atlanta was the stranglehold broken, by the XJR-5. Ford switched to a mid-engined GTP, the Mustang Probe, but this did not succeed, its 2.1-litre turbo engine being its major problem. Other new projects were a BMW GTP derived from the G Series cars and propelled by a 2.1-litre turbo derived from the BMW Formula One engine plus the long awaited

Chevrolet V6 turbo version of the T600. There was another Lola production too, this one fitted with the Nissan V6 turbo engine that won at Fuji.

The Lola T710 Chevrolet car had a body styled by GM and was known as the Corvette GTP while the Nissan T810 was another variation on the T600 theme for the Electramotive concern. It was notable for mid-mounted coolers fed via ducts running forward alongside the cockpit to pick up a cool, high-energy nose feed. T810 development work had taken Lola to Imperial College to further refine its full-length tunnel underwing package. This was now headed by a conventional splitter while the rear wing was still on a central post.

Thus, IMSA was still racing developments of the original GTP cars of 1981-2, aside from the interesting new Probe. The Probe was a clean sheet of paper design by Zakspeed's Paul Brown who ran over 200 20 per cent and 12.5

In 1986 TWR came out with a lighter, refined version of its XJR-6 Group C car and won here on home soil, at Silverstone. Often the V12-engined car was the fastest machine on race day.

per cent model runs in the Aachen University rolling road wind tunnel. A 100 per cent model was then run in the Ford Cologne fixed-floor tunnel. As with the Nissan-Lola, special attention was paid to turbo engine cooling requirements. On the Probe, the water radiator was placed in the nose while the aftercoolers were mid-mounted and shared the same nose intake, the car having tunnels alongside the cockpit in Nissan-Lola fashion. The underwing conventionally featured full-length tunnels, these recessed into the floor of the chassis usual GTP style.

The Probe's cooling tunnels were used to duct air to the compressor intake and to the brakes and cockpit, thereby keeping the car clean of all intakes aside from the nose intake which was set above the splitter. The car ran a conventional combination of splitter, Formula One-style tunnels and remote rear wing and with its lack of intake ducts was claimed to have an extremely good lift:drag ratio. Indeed, Zakspeed PR commented: ''it is believed to be the most aerodynamically efficient race car ever built''.

There is a saying, ''when the flag drops the bullshit stops'' and as 1986 got underway Porsche remained in charge on both sides of the Atlantic, though it was watching TWR closely. The XJR-6 had been lightened to achieve 1870 lb (850 kg) and its engine had been taken out to 6.5 litres for 700 bhp though it took some learning for TWR to be able to consistently run that Porsche-challenging power level to the fuel. It was an output achieved with the help of a funnel-type air intake that added a little drag. Otherwise the aerodynamic package was a refinement of the original design and did not resort to a nose wing or nose tabs as the entire car package was now working properly.

Porsche had moved to a 3.0-litre version of its 956 engine and phased in a fully water-cooled derivative in the face of the Jaguar challenge. The factory team ran a reduced programme but the 956/962 still won all but two of the season's races with the Brun team winning the new Teams Championship. Of the nine races in the WEC, three were new style short distance events adding

some variety. Lancia ran just two races without adding another win and then quit, but both the XJR-6 and the Mercedes-Sauber won a race. TWR won at Silverstone, Sauber at the Nürburgring.

The Sauber, with its Daimler-Benz supplied 5.0-litre turbo engine (featuring full engine management, like the Porsche, Lancia and Jaguar engines) had been revamped in the aerodynamic department by Leo Ress. A front splitter was evidence of a move away from the 956-influenced underwing of the C7, towards the Southgate approach. However, Ress did not yet have the budget for serious wind tunnel testing. In 1986 the Sauber team was much less of a threat to Porsche than TWR, undertaking only five races and winning once, in wet conditions that favoured its fat power curve. In the dry the newcomer disappointed Mercedes fans.

TWR's performance was also a little disappointing: the team had the equipment to achieve more wins, but made mistakes. Its keen competition stirred up the Porsche parade, pushing a faster 620 ml (1000 km) pace. However, it lacked experience of Group C and opportunities slipped from its grasp.

Of course, victory at Le Mans first time out would have been expecting too much, but Le Mans was the win Jaguar wanted above all. Tony Southgate's major effort for 1986 went into a specific Le Mans package. At the Le Mans test day the team presented a number of possible configurations for evaluation, including the intended race weekend package with pronounced low downforce and low drag wind tunnel readings. Southgate had spent four separate sessions at Imperial College looking for half the drag of the sprint car with adequate downforce.

In fast circuit trim the 620 ml (1000 km) car had a splitter cut back so that it did not extend outside the basic nose plan and a wing lowered so that it was still above the rear deck but was at wheel arch height. One car in this configuration was fitted with a single-element rear wing for the test while two others had experimental Le Mans packages; one with larger volume diffusers than the other, although not full standard

TWR Jaguar XJR-6 versus Porsche 962C at Le Mans in 1986. Note the low-set wing on each car. The Le Mans long-tail version of a Group C car these days was no longer than standard but produced less downforce.

volume. The complete Le Mans package consisted of nose, underwing, wing and tail modifications.

The Le Mans nose was of the regular form but lacked front wheel arch louvres and the regular lip across the front of the radiator exit. Underneath, adjustable size apertures were set in the radiator bay floor panel to bleed some of the high pressure air down into the underwing rather than letting it all exit over the windscreen. Further, this nose was run with the short splitter and without front wheel infill plates. The rest of the Le Mans underwing was characterized by smaller diffuser tunnels. The tail was lengthened, but only at the base, retaining the standard length of

rear deck. Meanwhile, a long-chord single-element wing was run so that the air saw it as an extension of the deck. It blended the over and underbody airflows and helped extract the tunnel but did not act as a conventional wing.

The car with the low tunnel Le Mans package predictably ran the Mulsanne fastest, at 221 mph while the version with interim underwing ran 214 mph. The 620 ml (1000 km) car porpoised and grounded along the straight and would not exceed 190 mph (still 10 mph more than seen at the fastest of other circuits, Monza and Silverstone). Although relatively slow on the Mulsanne, it was just about as quick as the other cars around the lap. However, it was harder

NORMAL

LE MANS — low wing, longer tail

Comparative drawing of the Jaguar XJR-6 in Le Mans and Sprint guise illustrates the tail modifications, which were matched by smaller tunnels for the French race. No splitter was run at Le Mans.

to drive to a good time, consumed 25 per cent more fuel and the unwanted downforce on the Mulsanne caused the driveshafts to run at an acute angle which led to cv failure.

Of the faster cars, the interim underwing version was fractionally quicker around the lap but its centre of pressure was too far forward, making it darty and unstable on the Mulsanne. It also burned more fuel. The full intended Le Mans package was adopted for the race, a race offering 2550 litres and in which the XJR-6 showed strongly. Alas, one car coasted to a halt with its fuel tank dry, another suffered cv failure and the third fell victim to a burst tyre.

Although Le Mans 1986 was about Porsche and Jaguar, it was also notable for the appearance of a private Cosworth DFL turbo Tiga (which lacked funding) and, more importantly, three Japanese factory teams, all of which appeared again at Fuji. Mazda additionally ran Silverstone with its new, Stroud-designed three-rotor GTP machine which sported a funnel-type underwing mouth and a

remote rear wing mounted on small fins. Toyota brought out two revised Dome chassis, the 86C, while Nissan had a new version of the March G Series, the 86-S. This Gordon Coppuck creation had a wedge nose and mid-mounted coolers and was run by the factory competition department.

Aside from this project, March provided BMW with a modified GTP chassis and eventually got around to supplying a 1986 specification for the Buick GTP project. Both IMSA cars were quick but only the BMW brought home the goods, and then only on one occasion. Other Camel GT winners were the Corvette GTP, the Ford Probe and the Group 44 Jaguar, which had been updated to XJR-7 specification and now carried a 6.5-litre engine. The Probe ran into constant reliability problems and tried a 2.1-litre version of the DFL turbo seen at Le Mans. However, politics killed the entire Ford GTP project and BMW likewise quit.

While the Corvette won two races and BMW, Ford and Jaguar one apiece, the

The Toyota 86C-L was produced in Japan and was propelled by a factory-supplied in-line four engine displacing only 2.1 litres. It had to be turbocharged to an uncomfortable extent to contest Group C races.

Descended from the Lola T600 of 1981 was this so-called Corvette, styled by GM. Produced by Lola, the car was seen in turbocharged and in normally aspirated form (as here with the Chevrolet V8 engine).

Porsche 962 won the remaining 12, retaining its grip on IMSA competition. However, it had a good number of challengers and although the Ford and BMW efforts ended, the Nissan-Lola effort was gathering strength. The car's aerodynamics were revised, away from the full length tunnel approach, and it started to look very strong. In 1987 it scored its first victory, at Miami. *Autosport* wrote: ''it often failed to go the distance, its aggressive red, white and blue appearance and storm trooper qualifying runs too often proving to be more bark than bite. The 1987 series' most exciting car was often its most disappointing''.

In 1987 the Corvette GTP Lola was just as much a let-down while a privately funded derivative of the Probe, the Maxxim – likewise designed by

Brown – was another flop, as was the Buick-March. All that left Porsche precious little opposition and the 962 won 13 of 16 events. Surprisingly, the XJR-7 scored two victories but this was the swansong for the Group 44 team. In 1988 TWR took over Jaguar's GTP effort.

It came in with a bang, winning Daytona with the XJR-9 GTP version of its familiar Group C car, then fighting Porsche hard at Miami and Sebring. On those occasions Porsche came out on top. Then in came Nissan with a revamped, stronger chassis, new tyres and further refined aerodynamics. The V6 turbo car took eight straight wins and went on to lose only two races in 11 starts. Porsche had been pushed aside, but not by Jaguar.

TWR was restricted to 6.0 litres rather than the anticipated 7.0 litres and

The Jaguar XJR-8 was an improved version of the XJR-6 with a full 7.0-litre engine and it dominated the 1987 World Championship. However, it did not manage to dethrone Porsche at Le Mans.

struggled throughout the season, taking only two wins. That was equal to Group 44's 1987 tally whereas Porsche took only three wins this year. Meanwhile, the Corvette GTP had a winless season, the rival Buick-March faded away and an attempt to revive the original Probe project was low key. Chevrolet V8 power returned with the Fabcar while a Spice ran virtually the same engine with a Pontiac badge but there was not enough power in the old push rod engine to pull its allotted weight.

In 1989 it was much the same story for the Electramotive-run Nissan GTP: 10 victories this year. TWR Jaguar phased in a new V6 turbo engine but this did not come good until the season finale. In total, TWR got three victories, Porsche two – and there were only 15 races.

It is worth noting, however, that this year's Daytona 24 hour classic gave Porsche its 50th GTP victory with the 962. Also of note was the Toyota-Eagle GTP car of Dan Gurney, fielded alongside a Dome Group C development chassis running the same 2.1-litre four cylinder turbo engine. The Eagle was the only new project but the GM-Spice effort showed renewed hope. Particularly since IMSA was keen to encourage the good old-fashioned pushrod engine through weight manipulation.

Over in Europe Spice was flogging another old horse, one that was only 22 rather than 34 years old – and equally in favour with backward-looking rule makers. By 1989 the FIA had committed Group C to a simple 3.5-litre displacement – shades of 1972 – and those antique dealers peddling the Cosworth DFR could do so free of fuel consumption restrictions and taxed to the extent of only 1650 lb (750 kg).

Of course, the Mercedes turbo engine doing all the winning was, at heart, just as ancient, for all Daimler-Benz' massive Group C investment.

The German effort had really gathered strength in 1987 when Peter Sauber fielded a revised C9 model with improved Jaguar copy aerodynamics and improved engine control. The 1987 car contested five races and showed good pace but only one finish was achieved, its transmission a major weakness. Meanwhile TWR got its act together,

a 7.0-litre XJR-8 version of the Kidlington car dominating the WEC just as Porsche had done in years past. In all the XJR-8 notched up eight victories. The only disappointment of the season was the failure of the team to win Le Mans. The Le Mans package was refined but a shunt at the kink though tyre failure, a cracked cylinder head and a gearbox failure accounted for all three entries.

The Porsche factory team won Le Mans once again and Britten-Lloyd Racing won the Norisring but those were the only successes for the 962C, which looked a spent force even with an improved, fully watercooled 3.0-litre turbo engine. Meanwhile, Courage wheeled out a new Porsche-propelled Cougar which was again fast on the Mulsanne and netted third place in the race for which it was primarily intended. Mazda, Toyota and Nissan came out once more at Le Mans and Fuji, Nissan with a new V8 engine and another revised March chassis but no substantial progress had been made by the Japanese.

Peugeot-WM fielded an entirely new Le Mans car aimed specifically at 400 km/h (248 mph) on the Mulsanne after 11 years with its traditional design. An engine management system helped the new, ultra-low-drag challenger. Sure enough it reached the target speed, but not on the official radar.

There was always 1988. This year WM made it official and this year TWR won Le Mans. Five cars started whereas Mercedes-Sauber – the surprise WEC force of 1988 – withdrew both its entries following unexplained tyre blow outs on the Mulsanne. Thus, Porsche was again the major obstacle to Coventry's coveted win and it ran the British close. However, elsewhere the Porsche 962C was uncompetitive. Jaguar's XJR-9, a direct descendant of the XJR-6 of 1985, was threatened only by the Sauber C9, which this year had the full backing of Daimler-Benz and Mercedes engines direct from the factory.

Regulation changes for 1988, however, had benefited Porsche relative to Jaguar since tunnel volume was restricted. Jaguar had been better exploiting tunnel technology than Porsche, of course. The new regulations demanded a larger flat-bottom area and a maximum tunnel height of 11 in (280 mm). The flat-bottom area now had to be 35.4 in (900 mm) long and to reach the full width of the car, the latter factor making the Southgate approach mandatory: there was no longer scope for full-length tunnels. For Southgate, the 35.4 in (900 mm) rule pushed the tunnel entrance back, while the lower tunnel restricted diffuser design.

In 1988 the Japanese still shied away from full WEC participation and the only exciting development from the land of the rising sun was a heavily revamped Nissan V8 engine which did not get the job done at Le Mans. Sauber won the first race of the season, then after Le Mans – round five – really gathered strength, winning four more races. During the second half of the season the new German challenger emerged as a stronger force than TWR. That much was shown in 1989 when Mercedes-Sauber dominated the results beaten only once, at Dijon. On that occasion a freak tyre advantage enjoyed by the Joest Porsche team gave Porsche another World Championship race win.

This year the standard race distance was 298 ml (480 km) rather than 620 ml (1000 km) and the minimum weight was up to 1980 lb (900 kg). As a result the C9 no longer carried a lot of excess kilos and with an improved, four-valve engine it had the legs of the opposition winning even Le Mans, which was outside the championship following political wrangling. TWR should have won Le Mans but reliability slipped. Given that, the strongest opposition for Sauber at Le Mans – as often elsewhere – came from the Joest Porsche team. The further revised regulations gave Porsche a new lease of life.

In sprint events TWR floundered, its V12 atmo engine no longer competitive against the turbos with their improved engine management systems and greater flexibility. The extra 110 lb (50 kg) cost TWR its weight advantage and presented it with new problem areas: brakes and tyres in particular. TWR phased in a Group C version of its IMSA turbo but it was too early to expect results.

Meanwhile, Nissan slotted a revised version of its V8 into a new Lola chassis and spent the year getting to grips with a new package and a full WEC programme, as did Toyota which had an in-house chassis and a brand new V8 engine. The other brand-new package of 1989 was an Aston Martin utilising a four-valve version of the old V8 developed in the USA and a new chassis built in Britain. It was a fabulous mid-field runner but no more. It was no less worthy for all that; a sporting effort, like the majority of Group C1/GTP cars of the Eighties.

Chapter Eight

High Load

By the late Eighties all the major Sports Prototypes (with the notable exception of a number of quick Porsches) had an underwing following the pattern of the Southgate Jaguars. This was the case both in Group C, before the regulations made a flat belly mandatory and in GTP, in spite of the greater freedom of underbody sculpturing afforded by IMSA regulations. That included the super-successful Electramotive Nissan GTP car.

The Nissan GTP's aerodynamics were the work of Yoshi Suzuka, a Japanese engineer working with Electramotive's own rolling road tunnel which accepted 15 per cent scale models. Suzuka had started the programme in 1984, working with Lola on 25 per cent models at Imperial College; then development work continued at Electramotive in California as the race programme got underway. The initial aim was to produce a GTP car with Le Mans potential, so low drag was considered important, as was generous cooling for the turbo V6.

Cooling considerations led to the distinctive nostrils collecting air at the nose for mid-mounted radiators and aftercooler. Additional cooling-induced drag was an inherent drawback of using a turbo engine rather than an atmo engine, such as the Chevrolet V8 with which Lola had established its GTP reputation. However, Electramotive insisted that charge cooling in particular should be in no way compromised, indeed that it should have top priority.

For the new T810 Nissan chassis, air feeds from the both nose and the horizontal section of the doors with exit channels through the top of the deck was the solution identified for minimum drag.

The basic aerodynamic package at the outset was fronted by a splitter ahead of a wedge nose. Underneath there was an underwing bubble between the front wheels, the flow then dividing into full length tunnels running alongside the cockpit floor and the powertrain. The diffuser sections rose towards a remote single element wing fitted with a Gurney and small endplates and mounted on a central post. The upper surface of the wedge nose sported those distinctive nostrils feeding the cooler channels which ran through the upper half of the sponsons. The compressor of the single turbo was fed via a periscope which emerged through the rear deck. There were also smaller rear periscopes for brake cooling.

This original package, as evolved at Imperial College, was capable of the production of around 3500 lb (1587.6 kg) downforce at 200 mph with a lift:drag ratio in the region of 3.5:1 and 35-40 per cent of the pressure at the front. Comparative figures for the XJR-6 which was evolved in the same tunnel around this time have not been released. However, it is clear that Southgate's new-style underwing produced significantly more downforce with a higher lift:drag ratio. On the other hand,

The Nissan GTP car was built initially by Lola but this 1989 Daytona car had a Californian tub. Its aerodynamic development was the work of Yoshi Suzuka working in the Electramotive wind tunnel.

Southgate was not looking for a Le Mans compromise at this stage.

The Electramotive race programme got under way in 1985 and by mid-1986 two cars were on the track. Although manufactured by Lola, they now carried much Electramotive technology and that included a Suzuka evolution of the original aerodynamic package. In 1988 Electramotive phased in its own chassis, designed by Trevor Harris and manufactured in California. However, this was an update of the existing model rather than a new design and the car retained the Electramotive aerodynamics developed over the period 1986-7 with only detail changes. The culmination of the work of Suzuka and Harris was not seen until 1990, in the form of an all new car.

Early on the splitter had been removed and by 1987, aside from the superstructure, just about everything had changed, although few of the modifications were very obvious. For

example, the top surface of the nose was a reworking for higher downforce but it looked the same upon casual observation. Underneath, the underwing was headed by an understated funnel-type intake and the basic approach followed the XJR-6 pattern using the entire expanse of the belly of the car to prepare the air from ahead and from the sides for its rush into the diffuser tunnels.

There was no longer a bubble, while the new diffuser tunnel entrance was narrower than the span of the old full-length tunnel and the diffuser upsweep was different. The deck was shorter while the wing (still the Lola original) was mounted further back relative to the deck and lower (though still above the height of the rear arches). Within the wheelbase the flanks of each sponson were bevelled at the lower edge to allow provision of horizontal side skirts.

Although the initial approach had been towards low drag, the team had kept on adding downforce and the car had kept on going faster. A high downforce approach was clearly important for GTP racing. During 1986, following the deck and wing position modifications, the wing endplates were greatly enlarged and were merged with the flanks of the body. Thus the wing was carried by its endplates, although there was still a central support in view of its width. The cooler air exits in the deck were closed off and a triangular cutout in each flank immediately ahead of the rear wheel let air escape. This modification improved the lift:drag ratio.

In 1987 the Electramotive package was characterized further by an unusual rear wing. Whereas the 1986 single-element wing had been mounted well clear of the deck, the distinctive new version had its leading edge at rear wheel arch height. The deck sloped away gently behind the arches, thus the leading edge of the wing was still higher than the trailing edge of the deck. The new wing was two element with a most unusual slotted flap which had an upward and outward curved trailing edge. It was a design by the famed Bernard Pershing, guru of American race car aerofoil design.

By 1987 the Electramotive Nissan, given the right ride height, was capable of generating 7000 lb (3175.2 kg) downforce at a 200 mph – no less than three times its own weight. Of course, Camel GT venues tended to be on the slow side and somewhat rough, given the available power 200 mph was rather optimistic while often the ride height had to be compromised. The lift:drag ratio of the high downforce 1987 car was in the region of 4.0 – 4.5:1, the latter a figure seen by few high downforce late Eighties Sports Prototypes. The Nissan GTP attained its own weight in downforce at around 120 mph.

Aside from the lift:drag ratio, Southgate agrees that these figures quoted by Electramotive were ''well within the realms of possibility'', pointing out that it is feasible to get more than 7000 lb (318 kg) at 200 mph given GTP high drag requirements. We have noted that a Prototype running the style of underwing he devised has around 5000 sq in active: to produce

7000 lb (318 kg) downforce then requires an average pressure reduction of only 1.4 psi at 200 mph – a realistic figure. Southgate doubts the lift:drag ratio but points out that different methods of measurement vary the result to a significant degree.

For 1988 modifications to the Electramotive package were subtle; most obvious being more pronounced tabs or dive planes on the nose, two-tier for slow circuit work and reminiscent of those run by the 1969 Ferrari 312P spyder at Brands Hatch. As usual the car was run with louvres in the front wheel arches and it was fitted with triangular lower sponson projections providing arch infill in the wake of the front wheels. The tunnels went essentially unchanged, the underwing the fruit of 2500 wind tunnel runs over a four year period. Rear wheel sealing plates were tried but showed little benefit while the side skirts had proved not very effective. The 1988 lift:drag ratio was quoted as around 4.5:1 while the aerodynamic split put from 30 per cent to 40 per cent of downforce on the front, according to set up.

Pitch and ride height stability were very important for maximum underwing performance, implying hard springs, but often soft springs had to be fitted for slow corner performance and in the face of frequently bumpy racing surfaces. For example, at Watkins Glen it proved impossible to achieve desired underwing stability. In general, the rear ride height was set a little higher than the front, the downforce tending to pull the tail down. Compared to the rival Jaguar V12 XJR-9 GTP car of 1988, the Nissan's drawback was its aftercooler requirement which had an adverse affect on its lift:drag ratio.

The TWR GTP car was a close relative of the team's contemporary Group C contender, this for logistical reasons. Thus, it shared the existing monocoque base while for 1988 the Group C car was converted to run 17 in (432 mm) rims front and rear in line with GTP regulations. The smaller rear wheels (down from 19 in (482.6 mm) angled out the top of the spring/damper unit which previously had been vertical and buried completely within the taller wheel well.

The TWR Jaguar XJR-9 had tunnels much lower than previous models following a regulation change for 1988. The revised car also ran smaller diameter rear wheels and thus had lower tail wheel arches.

For Group C that was not the disadvantage it might have been in view of the new low tunnel regulation. However, the GTP car could run higher diffuser tunnels and these needed an intrusive blister to clear the top of the angled spring/damper unit.

For both XJR-9 versions the use of 17 in (432 mm) wheels (as employed by the Nissan GTP) allowed a lower rear arch which was to the benefit of drag reduction. To accommodate the 120 litre tank eligible for GTP, the standard XJR-9 monocoque had its rear cockpit bulkhead further forward than had previously been the case. Since 1987 the monocoque floor had been altered so as to allow the tunnels to start further forward, at the back of the mandatory flat-bottom area under the fuel tank. The diffuser was then longer and more gently inclined, though the basic pattern of the underwing was the same and there was a choice of tunnel shape with slot-in panels allowing a shorter diffuser.

Another modification to the original TWR monocoque was a NACA duct-style engine air intake recessed into the roof moulding, this replacing the 1986 funnel inlet and reducing drag. The GTP version of the XJR-9 was, of course, ballasted to 1980 lb (900 kg) in view of the use of a 6.0-litre V12 engine. At Daytona the GTP car ran TWR's regular fast circuit aerodynamic package – as seen at Monza, for example – and the main problem was the conflict between the high tyre pressure needed to run the banking and the loss of traction on the tight infield circuit implied by such pressures. Nevertheless, the car took a memorable victory.

Meanwhile, in Europe the new regulations for 1988 had cut tunnel volume and hence maximum downforce potential. However, Group C cars did not require the greatest possible downforce, rather the right trade off in respect of drag. TWR experience in 1987 had suggested that its car had exceptional downforce at the expense of uncomfortably high drag, that some drag reduction could perhaps be worthwhile. The smaller rear arches were important in this respect.

The enforced lower diffuser tunnels still started under the fuel tank floor, although 4 in (100 mm) further back since they were again taken to the edge of the mandatory flat area. Careful shaping of the revised underwing and careful positioning of the rear wing

would regain much of the downforce cut seen when the 1987 package was tried against the 1988 regulations.

Further, for this level of downforce the lift:drag ratio was better, the car then running faster to the fuel. Southgate and others had found that the best approach to the mandatory lower diffuser tunnel was, effectively, to put a lid on the 1987 tunnel. In other words, the wedge angle was retained but once the new maximum height of 11 in (280 mm) was attained,

The 1987 Mercedes-Sauber C9 was a very strong runner at Le Mans but lacked the development necessary to survive the rigours of the 24 hour race. Sauber also needed time to learn how to set the new car up.

the tunnel roof was made horizontal. The Jaguar was notable for the fact that it maintained its balance well between high and low downforce settings and this characteristic was unaltered.

A similar response to the 1988 regulations was made by Sauber, which had developed a superficially similar underwing. Indeed, since 1987 the Swiss team had carefully copied the TWR approach. In 1988 the fixed-floor-tested Mercedes-Sauber, with its very strong turbo engine, proved the best package when fuel was spent accelerating from low to high speed, such as at Brno or Sandown, while the XJR-9 was superior when fuel was spent overcoming aerodynamic drag.

In general, TWR was hardest hit of all by the low tunnel regulation since it had been exploiting underwing technology best of all. In contrast, Porsche had stood to gain most, lower tunnels suiting its chassis architecture. By 1987 the Lloyd 962C – which gave Porsche its only WEC win of that season away from Le Mans – had been converted to central post-mounted remote rear wing since that allowed the wing to be positioned

for a better working relationship with the underwing. Further, it made for a shorter, lighter tail section which could be further lightened structurally since it was no longer called upon to handle wing loadings.

Nigel Stroud found that the new wing location allowed the car to run more wing without pitching its nose up, spoiling its balance. He also introduced wheel covers which improved the sealing of the underbody region, marginally reduced pressure within the rear wheel arch and marginally reduced form drag. The basic underwing remained to the earlier pattern. The car was also fitted with a more concave nose which was not a Stroud design. With the complete package Stroud reckons the aerodynamic split was in the region 30-70 front-rear, without a nose wing.

In view of the 1988 regulations, Stroud put the usual lid in the diffuser, lowering the wing an appropriate amount. At the front of the car, he countered the effect of the smaller diffuser by a combination of splitter and less pronounced bubble. As more downforce had been found, the Porsche teams had been running progressively stiffer and the consequent reduction in pitch change allowed the introduction of a splitter, which is more pitch sensitive than a funnel inlet.

The splitter allowed the Lloyd 962C to run lower ground clearance – with the funnel type inlet it had been necessary to ensure there was always an adequate tunnel feed. Running the funnel too close to the ground had been liable to cause a sudden stall of the full length central tunnel. Further, adjustment of the splitter proved a useful means of altering front end downforce without having a significant effect on the operation of the underwing.

The history of the development of the 956/962C was about the search for front end grip without spoiling the overall aerodynamic characteristics through the use of a front wing. With the splitter the Lloyd team enjoyed really good front end

The 1988 Richard Lloyd Racing Porsche 962C had a remote rear wing mounted on a single central post. This allowed the car to have a shorter, non-structural hence much lighter tail section.

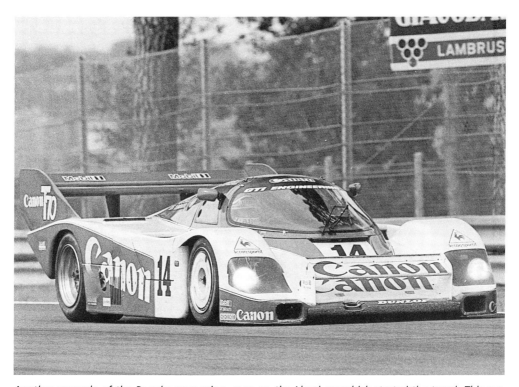

Another example of the Porsche nose wing, seen on the Lloyd car which started the trend. This car also featured a two-element rear wing. The nose wing spoiled the airflow to the tail but reduced understeer.

bite for the first time without a nose wing.

In 1989 there was a slight refinement of the Lloyd car's aerodynamic package after wind tunnel testing at MIRA and at Imperial College with 20 per cent models, this work following an evaluation of the actual car in the Paris-St Cyr full-sized fixed-floor tunnel. The refinement included bevelled bottom corners to the car's flanks to allow TWR-style horizontal side skirts. In its final form the car was measured as having a lift:drag ratio of 4.5:1 with a drag co-efficient less than Cd = 0.5.

Those figures are too good in comparison with those of rivals to take at face value: again different methods of measurement come into play. However, it was clear that much progress had been made over the original 956 Kurz package, though the co-efficient of drag was much higher than the Cd = 0.32 for the low downforce car used in the early Eighties which was not far removed from the Le Mans version. By the late Eighties

the factory Porsche 962Cs were running 3500-4000 lb (1590-1818 kg) downforce at a theoretical 200 mph whereas at the same speed the trick Lloyd car was running over 4000 lb (1818 kg), the XJR-8 over 5000 lb (2272 kg).

Of course, the Electramotive GTP was higher again while the comparative Group C figures were a lot closer at 100 mph than at 200 mph. In reality, 100 mph was regularly seen as a cornering speed, 200 mph (away from Le Mans and its Mulsanne kink) never. For Porsche, lack of front end downforce was a more serious problem than lack of overall downforce. The Lloyd approach was consequently echoed by the other top Porsche teams as the 962C refused to lie down and die in the face of blitz first from the direction of Kidlington, England, then from Porsche's home town.

The Mercedes-Sauber C9 that first appeared in 1987 was essentially a C8 with a revised weight distribution, new suspension and a new approach to

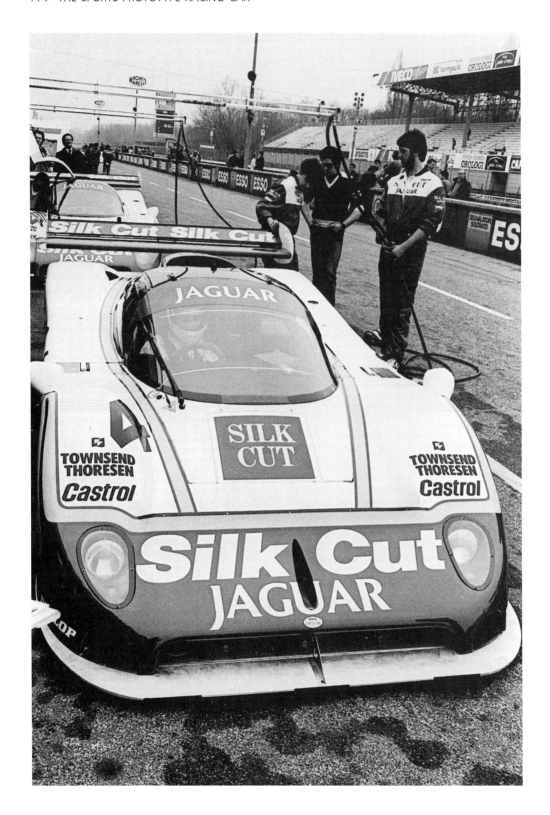

aerodynamics following the lead of the XJR-6. The new aerodynamic package was devised by Leo Ress working with ideas man Paul Pfenninninger on 20 per cent models in the fixed floor Daimler-Benz tunnel. Boundary layer air was sucked from the floor of the tunnel, although this was no substitute for a proper rolling-road facility. Overall, Ress gained 80 per cent more downforce. In so doing he rejected the Porsche-inspired funnel and bubble, filling in the base of the nose and fitting a splitter ahead of a Southgate-pattern underwing which was scavenged by the local effect of a remote single-element wing mounted on a central post.

Thus, the car's belly was flat while the air was channelled into diffuser tunnels with straight outer walls. There were only narrow side skirts in view of the width of the monocoque. The wing carried small endplates and a Gurney and slightly overlapped the deck, from which it was kept clear, exceeding the height of the rear arches, which were tall enough to accommodate 19 in (482.6 mm) rims. A spoiler was fitted to the tail: this was found to stabilise the car in the wet without adversely affecting its performance in the dry. The car retained a nose radiator with hot air exhausted over the windscreen behind a concave panel. NACA ducts in the flanks of the car fed twin aftercoolers, one for each turbo.

The 1987 season was a learning year for Sauber, finding out how to get the best out of the car in terms of pitch and ride height in particular. At the end of the year the 20 per cent model went back into the same tunnel to investigate refinements to the package and in spite of the 1988 regulations Ress says he retained the same level of downforce for 10 per cent less drag. Outwardly there was no obvious change aside from the lower diffusers. Two lengths of splitter were provided, rated fast-circuit and slow-circuit while the wing angle was the crucial tuning device at the track.

A new nose with a cut-down concave panel was introduced mid-way through the 1988 season. This caused a marginal deterioration in cooling efficiency but improved the airflow to the rear wing. For 1989 it was the original intention to phase in a new C11 design with aerodynamics developed in a rolling road tunnel but in practice complications with that car's carbon fibre composite chassis delayed its début until 1990. However, Ress was able to tweak the C9 aerodynamic package in the light of C11 studies and track testing.

An obvious external change was to the bodywork around the front wheels. The shape of the arch was modified with a wedge-shaped extension at the front of the sponson, following Nissan GTP practice. This modification would not have shown up in fixed floor modelling since it related to the rotation of the tyre. Another detail improvement was a fairing of the wing's attachment to its post. Otherwise, essentially the 1988 package was carried forward as most work went into the C11 and the C9 Le Mans package.

The Sauber had a lift:drag ratio assumed to be better than 4:1 but figures were suspect due to the fixed floor tunnel. Little value was found from rear wheel covers in the tunnel so these were not employed, given considerations of pit stop access and brake cooling. The major change to the car during 1989 was a modified nose to fully conceal the radiator in plan view, as per the regulations. This added a little drag since the rear wing no longer worked so well.

Of course, in 1989 the C9 was hugely successful, in spite of its lack of rolling road-designed underwing. Toyota also shunned rolling-road testing. It produced its 1989 car in Japan using full-size models in a fixed-floor in-house tunnel, comparing the results with track test data, reading suspension movement and taking measurements on a special load cell. Nevertheless, the resultant car did not have as sophisticated aerodynamics as those of arch-rival Nissan's new Lola Group C car which Broadley designed using the Cranfield rolling road, and which is described in Section Four.

How much downforce did the top 1988-9 Group C cars exploit? Genuine figures still tend to be a closely guarded secret. The following figures relate to a representative car running the usual XJR-6-inspired aerodynamic package. However, the identity of it must remain secret to protect our informant! Our representative car as tested in model form in a sophisticated rolling road tunnel produced around 4000 lb (1814.4 kg) downforce at 180 mph with 5218 lb (2366.8 kg) downforce at 225 mph.

Not as impressive as the figure quoted for the Nissan GTP but that is to be expected given the low-tunnel ruling and the greater importance of drag in Group C. Our car had a lift:drag ratio of 4.2:1 and its co-efficient of drag was Cd = 0.53. It produced 1742 lb (790.2 kg) downforce at 130 mph – not far off its own weight. Again, we put these figures to Southgate and he feels they are in line with the results he would expect from his own wind tunnel work at Imperial College.

In terms of drag, we can see that our car pulled 952 lb (431.8 kg) at 180 mph and not much over 1000 lb (454 kg) at 200 mph at which speed the Nissan GTP would be pulling 1555.5 lb (705.6 kg). In Group C the challenge was to attain maximum downforce for an acceptable amount of drag. How much was acceptable related to the overall car package and the circuit, and Le Mans demanded less than anywhere else. The problem was, the lower the downforce the harder it was to achieve a high lift:drag ratio. This fact might help explain the inferior lift:drag ratio of our representative car compared to the Nissan GTP, although Southgate feels the GTP figure is unrealistic in any case.

Throughout the Eighties, the story of Group C aerodynamic development was one of improvement in terms of lift:drag ratio rather than ever increasing downforce. As we have seen, back in the early Eighties Southgate's Ford Group C car could produce 4000 lb (1818 kg) downforce at 200 mph but with a lift:drag ratio of 3.3:1 hence drag at that speed of 1212.1 lb (549.8 kg) compared to the 952 lb (432.7 kg) of our late Eighties car when running 4000 lb (1818 kg) downforce. In essence, over the decade the drag load lightened, consequently the cars could run more

power for a given amount of fuel.

In terms of aerodynamic split, our representative car had 44 per cent of its downforce at the front axle, though this split was easy to alter by playing with the various options within the package and up to 50-50 was possible without greatly compromising the overall lift and drag figures. Although the maximum air acceleration and hence the lowest local underbody pressure was experienced as the air rushed into the diffuser tunnels, as we observed in the case of the XJR-6, the overall effect of the aerodynamic package of a car with this type of underwing was to locate the centre of pressure much further forward than that. At least 30 per cent of the downforce was on the front and clearly a higher percentage was typical.

We also noted that the height of the rear wing in relation to the diffuser exits and the deck affected the location of the centre of pressure. Lowering the wing relative to the deck put more emphasis upon its role as a tunnel extractor and drawing more air from the underbody put more downforce on the front of the car. Taken to extremes, there was a danger of over-extraction pulling the nose down too far for comfort.

On the other hand, putting more emphasis upon the use of the wing as a downforce producer in its own right moved the centre of pressure back at the cost of higher drag. Southgate notes that lack of front end downforce was an inherent problem of Prototypes throughout the Eighties. In terms of general approach, he tried to get too much on the front, then backed off.

Some cars favoured a rear spoiler, which created a little extra pressure over the body as a whole. The spoiler had the advantage of not being sensitive to pitch to any great degree. Further, like the wing it helped draw air from the tunnels. It was commonly run by Porsches. It is clear why the nose wing did not catch on. It was a fix for the 956/962C which had an inherently poor aerodynamic split in its traditional guise.

The nose wing which appeared briefly on the XJR-6 was to help overcome an early problem with mechanical grip caused by the weight distribution difficulties posed by a long, heavy and top heavy engine. The nose wing clearly spoiled the entire airflow over the car and played no part in an efficient package since by spoiling the airflow to the rear wing that in turn adversely affected the operation of the underwing.

As we have noted, everything on the car that had an aerodynamic effect influenced everything else. It is worth pointing out that even nose overhang had an importance influence on front end downforce. The bubble is an interesting device, not seen in Southgate's work but appearing on cars such as the new 1989 Nissan and Toyota designs both of which featured a TWR Jaguar-style underwing. Unlike Southgate, Broadley championed the bubble in the mid to late Eighties and a muted bubble was even evident on the 1989 Nissan Le Mans car.

Why a bubble? Clearly it creates a short primary underwing, theoretically producing additional downforce at the front. Equally as significant, the bubble shortens the length of the main throat which is then less likely to choke as the wedge-shaped boundary layer thickens and is logically less pitch-sensitive. It is also worth noting that it provides the underwing space lost through the intrusion of the front wheels. Further, it can be seen as a form of vortex generator, re-energising the boundary layer as a turbulent flow less inclined towards separation.

Clearly, bubble or no bubble, the form of nose entry is important, the splitter being the popular choice. However, Electramotive made a form of understated funnel-type inlet work as an alternative frontal feed to the flat belly-type underwing while also employing side skirts. The funnel was less pitch-sensitive than the splitter (which might be cut right back for fast circuits) but required more ride height. Running a funnel might cost a little pressure at the front.

The overall nose form was another important consideration. Aside from the trick Porsches, cars running a splitter tended to have a front radiator. However, teams employing a splitter without a nose radiator included Mazda and Cougar, both of which opted for an air dam-type nose. Nissan went for an air dam plus a funnel but the increasing use of dive planes on the car suggest that a splitter might have worked better. Suzuka moved towards a splitter for his all-new 1990 car, which had a front radiator.

Teams running splitters invariably had at least two lengths to chose from, aside from a Le Mans option. The splitter length affected the pressure created on its top surface. The wing had to be the other key method of juggling the aerodynamics, aside from considerations of ground clearance and wheel control, although as we have seen TWR developed alternative diffuser entrance profiles. Since the wing was primarily a device to extract air from the underwing the remote wing was appropriate, with the wing/deck/underwing spatial relationship always a crucial consideration. The rear body form was also important. With a fully enclosed car it was possible to enhance the operation of the wing through manipulation of its feed whereas a single-seater's fuselage was merely a nuisance.

Thus, shaping of the superstructure and the deck had to recognise the general aim of drag reduction and the requirements of the wing. It was noticeable in the wet at Francorchamps in 1988 that the Sauber C9 got dirty on its cockpit roof, its high rear arches and the upper surface of its wing, whereas its dorsum remained shiny silver. Was the air separating at the back of the cockpit then re-attaching itself to the wing? Boundary layer separation can be a temporary phenomenon if the flow conditions are right.

We have seen how wheel arch size played an important role in drag reduction, this effect less through reduction of frontal area than through enhanced feed to the wing. Indeed, Nissan found smaller front arches – which affected the frontal area not at all – reduced drag through enhancing the flow to the rear of the car. The question of drag reduction is considered at greater length in the following chapter.

A lot of less obvious items affected lift and drag to a surprising degree. For example, in 1988 TWR converted the XJR-9 oil cooling system from an oil radiator in its flank to a oil/water heat exchanger. The heat exchanger called for increased water radiator cooling capacity which in turn called for a larger nose inlet. That added a measurable amount of drag. However, sealing the flank added downforce.

A common practice was the provision of louvres in the top of the front wheel arch, this an old practice dating from the Sixties. The louvres provided an air bleed. Pressure within the arch tended to be higher than that above, thanks to the effect of tyre rotation. Balancing the pressures above and below added both downforce and drag. The 1989 Aston Martin AMR1 had a radical aerodynamic package with wedge-shaped sponsons that left the front arches open behind the tyre. That was taking it to extremes.

For the AMR1, other radical measures included an inboard gearbox within a tilted drivetrain designed to allow a single central diffuser upsweep. As seen in 1989, the car was not a success. It had a poor lift:drag ratio. Ray Mallock did some development work which got no further than the wind tunnel due to the premature demise of the project. He was able to cut 25 per cent from the drag while retaining a competitive level of downforce. That illustrates how poor was the original package. An interesting experiment was exhaust activation for the diffuser as the team struggled to make it more efficient. No other team found exhaust activation worthwhile.

As we have seen in the case of the earlier Aston Martin-Nimrod, it was, in principle, desirable to keep the wheel arch as close as possible to the tyre for minimum drag while rear wheel covers could play a major role in the operation of a high downforce underwing as well as reduce drag. Underneath, the aim was to seal as much as possible of the plan area, leaving just enough room for the wheels to operate.

Given that the lateral feed was as important as the nose feed to the operation of the underwing, side skirts

One of the most radical prototypes of the Eighties was the Aston Martin AMR-1 with its engine tilted to allow a single central tunnel and its massive wheel arch vents. It created too much drag.

logically needed to extend right to the tail, XJR-6 style. Horizontal side skirts were an obvious advantage of the Southgate Jaguars which others, with older chassis, found difficult to copy. Another structural consideration was the sheer strength of the aerodynamic surfaces. Diffuser tunnels had to be strong: TWR made them out of carbon fibre composite and used them as part of the chassis.

Compared to a single-seater, the wide body of a prototype ahead of the cockpit area called for additional ground clearance. Further, its bigger plan area made the car inherently more pitch-sensitive. On the other hand, the angle of attack of the flat-bottom area was less critical than that of a contemporary single-seater since the tunnels were less constrained in terms of volume. In general, the bigger the tunnel the more constant the downforce and the more stable the centre of pressure.

Changing the pitch of the car altered the centre of pressure while both the pitch and the ride height affected the operation of the underwing. Ideally, the car wanted to run at the same ride height front and rear throughout its cornering speed range, hence the static rake towards the front. In general, the ride height wanted to be low and the car wanted to be free from pitch change. The driver could feel the difference in a millimetre or so of ride height.

In view of the pitch sensitivity, wheel movement could be restricted to a couple dozen millimetres, half of which could be down to tyre deflection rather than suspension movement. It was a case of running as hard as was feasible. Nissan started out with too little suspension travel on its 1989 Group C car and found it had to make its suspension more supple, more driver-friendly, trading aerodynamic performance for driveability. Further, a car could be run too low, throttling the essential throughflow.

For reasons of ride height control, radials were preferred to crossply tyres, the latter growing at speed. Early on TWR pressed crossply-maker Dunlop for Kevlar ply tyres to help alleviate this problem, and by 1989 the firm had moved to radials. Of course, the problem

of ride height and pitch control has a potential solution in Active or Reactive suspension, the former as used by the 1987 Honda-Lotus of Ayrton Senna. Computer control of wheel movement to maintain an optimum ride height front and rear (and absence of roll if so desired) under all conditions, including braking and accelerating, promised major gains.

Those gains were not realized by Lotus in Formula One. In practice there were logistical problems while it was found that such a large proportion of contemporary Formula One suspension was contributed by tyre-wall flex so that the Lotus Active system only paid off on unusually bumpy circuits. Street circuits were the obvious application for Active and Senna won at Monaco using the system. Given the greater wheel movement required by a wide-bodied Prototype, and the need to alleviate driver fatigue, TWR looked seriously at Lotus Active but the major stumbling block was finance.

As Southgate put it to Allan Staniforth: "The Jaguar is almost antique compared to computer control. I tried to buy Lotus Active on behalf of TWR but they wanted a million pounds or something for the principles, let alone buying the hardware." Of course, IMSA's bumpy circuits presented an even greater case for Active and following the acquisition of Lotus by GM, the Active system appeared on the GTP Corvette. Alas, by 1987 the Corvette project was on the way out and the experiment did not last.

Aside from set-up, there is that crucial question of the trade-off between lift and drag. Downforce can get a car around the corners quicker but there is no point in that if the cost in drag is such that the fuel will run out before the end of the race. IMSA regulations did not make fuel consumption of paramount importance, hence high downforce was the characteristic of the GTP car, particularly in view of many slow circuits. In view of that, Nissan did not bring its GTP car to Le Mans after all, not wishing to make the mistake that Jaguar had made with the XJR-5.

Low drag was a major consideration in Group C. The underwing, as we have noted, is more efficient as a means of producing downforce than the conventional aerofoil, hence lift:drag ratio can only be optimized through ground effect technology. However, striking the right balance between lift and drag is another matter altogether and in the final analysis it can come down to some very subtle trade-offs.

Part of the overall equation is the trade-off between the engine intake and car drag. An engine wants cool, high-pressure (hence dense) air and even a turbocharged engine can benefit from receiving pressurized air at the compressor eye, for then the turbo has an easier time and back pressure is less for a given level of boost. Air for the intake has to be taken from a high-pressure region – too many Prototype engines have been starved of air at high rpm, particularly on the Mulsanne.

In the case of the turbo, charge cooling is a major consideration which has an even more significant impact upon drag. It is also worth noting that the entire airflow across the car will be warmed by a nose radiator. It is not only the charge and the engine coolant and lubrication that have to be cool but also the brakes, sometimes the shock absorbers and always the driver.

At the front, the collection of air to cool the brakes is straightforward but the air still has to be properly ducted to the eye of the disc through the upright. At the rear, air collection is a greater problem, particularly where carbon-carbon discs are employed and snorkel-type intakes are often favoured, these projecting through the rear deck. Wheel covers add another dimension to the problem and TWR found it had to fit a NACA-type duct into its covers to avoid excessive brake and wheel bearing heat.

Cooling the driver can be equally as demanding, particularly where the car

Brake cooling ducts typically were of the periscope type at the rear, reaching up through the deck to collect cool air. This air was then ducted down through the upright to the centre of the disc.

has a nose radiator. With a well enclosed tail such as that of an effective ground-effect car, a lot of heat is retained in the engine bay and this tends to make the cockpit a very hot environment. TWR put silver foil on its rear tub bulkhead to reflect heat away from the fuel tank and cockpit. The problem is not new – Porsche had a serious cockpit temperature worry with its 917, the drivers having to wear special cool suits. However, when the back was opened up to form the 917K a much cooler working environment was created while the reduction in engine bay temperature was considered a major gain in terms of reliability.

Where a car has a nose radiator the cockpit cooling intake has to be arranged ahead of the radiator and this led to the distinctive central scoop on the Sauber C9. However, experience has shown that no amount of cold air collection will be truly effective unless provision is made for a cockpit through-flow. Since air is reluctant to climb to a higher pressure the appropriate air outlet must be provided where there is a zone of suitably low pressure: perhaps over the driver's head, as observed in Chapter One.

Chapter Nine

Target 250 mph

When Bernd Rosemeyer became the first man to exceed 250 mph on the public road in the fully enclosed, mid-engined 1937 Auto Union he had at his disposal 545 bhp while the slippery shape of his car can be illustrated by a drag co-efficient of less than Cd = 0.3. Rosemeyer's speed was highly impressive when one considers that the 1988 Peugeot-WM had a comparable frontal area and a drag co-efficient claimed to be as low as Cd = 0.28 yet required in excess of 800 bhp to become the first car to break 250 mph (400 km/h) on a French highway. Of course, it can be misleading to try to compare the drag of two cars half a century apart with any degree of accuracy.

What is certain is that when Auto Union shot for speeds close to the Land Speed Record on Germany's new autobahns, its tortoise-shell car had very little drag and no downforce. Indeed, it tended to go light at speed, while instability in the face of crosswinds appears to have been the root of Rosemeyer's tragic accident in 1938. The Peugeot-WM had a muted ground effect underwing and created a significant amount of downforce at 250 mph helping it negotiate the Mulsanne kink. Induced drag came into the equation, as it did for the Mercedes-Sauber and Toyota, both of which ran over 250 mph (400 kph) on the *Ligne Droit des Hunaudières* in 1989.

The Sauber C9 enjoyed 820 bhp, the Toyota 950 bhp, neither having a drag co-efficient anywhere near as good as that claimed for the WM P87. In fact, Toyota claimed a drag co-efficient of Cd = 0.43 with a lift:drag ratio of 3.2:1. Both those figures are high for a late Eighties Le Mans package and the Toyota was far from typical. It pulled a lot of downforce. By Le Mans standards the Japanese machine had high drag and high downforce but then it could afford to run a lot of downforce with so much power at its disposal. Like that of WM, its claimed drag number was a measure from a fixed-floor tunnel.

Running low downforce for high Mulsanne speed is only part of the Le Mans compromise. The Peugeot-WM set a new record for *Mesures de vitesse instantanée* on the *Ligne Droit des Hunaudières* but was left behind around the rest of the circuit. The Toyota was quick around the entire lap but burned a lot of fuel. The lower downforce Sauber was more typical of a late Eighties Le Mans package. The Sauber was designed to be fuel-efficient with a view to winning the race; the Toyota was a pole position special.

With Group C power levels generally in the region of 750-800 bhp, top speeds in the vicinity of 230 mph were commonplace towards the end of the Eighties. Lower power in the mid-Eighties saw a record speed in 1985 of 231 mph – and that was the first time the 230 mph barrier had been broken

The 1987 Jaguar XJR-8 in Sprint and Le Mans guise. Note the difference between this and the Le Mans package fielded in 1986 as illustrated in Chapter Seven. Again, there was no splitter at Le Mans.

since 1978. It was a speed clocked by a 650 bhp Porsche-Cougar, a Le Mans special with a narrow track for a low frontal area.

At 230 mph the Le Mans version of the typical 1987-9 Group C car would produce at least one and a half times its own weight, often more. It is worth emphasizing that a high lift: drag ratio – better than 2.5:1 – is relatively hard to achieve given this low downforce set-up. A lift:drag ratio of 2.5:1 for a fuel-efficient, low drag package at Le Mans is good, anything higher is excellent; whereas elsewhere 4.0:1 is good, anything higher is excellent.

Let us go back to our aforementioned representative Group C car. This had a drag co-efficient of Cd = 0.41 in Le Mans trim and ran 237 mph given 700 bhp at the rear wheels – say 750 bhp at the flywheel – at which speed it produced just over 4000 lb (1814 kg) of downforce: twice its own weight.

Southgate accepts that figure is realistic given a speed of 240 mph, which Jaguar ran. Of course, that was downforce well in excess of what was required to keep its feet planted firmly on the tarmac. It was as much as it saw in regular high-downforce trim on most circuits. For

Mulsanne running it represented unnecessary induced drag: that was the penalty of the minimum downforce required to get from Mulsanne corner back to Terte Rouge at an adequate rate.

Let us compare our representative car in its compromise Le Mans package more closely with its regular sprint trim. In the last chapter we noted that it had a drag co-efficient of Cd = 0.53 in high-downforce guise and a lift:drag ratio of 4.2:1 and put 44 per cent of its downforce over its front wheels.

In Le Mans trim we find our car, with its drag co-efficient of Cd = 0.41, having a lift:drag ratio of 3.7:1 – such an excellent Le Mans ratio our informant was moved to double-check it. Southgate does not accept that it can have been so high but suggests the drag co-efficient is high. More realistic was the fact that our car put 30 per cent of its downforce over its front wheels. That percentage could be decreased without upsetting the overall fuel efficiency, but could not be increased without resort to higher drag settings.

Given the same power as Rosemeyer's car – 545 bhp (say, a 3.9-litre Cosworth DFL) – we can calculate that this representative 1988-9 Group C car would run to 220 mph. The rolling road model tests tell us that at 220 mph this Le Mans package would produce approximately 3500 lb (1587.6 kg) downforce, hence 946 lb (429.1 kg) drag. Of course, the fact that Rosemeyer's car would be significantly faster is down to its lack of induced drag. Running the same power, Rosemeyer would have pulled comfortably ahead of this hypothetical DFL version of our representative Group C car on top speed but he would have had a real problem at the Mulsanne kink.

Playing with figures and history aside, it is obvious how Eighties Sports Prototypes got into trouble with excessive downforce on the Mulsanne, just as lack of downforce had been a threat in the Thirties. We referred earlier to the porpoising of the Rondeau M.482 design on the Mulsanne. According to the factory, this machine had a drag co-efficient of Cd = 0.35 and, fitted with the 3.9-litre version of the Cosworth DFL, the factory calculated a theoretical top speed of 222 mph.

Of course, that speed equates to the theoretical speed run by our representative car given the same engine. In fact, Rondeau was misled by fixed-floor wind tunnel testing by Max Sardou and found excessive downforce on the Mulsanne: quite how much is anyone's guess. It could have been anything from two to three times the car's own weight. The 1986 XJR-6 in virtual Monza/Silverstone trim started porpoising at around 190 mph on the Mulsanne at which speed it must have been producing well over twice its own weight in downforce.

Porpoising is only one drawback of excessive downforce. Most serious is general component stress. Peter Sauber suffered more than most from Mulsanne dramas in the Eighties, first with the 1985 somersault then with the shock 1988 withdrawal following Michelin tyre failures. The somersault is thought to have been caused by downforce pulling the undertray of the car loose. The car took off at the Mulsanne brow (soon after the kink) and, although it landed back on its wheels, damage was too heavy to reveal the true cause of the

Large tunnels for the Rondeau M.482 bearing the hallmark of Max Sardou, also responsible for the BMW M1/C. The car produced excessive downforce at speed on the Mulsanne.

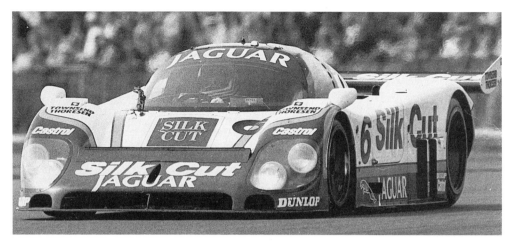

The Le Mans winning Jaguar XJR-8 featured a sophisticated aerodynamic package designed to strike the optimum balance of downforce and drag for the special demands of the French circuit.

incident. Likewise, the 1988 tyre failures were not necessarily due to excessive downforce loading but there the finger of suspicion points.

The Mulsanne had been resurfaced and the new surface was proving more abrasive while the loss of bumps was providing more downforce. A number of competitors were finding tyres hot and blistering, including TWR which was able to control the problem only by raising the pressure in its Dunlops. Meanwhile, Sauber had seen high temperatures on its Michelin rubber and one car blew a tyre just after the brow, thankfully without crashing. Since Michelin could give no reassurance that the problem would not recur, the team withdrew.

Leo Ress reported that subsequent runs over a load cell on the Michelin test track suggested that the level of downforce should not have been high enough to cause tyre overload. However, it was significant that the following year the C9's downforce was carefully trimmed back to a limit set by Michelin. Thus, in effect, the danger of stress on the Mulsanne effectively set the limit on the amount of downforce that could be run elsewhere on the circuit. Nowhere would a moveable aerodynamic device be more useful than at Le Mans. Without it, a low drag compromise is safest.

On the other side of the coin is the benefit of low drag in terms of improved fuel consumption. "Langheck development was always for fuel consumption," Ferdinand Piech said of the 917 programme and the fuel economy gain was the prime reason for the low-drag LM versions of the TWR cars, as we have seen. The 1987 version was designed to have its centre of pressure further back, the 1986 car having been too darty on the Mulsanne. Of course, this implies less downforce on the front end. With its classic 20-80 weight distribution, the Porsche 956 put plenty of feathers on the arrow but a high degree of understeer was the unwanted by-product of that.

The 1987 XJR-8LM had an angled drivetrain to avoid working its driveshafts through an angle (in the interest of cv joint longevity) and a revised aerodynamic package that featured a shorter tail and a long-chord single-element wing at deck height. In spite of its outward appearance, the air saw the 1987 car as a long-tail car, the wing size and position reducing drag in Langheck fashion while working as an underwing air extractor. The net result was a slight gain in downforce following some underwing refinements, yet a 13 per cent drag reduction.

The following year there was a further improvement thanks to the smaller rear arches while the smaller rear wheels also did away with the need to angle the powertrain, which had made the car more of a handful to drive through the corners. It had also been found to lack downforce to tackle the Porsche curves in particular, so Southgate amended this for 1988 with subtle alterations. The lower arches were only one of perhaps two dozen alterations to the 1987 package, few very visible.

In 1987 TWR had found it had fuel to spare, so on the face of it Southgate could afford to give the drivers a little more grip. In round figures, however, Southgate found 13 per cent more downforce while achieving a further 5 per cent drag reduction. Given the small tunnel central to his LM package he was unaffected by the 1988 regulation changes while he retained the long-tail effect of the wing at deck height, merging the under- and over-body flows without boundary layer separation. It was the details which differed, aside from the obvious return of wheel covers, left off the 1987 package. That was significant, as were ongoing changes to ducting drag, the often overlooked component of the lift:drag ratio.

That was one approach to a Le Mans package, another was to run a shorter-chord single-element wing higher than the deck. It should be noted that lowering a wing to deck height was not, in itself, a means to produce a good Le Mans package. According to the characteristics of the overall package, lowering a standard wing could create too much downforce at the front and/or could cost revs.

That much was established by empirical means: not all teams could afford costly wind tunnel programmes. Extensive rolling road wind tunnel testing by Mazda suggested that the Southgate approach was particularly effective but that the shorter-chord higher-wing alternative could be make to work well. Mazda followed TWR and found useful additional Mulsanne speed without loss of pace elsewhere on the circuit. Meanwhile, Sauber continued to exploit the shorter-chord wing option and Porsche refined its regular long-tail package.

The classic Porsche underwing was more effective at Le Mans than in sprint trim, given the usual widening of the throat area. The refined version that Porsche created for the 1988 Le Mans race was a match for the Jaguar XJR-8LM with similar drag and similar downforce. Thus, downforce was in the region of 1800 lb (816.5 kg) at 180 mph rising

towards 4000 lb (1814.5 kg) at 240 mph while the lift:drag ratio was around 2.5:1, hence top speed Mulsanne drag was around 1600 lb (725.7 kg). Following the early withdrawal of Sauber the race was TWR versus the Porsche factory team: it was closely run.

Following its unhappy experience at Le Mans in 1988, Sauber conducted tests of its usual 20 per cent model and a full sized replica in Daimler-Benz fixed floor wind tunnels trying different wing sizes and positions. In the end it decided to put its regular single-element wing as high and as far back as possible while producing shallower tunnels and modifying the splitter. The wing was set at almost zero angle of attack and the regular splitter was replaced by a

Porsche produced a revised long tail for late-Eighties Le Mans races, one that offered low drag with adequate downforce. The Le Mans 962C was a tough rival for Jaguar in 1987 and 1988.

wooden rubbing strip that did not project further than the nose. The spoiler came off the tail and regular air bleed holes in the front arches were concealed.

According to tunnel readings, the lift:drag ratio was better than 3:1, whereas the regular car had a lift:drag ratio better than 4:1. The co-efficient of drag was not disclosed. With the high speed attained at Le Mans, Ress notes that the influence of pitch was more important than ever and the car ran the angle of rake identified as optimum in the fixed-floor tunnel testing. The upshot was that 250 mph clocking but while the C9 could keep up with the Toyota Q-car on the straight, with less downforce, hence less grip and less power, it was not as quick around the lap. Of course, the race was another matter altogether.

Aside from the Toyota, another

powerful Japanese challenger at Le Mans in 1989 was the Nissan-Lola with its 800 bhp V8 turbo engine. The Nissan was a relative of the Electramotive GTP but was all-new and designed specifically for Group C. It had a combination of nose radiator and mid-mounted aftercoolers, the latter having intakes alongside the windscreen in familiar GTP-fashion. Underneath was a conventional late-Eighties underwing headed by a splitter and with unusual side skirts in the form of a lip at the base of a carefully sculptured lower flank indent.

Like Jaguar's 1988 winner the low drag Le Mans version of the Nissan RC89 had rear wheel covers and it had both front and rear wheel horizontal sealing plates at Le Mans. With a high lift: drag ratio harder to achieve at Le Mans, Nissan saw the covers as beneficially reducing drag.

Early-Eighties WM with narrow track and flat bottom and powerful turbo engine had high Mulsanne speed. Note the faired-in rear wheels, helping minimise drag, a technique followed by TWR.

Compared to its regular car, the diffuser tunnels were lower and started some 9.8 in (250 mm) further back, while the wing was lower. The wing was a single-element aerofoil with an intermediate chord length while the splitter did not project beyond the length of the nose but a low bubble was retained.

The short tunnel's later start moved the centre of pressure back in spite of the low wing but this shift was found not to be enough: the wing had to come up to get the centre of pressure far enough back. The RC89 put 32 per cent of its downforce on the front wheels with the wing height originally intended and according to tests at Cranfield produced approximately 2400 lb (1090 kg) downforce at 200 mph whereas the sprint machine enjoyed over 4000 lb (1818 kg) at the same speed. At 240 mph on the Mulsanne the Nissan apparently experienced 2900 lb (1318 kg) of largely unwanted downforce.

We do not know how much downforce was experienced almost a decade earlier by the fastest car of 1980, the Peugeot-WM. Certainly very little. Running 500 bhp this flat-bottom device (carrying a splitter and a small single-element rear wing) clearly enjoyed untypically low drag, partly due to its narrow track, and was fastest of all on the Mulsanne at 217 mph. By 1984 its V6 turbo engine was up to 600 bhp and that year driver Dorchy passed the Lancia of Bob Wollek to take the lead on the Mulsanne early in the race, exploiting a top speed officially as high as 227 mph. Of course, the following year the similarly narrow track Porsche-Cougar replied with almost 10 per cent more power and 231 mph.

By 1986 WM had found its way to a helping of well over 600 bhp and it duly replied to Cougar with a speed of 232 mph, higher than any previous official record, although the 917 Langheck of 1971 had gone 240 mph unofficially. However, that was not the 1986 record – a Joest Porsche went 233 mph with a similar power level. Joest had not beaten the Porsche factory at Le Mans in 1985 by standing still on the Mulsanne!

At this stage, with 230 mph to its credit, WM set about Project 400. A new car was conceived; low, low drag its

aim – without loss of directional stability. Peugeot agreed to sponsor wind tunnel time for the team and 10 per cent models were evaluated at St Cyr. A longer-wheelbase, wider-track car was conceived, the additional width to provide arch overhang – shades of the Porsche 917/20 of 1971. The aim of the overhang was to allow partial enclosure of the front wheels and to reduce interference between the flow along the sides of the car and the air whipped around by wheel rotation. The rear wheels were fully concealed.

The internal ducting was ingenious. WM required a good deal of cooler surface given the horsepower it planned to extract from its V6 turbo engine. Air was taken in at the nose, was channelled over the front arches and then fed through mid-mounted coolers. The hot air was then invited to escape through a central exit in the dorsum, where the flow over the superstructure had detached, hence there was low pressure.

The new car carried a low-downforce underwing to keep it planted on the track (particularly at the kink) plus a short-chord aerofoil just above deck height, primarily acting as a trim tab. The nose and underwing were of the TWR Jaguar pattern. Careful massaging of this package registered a drag co-efficient of Cd = 0.26/28 (according to wing angle) in the fixed-floor Parisian tunnel. The car produced no more than 1100 lb (500 kg) downforce.

An alternative higher-downforce package was evaluated for 1989 with a new underwing, a new wing and 7 in (180 mm) overhang added to the front, taken from the rear. With a drag figure of Cd = 0.38/0.41 this gave twice the downforce, running only to 225 mph. This was still a low figure by even Le Mans standards, and offering a lift:drag ratio no better than 2.4:1.

In 1987, with more boost and more revs than in 1986, the Project 400 Peugeot engine was coaxed to give 850 bhp. Dorchy ran 217.9 mph at the Le Mans weekend – the speed our aforementioned representative Le Mans car would have run given Rosemeyer's 545 bhp. Of course, our baseline car had very sophisticated, rolling road wind tunnel-developed aerodynamics – and its

545 bhp performance was unproven.

Out there rattling the shutters of the *Restaurant des Hunaudières*, Dorchy knew he had plenty more to come. He did some more sorting on the Bugatti circuit a few weeks later, then took the car to a six-kilometre stretch of unopened autoroute between St Quentin and Rheims. This time François Migault drove. He took the controls for a single run on a moist surface under threatening dark clouds in front of French TV cameras. He watched the digital speed read out climb to 242 mph (390 km/h) then concentrated on driving. The car flashed through WM's police radar at 258 mph (416 km/h). ''It was easy, the car felt very safe'', Migault told his audience.

Subsequently Dorchy ran 250 mph (404 km/h) on the Michelin test track where there was a one-kilometre straight followed by a fast turn. In Wednesday qualifying at Le Mans there were engine bothers but on Thursday the team clocked 252 mph (407 km/h). Mission accomplished? Not according to the officials who registered only 236 mph (381 km/h) as Dorchy howled through the speed trap on full boost and maximum revs at 7.38 pm.

Dorchy told the author the behaviour of the car was ''acceptable but not comfortable'' since it had drifted across the road somewhat, which it had not done on the autoroute. Understandably, he found it necessary to lift for the kink. His attempt to go for an official 248 mph

The late-Eighties WM was specifically targeted at 250 mph (400 km/h). It had extremely low drag with a muted ground-effect underwing to ensure stability in the Mulsanne kink.

(400 km/h) clocking was thwarted on Saturday by an early engine detonation problem, similar to that which knocked out a number of top Porsches. The common factor was the fuel supply.

Thus, 236 mph (381 km/h) stood as a new record. However, the Porsches and Jaguars were not far behind. WM immediately began construction of a second car, this having modified rear suspension for a lower and wider diffuser package. The engine was coaxed to produce around 900 bhp. In qualifying for the 1988 race Dorchy went 252 mph (407 km/h) according to the information recorded by the ECU log. The official radar did not acknowledge that. Between qualifying and the race a more accurate radar system was introduced.

Again engine problems intervened. However, the radar was registering 244-5 mph (394-6 km/h) when the car was running. The team was duly informed. Dorchy turned up the boost in response. Thankfully, at last he got an official endorsement of the conclusion of his project: 251 mph (405 km/h).

On target.

PART TWO

MOTIVE POWER

Chapter Ten

The Famous Five

Five very different engines shared the major honours in Eighties World Championship and IMSA Prototype racing: the Chevrolet V8, the Porsche flat 6, the Jaguar V12, the Mercedes V8 and the Nissan V6. All were stock block engines and the Chevrolet and Jaguar engines had their roots in the mid-Fifties. The unsophisticated pushrod 5- to 6-litre Small Block Chevrolet had grown into an American motorsport institution, primarily due to the availability of aftermarket parts. It was possible to build a full race version via a mail order catalogue and on American high-octane fuel as permitted by IMSA it was a durable competition option.

That much had been demonstrated by its use in the most popular competition on the North American continent, NASCAR Grand National Stock Car Racing which had downsized in the Seventies, forcing a switch from 7-litre engines to smaller units such as the 358 cu in Small Block. Running a single four-barrel carburettor and 107 octane fuel, on a 14:1 compression ratio the late Seventies NASCAR dominating 358 cu in Chevrolet V8 produced approximately 620 bhp at 7750 rpm.

For a pushrod V8 engine 8000 rpm was reckoned to be about the limit due to valve train inertia, with 7000 rpm the level for long-distance running. NASCAR's success in running the Small Block for three to four hours at 7,000 rpm was one of the factors that had influenced the way IMSA had created its GTP class. IMSA had always championed the cause of the amateur racer. So it was that GTP regulations welcomed the Small Block and a Bosch mechanically injected 350 cu in version nestled in the back of Lola's trailblazing GTP car, the prototype T600 of 1981.

The Small Block race engine was based on a 90° vee linerless iron block essentially unchanged since its introduction in 1955, aside from four-bolt main bearing caps. Extending from deck to crank axis, the block was of compact and relatively lightweight design running a short, stiff five-bearing crank. Plain bearings were run throughout and as standard the steel crank was of two-plane configuration with extended counterbalance webs for primary and secondary balance, at the expense of exhaust-pulse tuning potential compared to a flat-plane crank. Flat cranks were, however, available from factory and aftermarket sources.

The stock Chevrolet con rod was of typical I-section but the most popular race engine rod was the H-section steel Carrillo rod. The piston was attached by a conventional steel gudgeon pin, retained via circlips. Typically the semi slipper-type piston was an aftermarket forging – from the likes of Diamond Racing and TRW – with three rings, these often supplied by Sealed Power and the top ring Moly coated. The desire for a high compression ratio often saw a dome

The Pontiac V8 was a re-badged version of the classic Chevrolet Small Block. Its push rod operation restricted engine speed to less than 8000 rpm.

on the piston crown, reaching up into the classic wedge-shaped combustion chamber with its side-by-side valves and extensive squish area.

Head design and preparation was reckoned to be the key to Small Block performance. For GTP the stock iron casting could be replaced by an aluminium aftermarket item. Most aluminium two-valve race heads followed the general pattern of the stock head, perhaps with an angled plug and invariably with enlarged ports. Heads were attached by 17 studs with a steel shim gasket at the block interface.

The single camshaft ran deep in the valley of the block and operated the valves (often titanium) through traditional pushrods and rockers. Valve train inertia being a major consideration, lightweight tubular steel pushrods and machined aluminium rockers were employed. Roller lifters replaced the stock hydraulic items while the rockers were also of the roller type and were carried on needle bearings, sometimes shaft-mounted, whereas stock heads carried rockers on individual studs with ball joints. Invariably at least two springs were run, together with an appropriate titanium retainer.

The camshaft was chain-driven on the stock engine (from the front). Some race engine builders preferred the precision of a gear drive whereas others sought the cushioning effect of a chain, and chain drives were highly developed. Dry sump systems were likewise available from many aftermarket sources. Usually there was a scavenge pump for either end of the crankcase plus a single pressure pump. Ignition was of the CD type for serious racing, supplied by the factory, with crank trigger and conventional distributor.

With his injected Chevrolet, Redman swept aside the massed ranks of Porsche 935s to clinch the 1981 Camel GT crown. The following year's Champion John Paul Junior used a Small Block-T600 for the sprint races while 1983 Champion Al Holbert used one before an alternative

Porsche- March 83G was ready. Holbert had the Porsche 962 for 1984 but before that was up to speed Randy Lanier had taken an unassailable points lead in yet another 350 cu in Small Block V8 GTP car, the Blue Thunder Chevrolet-March 84G.

By the mid-Eighties the 3.2-litre Porsche turbo engine was starting to get a firm grip on GTP racing and Chevrolet enthusiasts looked in vain for a new turbocharged engine to continue the fight. Porsche's GTP engine was almost as old as the Small Block, having its roots in the classic Porsche 901 engine of the early Sixties, which in turn had been influenced by the VW Beetle. The Beetle was, of course, a product of the Porsche Design Office and the 901 retained its characteristic boxer configuration and air cooling.

The original 901 road car engine displaced 2.0 litres and was very light with aluminium crankcase, cylinders (carrying iron liners) and heads. The crankcase was split vertically and carried individual cylinders and heads, the separate heads on each side joined by a magnesium cam box. This carried a sohc chain driven off the front end from a layshaft running under the relatively high mounted crankshaft and geared to it. The short layshaft was supported by two bearings and a shaft was screwed into the back of it to drive the oil pump which was situated at the back of the centrally scavenged sump.

Each camshaft actuated two valves per cylinder through rockers to allow the valves to be disposed either side of the cylinder axis in a hemispherical combustion chamber. The piston crown was domed to match (with light valve clearance notches) forming a classic orange peel chamber. Ignition was via a single plug per cylinder while each cylinder was fed through its own Solex carburettor. The inlet manifold fed down into the head with the exhaust tucked underneath the engine.

Conventional reciprocating parts drove an eight-bearing steel crankshaft, each con rod having its own crankpin and there being an additional bearing to steady the layshaft drive gear and to provide an oil feed to the crankshaft. On the nose of the crankshaft was a pulley which drove the belt powering the fan which had the alternator mounted in its hub. The fan was vertically mounted ahead of the cylinders with glassfibre ducting to direct air to the barrels and the generously finned heads, VW Beetle style.

The Porsche flat six was designed to be rugged and to allow for future capacity increases. As early as 1966 a derivative was powering the marque's Sports Prototype racer, the 2.0-litre Carrera 6. This featured chrome plated bores allowing all-aluminium cylinders and also had a lightweight magnesium crankcase, as later used for 911 road cars. Its stock heads were ported and were fitted with larger valves while it also had a higher compression ratio (10.3:1), forged pistons and titanium con rods. With a tuned exhaust, two plugs per cylinder and high pressure mechanical injection (from a six plunger Bosch-Kugelfischer pump) it produced 220 bhp.

The six-cylinder Sports Prototypes soon gave way to larger capacity eight-, then twelve-cylinder contenders, the latter the famous Type 917 which was a 180° vee rather than a boxer to minimize pumping losses. Nevertheless, in the Seventies turbocharging gave the 901 engine a new lease of life. The first 2.1-litre turbo engine surfaced in 1974 as an alternative to a 3.0-litre four-valve water-cooled head atmo engine.

The so-called ATL engine had Nikasil cylinders bolted to its magnesium crankcase and a Bosch CD system firing twin plugs, but otherwise retained the characteristics of the Carrera 6 engine of 1966 and even had the same 2.5 in (66 mm) stroke steel crank, and borrowed Carrera 6 titanium con rods. The most obvious concessions to turbocharging were the fitting of a cylinder head O-ring seal and sodium-cooled valves, Nimonic on the exhaust side. The output of the cooling fan was also stepped up and later versions were equipped with a horizontal fan, driven through the usual belt then a pair of shafts connected via bevel gears. In this case the alternator was mounted on its own bracket and had its own drivebelt.

The ATL's compression ratio was lowered to 6.5:1 and up to 2.4 bar pressure was felt in its single central plenum thanks to a single KKK turbocharger which blew through an air:air aftercooler. Each cylinder's intake pipe had its own butterfly valve, and a single injector. Bosch mechanical injection was again employed with the pump made sensitive to boost pressure as well as throttle opening and revs. The pioneering engine was rated 490 bhp/7600 rpm on 2.35 bar.

At the end of 1974 Porsche launched its turbocharged 930 road car as the homologated base model from which its silhouette (Group 5) racer could be derived. The 930 had a 3.0-litre engine with a 2.7 in (70.4 mm) stroke and this was combined with a 3.6 in (92.8 mm) bore for the Group 5 racer to provide the maximum permitted capacity of 2856 cc. The only major departure from the 901 ATL race engine (aside from displacement) was an aluminium crankcase. As loadings increased, magnesium had been found wanting.

Thus, the cylinders were still Nikasil while the top piston ring was chrome-plated. The Mahle forged piston was of the oil gallery type fed by a single spray and had a domed crown. The hemispherical chamber's valve angles measured from the cylinder axis were inlet 25° 30', exhaust 30° 15'. Valve seats were intake FCN 335, exhaust Como 12. The sodium-cooled valves ran in bronze guides and had dual steel springs

Early 2.1-litre 2-valve Porsche boxer engine descended from the 911 road car. Turbocharger shown without intercooler installation.

and titanium retainers and were operated directly by the rockers.

As always, the individual heads were tied together by a one-piece magnesium cam box which provided three camshaft bearing supports and also individually supported both ends of each rocker arm's individual pivot shaft. The camshaft ran right through the centre of the cam box articulating three rockers each side. The chain-driven camshaft's bearings were integral and were of large enough diameter to allow the steel shaft to be slipped into the box from one end. The cam box was closed by magnesium rocker covers.

The 930 was in fact the basis of both Group 4 (934) and Group 5 (935) racers, the former having a single-plug, Bosch K-Jetronic-injected engine for homologation reasons. This engine was known as the Type 930/71 and had the production 3.0-litre displacement (with a 3.7 in (95 mm) bore). It was rated a whisker under 500 bhp whereas the slightly smaller capacity but twin plug Type 930/72 engine of the 935, with its full race mechanical injection system and

CD ignition (allowing higher revs), was rated over 600 bhp.

A twin turbocharged version followed for improved throttle response. It officially produced 630 bhp/8000 rpm on 2.4 bar absolute. For IMSA's GTP class Porsche produced a 3164 cc engine (having a 3.7 in (95mm) bore plus a 2.9 in (74.4 mm) crankshaft) to run at the heaviest, 409 lb (900 kg) weight break. Although restricted to single plug heads and a single turbocharger this large displacement Type 930 engine produced over 700 bhp on 2.4 bar absolute and, in a March chassis, it was the engine which helped Al Holbert win the 1983 Camel GT title.

In 1984 Porsche introduced its own 962 with a 2869 cc (3.6 in (93.0 mm) bore/standard 2.7 in (70.4 mm) stroke) version of the GTP engine, taking advantage of the fact that its lighter chassis could then be run at 527 lb (850kg). However, as we have seen, track experience suggested that the 3164 cc alternative engine, although having to pull 558 lb (900 kg), was a more competitive proposition.

For 1985, 962 customer cars were available with the smaller Type 962/70 engine or (ballasted to 558 lb (900 kg)) with the Type 962/71, which retained the 1983 bore and stroke dimensions. The two versions were otherwise identical (right down to valve sizes) aside from the longer-throw crankshaft 962/71 needing a 4.9 in (125.8 mm) rather than a 5 in (127.8 mm) con rod to maintain the same deck height. They both ran a horizontal fan and were fitted with a Bosch Motronic engine management system, as developed through the Group C programme.

The wastegate was mechanically operated, its setting being adjustable from the cockpit while the Bosch Motronic MP 1.2 system controlled injection timing and duration and ignition timing, the conventional single ignition system incorporating a Bosch CD coil, distributor and plugs while there were two injectors per cylinder. The firing order was 1-6-2-4-3-5, while the injection pressure was 5.0 bar. The Motronic control unit took readings of rpm, throttle position, charge air pressure and temperature, oil and water temperature and ambient temperature and there was a manual mixture control facility in the cockpit, weakening or enriching the mixture up to 7 per cent.

Both versions of the electronic Type 962 GTP engine ran a 7.5:1 compression ratio and were boosted to a maximum of 2.4 bar absolute by the mandatory single turbocharger. The smaller engine was rated 680 bhp/8200 rpm at 2.4 bar absolute and revved to 8450 rpm while the larger engine was red-lined at 8000 rpm and on maximum boost officially produced 720 bhp/7300 rpm. Of course, this was on IMSA legal high-octane fuel. Commonly a single air:air aftercooler was mounted conveniently between the plenum chambers, over the fan. This shortened charge plumbing to the benefit of response.

The Type 962/71 engine dominated IMSA GTP racing over the 1985 and 1986 seasons in the hands of customers and the factory-supported Holbert Racing car. Porsche Motorsport North America, run out of Warrington, Pennsylvania by the late Al Holbert, serviced the GTP cars. Porsche's domination was in spite of the outlawing of the cockpit boost control and the imposition of an extra 158 lb (72 kg) handicap for 1986 – during 1985 IMSA had admitted: "the 3.2 litre Porsche engine is stronger than we expected".

In response to the 3.0-litre displacement limit of 1987, Porsche developed a revised engine taking advantage of the fact that it could now run twin ignition. The 962/72 engine ran the 5 in (127.8 mm) con rod and 2.7 in (70.4 mm) crankshaft of the Type 962/70 engine together with a 3.7 in (95.0 mm) bore for 2994 cc. While twin ignition had been run on the Group 5 engine, timing was now controlled by the Motronic system. Running a 7.5:1 compression ratio the 962/72 engine was strong enough to continue Porsche's IMSA GTP domination.

Not until 1988 was the reign of the 962 overthrown, by the Electramotive Nissan turbo. For 1988 IMSA forced turbo engines to run a 2.2 in (57 mm) air inlet restrictor and Porsche responded with an 8.0:1 compression ratio and an engine tuned to offer far more torque if less top-end power, under 700 bhp. Response was faster, power building up very quickly – then the air restrictor cut in, flattening out the power curve.

Porsche did not have the advanced Motronic MP 1.7 engine management system introduced for Group C in 1988 available for IMSA. That system incorporated electronic wastegate control as featured on the Nissan GTP. Consequently some Porsche teams developed their own wastegate control systems. Nevertheless, Nissan-type performance remained out of reach. The Nissan engine is fully described in Section Four.

Meanwhile, the Porsche Group C engine had also been overthrown. Unlike the GTP version, this was a four-valve engine, as first used for the 935 programme. The single central plug four-valve head featured a narrow valve angle (30° included) and was run together with flat-top pistons. The inlet valve was set at 14° from the cylinder axis, the exhaust at 16°. The (still individual) four-valve watercooled heads were welded to the cylinder barrels, overcoming any potential gasket problem. Two-valve

The heart of the machine the Bosch Motronic MP1.2 engine management system's black box. In here the engine operating conditions are monitored and the engine is controlled according to the map.

heads could not have been welded in place since it then would have been impossible to insert the valves.

The cylinders were still Nikasil and the production aluminium crankcase was retained, although with provision for larger main bearings and larger crankpins. A new magnesium cam box carried twin camshafts per bank which actuated the valves through conventional steel bucket tappets. The Type 935 four-valve engine was designed for 9000 rpm operation and was gear- rather than chain-driven. In effect, two intermediate gears (mounted on plain bearings) replaced each chain.

Since it now cooled only the cylinder barrels, the fan was again vertical, as usual belt-driven off the nose of the crank. It was smaller in diameter, absorbing far less power and, with all its output directed on the cylinders, these ran cooler. Again the alternator was mounted on its own bracket and was belt-driven from the fan-drive pulley.

Each bank of heads had its own water cooling system with the pump driven off the front of the respective exhaust cam. The CD trigger was now mounted on the rear of the right-hand intake camshaft, rather than the crankshaft, for less vibration while the distributor was positioned symmetrically on the opposite bank. The original 3.2-litre twin turbo 935/71 engine ran a 7.0:1 compression ratio and was reckoned initially to produce the power of the two-valver at 0.15 bar less boost. Standard manifold pressure soon became 2.5 bar and at that the engine was rated 750 bhp/8200 rpm while at 2.7 bar qualifying pressure it offered around 800 bhp.

Concurrently with the 3211 cc engine Porsche devised a 2140 cc (3.0-litre FISA equivalent) four valve Sports Prototype engine (935/73), essentially similar, and this offered 580 bhp/8500 rpm at 2.5 bar absolute and 625 bhp in qualifying pumping 2.7 bar. Then came 935/72 – a 2650 cc derivative with single turbocharger and without aftercooler as per Indy Car regulations. However, since

the oval racer ran on alcohol, Porsche was able to dispense with the cooling fan. Engine Type 935/72 had the classic 2.4 in (66 mm) stroke crankshaft together with a 3.6 in (92.3 mm) bore (for 2649.65 cc) and, with a compression ratio of 9.0:1 was rated 630 bhp at 9000 rpm on the USAC regulation maximum 2.03 bar absolute.

Although stillborn, the 2.65-litre engine was perceived as having the ideal capacity for a twin turbocharged unit to meet the requirements of Group C. Thus the combination of 2.4 in (66 mm) crankshaft and 3.6 in (92.3 mm) bore surfaced at Le Mans rather than Indianapolis. The 935/76 engine for Porsche's 1982-launched 956 Sports Prototype was first race-tested at Le Mans in 1981, then its specification was finalized.

The 935/76 Group C engine remained essentially to the specification of the 935/71 unit, with twin KKK turbochargers (one per bank) and Bosch mechanical injection (one injector per cylinder) and CD ignition, but it ran air:air aftercoolers, one for each bank (each having its own plenum chamber). Of course, the familiar vertical fan seemed somewhat incongruous in a state-of-the-art Eighties Sports Prototype! The compression ratio was set at 7.2:1 and (given Group C fuel consumption regulations) on a typical 2.2 bar race boost power was quoted as 620 bhp/8200 rpm with maximum revs of 8400 rpm.

Above and opposite: *The four-valve version of the Porsche boxer seen in* Typ *935/82 and* Typ *935/83 guise. The former has a fan-cooled crankcase, the latter is fully watercooled. Both have twin turbos.*

Over the period 1982-6 Porsche had a virtual stranglehold on Group C racing, shrugging off threats by Cosworth-Ford and Ferrari-Lancia, then by Jaguar and Mercedes. Development saw the introduction in 1983 of the Bosch Motronic engine management system. This was the MP 1.2 system, as described for the GTP engine. It allowed the four-valve engine's compression ratio to rise, first to 8.0:1, then 8.5:1 over the 1983 season, power rising to 650 bhp without an increase in race boost. Subsequently, the ratio went to 9.0:1.

With the Motronic system the Group C engine was known as the Type 935/82. Pioneered by the factory team, it was offered to Group C customers from 1984 onwards. Nevertheless, Joest Racing won Le Mans in 1984 and 1985 running a mechanical injection Type 935/76. Both versions were produced in 2.65, 2.8, 3.0 and 3.2-litre displacements, the bigger displacement versions at first run in German national sprint races, though some customers tried them in World Championship races in the mid-Eighties. John Fitzpatrick was one of the first to race a 3.0-litre engine in the World Championship, a 935/76 version which was run in selected 1984 events. Joest followed a similar route.

Converting a 2.65-litre to a 2.8-litre engine was simplicity itself: it was a case of buying the appropriate stroke crankshaft and con rods to suit. The 2.8-litre version ran a 2.7 in (70.4 mm) stroke. To produce a 3.0-litre version it was then simply a case of taking the bore out to 3.7 in (95.0 mm) with a set of new pistons and rings.

Having run 2.65-litre Type 935/82

engines throughout 1984 and 1985, the works Group C team started using the 3.0-litre version for qualifying during its short 1986 programme. In 1987 the works team switched to 3.0-litre fully water-cooled Type 935/83 engines but the 935/82 remained the mainstay of Porsche's big customer 962C fleet, looked after by the Weissach-based Porschesport operation. In the late Eighties customers generally ran 2.8 or 3.0-litre versions in World Championship events. However, the Type 935/82 was no longer a consistently competitive proposition, given the standard set by Jaguar and Mercedes.

The Jaguar engine which rose to prominence in 1987 had been mapped out in the mid-Fifties but had not been seen in the metal until 1965 when the marque rolled out its XJ13 Le Mans challenger, rated 502 bhp at 7600 rpm. It was a 60° unit with a deep aluminium monobloc that extended from the deck

Road car basis for the TWR Group C engine of the late Eighties. The Jaguar V12 was based on a design from the mid-Fifties and was somewhat heavy, with a lot of weight high up.

to just below crank depth. Aluminium two-valve heads incorporated traditional Jaguar hemispherical combustion chambers, the valves were operated by chain-driven twin overhead camshafts. A seven bearing crankshaft provided a 2.7 in (70.0 mm) stroke: with 3.4 in (87.0 mm) bore cast iron wet liners the total displacement was 4991 cc. Fed via Lucas mechanical fuel injection, the dry-sumped engine was safe for up to 8500 rpm.

Alas, it never roared in anger. Early in 1965 Jaguar had a sudden change of heart: the marque would not return to racing, after all. However, all was not lost since the V12 race engine was perceived as an ideal base for a prestigious new road car power plant. Like a straight six (with which it shares a six-pin 120° mirror image crankshaft configuration), a 60° V12 engine is inherently well balanced. With six equally spaced firing impulses per revolution it is not only free from serious torsional resonances but is also smooth-running.

The development of the road car V12 became the responsibility of Walter Hassan who took overall charge of Jaguar engine development in 1969, assisted by Harry Mundy. A wet-sump version of the race engine was Hassan's starting point. A major departure, however, was an early decision to switch to narrower single-cam heads to keep the unit as light, compact and quiet as possible. On the road the V12 was not required to rev so high and Hassan's single-cam head offered in-line valves of adequate size for efficient breathing up to 6500 rpm. The new alloy head was developed in conjunction with shallow, large diameter bowl-in-crown combustion chambers; Hassan considering this type of chamber ideal for an over square multi-cylinder road engine.

Hassan took the iron liners out to a 3.5 in (90.0mm) bore which, retaining the original 2.7 in (70.0 mm) stroke crankshaft gave a total displacement of 5343 cc. Power was officially 272 bhp/ 5850 rpm. TWR started its racing involvement with this engine through a Group A XJ-S. Group A imposed restrictions on inlet valve size and valve lift and the original exhaust manifold had to be retained, although pistons,

camshafts and other engine internals were free. The 1982 débuted TWR XJ-S was fuel-injected as per the standard car and a wet sump was retained, as demanded by the regulations, with complex baffling to keep the oil under control.

The ultimate Group A engine had been achieved by the time of the 1984 season following porting and camshaft work, and the introduction of revised pistons which were run with a slightly higher compression ratio. The production injection had given way, first (in 1983) to an analogue Zytek/Bosch injection system, then to a digital system and 450 bhp/7300 rpm had been attained within the strict breathing restrictions.

For Group C, TWR Engine Division Manager Allan Scott, unhindered by mandatory engine specifications, could make a fresh start. He knew the two-valve V12 well and (unlike some of his colleagues) felt sure it could form the basis of a competitive Group C engine, though a four-valve engine should inherently be more fuel-efficient. Scott offered his own thinking on combustion chamber design.

Jaguar had two production versions of the V12: the classic flathead, plus an HE (high efficiency) version exploiting the May Fireball combustion chamber. The May Fireball had been designed by Swiss engineering genius Michael May (the same Michael May who had first run a wing on a race car, back in the mid-Fifties!) to reduce fuel consumption and unwanted exhaust emission. Developed in the mid-Seventies, Jaguar was the first manufacturer to productionize the lean-burn design, which ran a flat-top piston together with a complex chamber in the head.

Clearly, Scott was free to develop a flathead design as Group 44 had done for its IMSA GTP plus Le Mans programme, a flat piston crown design (not necessarily along May Fireball lines), or to devise a chamber partially in the piston, partially in the head. He understandably would not divulge his design, which was the key to the performance of the TWR Group C engine. It was not a straightforward development of his earlier Group A engine and it did not follow the Group

44 path.

Indeed, there was no input from the Group 44 engine programme. Scott went his own way on the basis of what he had learned in Group A plus his own, fresh ideas and he continued to work with Zytek engine management rather than use the factory-commissioned Micos system. Group 44 relied on a Jaguar-appointed Lucas expert: Scott felt it was essential to keep the vital engine management system in house, and this he was able to do working with Bill Gibson and Brian Mason's small, flexible concern.

Having opted to work with the two-valve Hassan head, Scott is unreserved in his praise for its porting. He says it flows extremely well: "somewhere between the best of any other two-valve and a four-valve head." Its semi-downdraught inlet port design (with only a gentle S-bend between overhead inlet manifold flange and valve seat) must take much credit for this and Scott says he was able to develop a Group C engine offering 100 per cent volumetric efficiency over the maximum torque period. The major drawbacks of any two-valve head are the location of the spark plug (unavoidably offset) and less valve area than it is possible to attain given four valves in the same area. To get more valve area Scott went for a bigger bore.

Whereas over in the USA Group 44 was confined by GTP regulations to a 6.0-litre displacement in 1985, Scott went for a same 3 in (78 mm) stroke crankshaft (this TWR employed in an XJ-S road conversion) but for a bigger 3.6 in (92 mm) rather than the traditional 3.5 in (90 mm)) bore to achieve a displacement of 6.2 litres.

The prototype TWR Group C engine ran a 11.8:1 compression ratio (compared to 11.5:1 for the Group A engine) and offered 640 bhp. By the time the TWR campaign commenced Scott's Zytek-managed engine was running a 12.0:1 compression ratio – in spite of the relatively low (maximum 102) octane Group C fuel – and offered 650-60 bhp at 7000 rpm. In 1985 Group 44 claimed a similar output at slightly higher rpm and from a slightly smaller capacity: a reflection of its far higher octane fuel.

Of course, the GTP car did not have to pay the same attention to fuel consumption. At first, in 1985, the XJR-6 was overweight and, with an eye to the fuel allowance, generally raced at 6500 rpm. However, with development, weight came down to the limit and Scott was able to run more power, introducing a yet larger bore at Monza in 1986: 3.7 in (94 mm), which gave a 6.5-litre displacement. That provided an extra 40-50 bhp – power was now in the region of 700 bhp at 7000 rpm which was the regular race rpm in 1986. Porsche power had gone up from 650 bhp in 1983-4 (when the TWR engine was designed) to 700 bhp, primarily through the switch from mechanical to fully electronic injection.

In 1986 TWR learned how to fine-tune its 6.5-litre engine and its sophisticated chassis from circuit to circuit for the best fuel efficiency and for 1987 Scott went up again in capacity, to 7.0-litres, having moved to a longer-stroke crankshaft. The key to the move was additional torque: with more torque there was less gear-changing, the car pulling higher gearing and saving fuel.

The 3.3 in (84 mm) stroke 7.0-litre engine was tuned so as to give only an extra 15-20 bhp at the top end, while pumping out an extra 45 bhp at 5500 rpm. The 7.0-litre engine boasted massive mid-range torque. Maximum torque went from 570 lb ft to 605 lb ft at 5250 bhp and Scott achieved a very flat torque curve: from 4750 rpm to 6250 rpm it was within 3 per cent of a straight line.

The 7.0-litre engine underwent no fundamental change prior to its 1988 Le Mans success, but with development the peak torque figure was attained at 6000 rather than 5250 rpm. For 1988 Scott had looked to achieve 750 bhp: by mid-season the TWR engines were running 745 bhp/7250 rpm with peak torque of 615 bhp/6000 rpm. Maximum rpm this season was 7400 rather than 7000 rpm.

Generally, development of the TWR V12 had consisted of lightening wherever possible, and of subtle evolutionary changes to the exhaust system (pipe diameters and lengths) and the camshaft together with progress in terms of mapping. Of course, the head and piston had changed to accommodate the changes in capacity but Scott's original combustion chamber concept remained.

Scott's 7.0-litre Group C engine was based on a remachined production block and steel four-bolt main bearing caps replaced the cast-iron production items, while TWR fitted a magnesium dry-sump pan as a stiffening structure, albeit retaining the stock sump fixing points. As with the block, Engine Division worked from Jaguar-supplied aluminium head castings, the heads having a separate tappet block which was closed via a TWR-produced magnesium cam cover. Again production fixings were retained, each head thus attached via 26 studs: each cylinder was surrounded by a six-bolt pattern with adjacent cylinders sharing a pair of studs.

TWR additionally doweled the heads to the block to avoid any danger of shifting – important since the engine was run as a heavily stressed chassis member. Although the V12 was long and heavy it was sufficiently robust to accept the major proportion of the chassis load: it was bolted firmly to the rear bulkhead and in turn the transaxle was primarily bolted to it.

The iron liners were located as per standard, via a flange situated just over 1.7 in (44 mm) down the depth of the bore which left the hottest part of the liner in direct contact with the coolant. Flange sealing employed a sealing compound and had never proved a problem. Sealing at the deck employed sealing rings and a perimeter gasket, the detailed design of which was a closely guarded secret.

The crankshaft was another TWR development. It was very similar in design to the production item but was significantly lighter. It was a special nitrided EN40B steel forging produced using TWR's own tooling. Tony Vandervell supplied the plain bearings while H-section forged steel con rods were machined outside to TWR requirements. The bushed small end carried a fully floating steel gudgeon pin retained by Teflon buttons.

The piston was a Cosworth forging and it carried three uncoated rings. The design of the oil spray-cooled piston was one of the factors allowing a high compression ratio to be run in spite of poor quality fuel. The head retained a production plug location and TWR achieved excellent results from its flow work thanks to the excellence of the stock port design.

The valve seats and guides were bronze-based while the vertical valves were solid stainless steel, the precise material specifications very carefully chosen. Dual Schmitthelm springs and steel bucket tappets were fitted. The steel camshaft was lighter than standard, was machined from solid and heat-treated. It ran directly in the head, retained, production-style, by aluminium caps. The camshaft drive sprocket was connected via the Jaguar production system which offered timing adjustment via fine internal and external teeth. The Duplex chain drive powered the distributor via a jackshaft in the centre of the vee while the pumps were driven by a pulley from the nose of the crankshaft.

As we have seen, exhaust tuning had been a continual process. TWR used a three-into-one then two-into-one system for each bank whereas Group 44 had tended to favour further blending into a single tail pipe. The TWR engine ran a fixed length of inlet trumpet for all circuits, the trumpets fixed to a throttle slide bank sitting atop short individual inlet tracts. The injectors (one per cylinder) were positioned in the trumpets just above the slides, feeding downstream (this arrangement having been standardised by 1986). New for 1988 was a fuel return line running just below the slides within the body of the manifold, this passage offering a chilling effect which saved the weight of a fuel cooler.

TWR's Zytek engine management system controlled Bosch-supplied solenoid injectors and a Lucas CD ignition system which fired a single 0.5 in (14 mm) Champion plug per cylinder. There was a back-up crankshaft trigger but the team had never had recourse to use it. Developed from the Group A programme, the Zytek system was housed in a single box and had never suffered noise problems. The major development in Group C guise had been a switch from Group A-type non-sequential to more precise, fully computer-timed sequential injection.

The TWR Group C engine devised by Allan Scott was capable of producing a solid 750 bhp to the fuel, having a 7.0-litres and running to 7250 rpm. Maximum piston acceleration was just over 100,000 ft/sec².

The main ECU inputs were speed and throttle angle and for 1988 the latter was measured via a high quality linear potentiometer attached to the slide and better able to keep up with it. This allowed improved fuelling under transient throttle conditions. While speed and throttle angle were naturally the key inputs, Scott was cagey about other readings. However, it was no secret that TWR had a driver-adjustable mixture control, according to the setting of which the ignition curve was programmed. It is possible that the team ran a Lambda probe on occasion.

After Le Mans 1987 the ECU became programmable directly from a portable micro rather than via a plug-in EPROM, Zytek ever striving to make its system more user-friendly. Engine Division did its own software development with support from Zytek and mapping was a continual process at its well equipped Kidlington 'shop. By 1989 that facility was dedicated to the new turbo programme as Daimler-Benz moved ahead in the power stakes using the Mercedes turbo engine described in the following chapter.

Chapter Eleven

The Swiss Connection (Mercedes Two and Four-Valve Turbo Engines)

Swiss race car constructor Peter Sauber's C6 and C7 cars were designed with the assistance of a number of Daimler-Benz Research and Development engineers working in their spare time, these including Rudiger Faul and Leo Ress. Faul was in charge of aerodynamics and had been able to get Sauber time to test scale models of the projected C6 shape in his employer's fixed-floor wind tunnel. Ress subsequently moved to BMW then joined Sauber full time as Technical Director in charge of Mercedes-powered developments of the C7.

The contact between Sauber and the Daimler-Benz R&D department had led to the availability of a Mercedes V8 turbocharged Group C engine. Sauber's efforts with the C6 had impressed the R&D hierarchy while Sauber had seen the potential of the all-alloy, chain-driven sohc, 16 valve M117 engine as the base for a powerful and reliable turbocharged Group C power plant. The M117 was the latest in a succession of Mercedes V8 engines stretching back to 1963. The original 6.3- (later 6.9-) litre V8 had been followed in 1969 by a new generation 3.5-litre M116 V8 from which the M117 was directly descended.

The M116 had iron block and alloy heads with chain-driven sohc. Its two valves per cylinder were offset 20° from the vertical in a wedge-shaped combustion chamber surrounded by generous squish area, run in conjunction with a flat-topped piston. Although the offset

valves were set in parallel they were operated through finger cam followers which pivoted on spherical-headed adjuster studs. The M116 engine was taken out to 4.5 litres and then, 10 years after its introduction, was replaced by the alloy block M117.

While the M117 generally followed the pattern of the iron block engine (retaining the wedge heads) the most important difference was a massive weight saving in the order of 275 lb (125 kg) This was made possible through a new production technique offering a linerless block, as introduced by General Motors with the famous Vega 2300 engine. In fact the Reynolds Aluminium developed process and material had been pioneered through racing having first been employed as a means of producing blocks for the works Chevrolet-McLaren Can Am car. Reynolds' replacement for the traditional cast-iron Chevrolet big block was able to offer increased capacity (8.1 litres) since it was linerless and it was, of course, a lot lighter.

The new generation linerless block was subsequently adopted by both Daimler-Benz and Porsche as a means of producing new lightweight V8 engines. The process saw the block diecast by the new Accurad method in a new aluminium alloy, Reynolds A390, which combined good fluidity in the molten condition with a fine dispersion of silicon after heat treatment giving good bearing properties and ease of machining. After machining, an electro-chemical etching process was used to expose the glass-hard silicon particles on the walls providing a wear-resistant and oil-retaining surface. This was run in conjunction with an iron-plated piston skirt to prevent any possibility of aluminium-to-aluminium contact since that would cause galling (thus reversing the usual combination of alloy piston on iron bore).

Although Daimler-Benz' M117 production engine was not turbocharged, the research engineers at Stuttgart were already familiar with the challenge of forced induction, having worked with turbocharged engines for 15 years. Working in the Advanced Engine Research Division at Stuttgart-Unterturkheim, engineer Withalm had investigated all forms of supercharging for both petrol and diesel engines with fuel consumption a high priority and it was felt that an efficient turbocharged version of the M117 could be produced for Group C. The engine was designed by Müller and developed by Gert Withalm under the project leadership of Doctor Hiereth.

Initially one engine was produced and, since the project was not officially recognised by the Daimler-Benz board, the parts and technical information for additional units were supplied to Heini Mader. The project echoed that of Aston Martin, on behalf of which offshoot Tickford Engineering had toyed with a Group C V8 turbo engine early in 1984. The longer-lived Mercedes challenger was a superficially similar, large capacity, lightly blown 90° V8. Likewise, it was essentially stock and consequently had a two-plane crankshaft for smooth running. Of course, the two-plane configuration made for a very smooth engine at the expense of exhaust-tuning potential. However, that was not a serious concern given that forced induction and the smooth, well-balanced nature of the unit was considered ideal for an endurance car.

The prototype engine first ran on the dyno around Christmas 1984 and started track testing in March 1985. Initially the head gasket gave problems but once the Stuttgart engineers had solved this it ran well. The solution was in a modified gasket and a stiffer head, the latter involving a modification to the casting which was carried through to the production car line.

The Mader-fettled engine benefited from a dry sump, porting and camshaft work, increased water circulation, special heat-resistant valves and oil-sprayed pistons. Type 27 turbochargers were supplied by KKK off the shelf and these were governed by mechanical wastegates which were modified Porsche road car items. The appropriately revised induction system included air:air aftercoolers while injection and ignition were incorporated in the Porsche Group C-type Motronic M1.2 package which was supplied by Bosch. Daimler-Benz had worked closely with Bosch for many years. Together they had pioneered fuel injection for road car engines and engine management systems.

The Mader-assembled 5.0-litre Mercedes engine was pressurized to a maximum of 2.0 bar absolute in qualifying, at which power was in excess of 700 bhp. Race boost was 1.8 bar absolute for 680 bhp while for maximum power the drivers had to look no further than 6600 rpm.

Sauber went in at the deep end, the Mercedes-Sauber C8 débuting at Le Mans. Qualifying was encouraging until, warming up for a serious attempt to post a grid time, it took off over the brow after the Mulsanne kink. It somersaulted a couple of times and was wrecked, thankfully without injury to driver Gunnar Nielson. Daimler-Benz kept faith with Sauber and a short, five-race programme was undertaken in 1986, the highlight being victory in the wet at the Nürburgring, aided by the tremendously fat power curve of the low-revving, big-displacement engine.

In the dry the Mercedes-Sauber was less impressive but with continuing engine development work and an improved chassis, the C9, the package was a real contender in 1987. Again the season was only five races long and this time the highlight was pole at Francorchamps. For 1988 Daimler-Benz came out and gave the effort factory support for a full season and engines were supplied directly from Stuttgart. The commitment was immediately rewarded with a win at Jerez. Following a disappointing withdrawal from Le Mans in the wake of

Daimler-Benz' Mercedes M117 Group C engine had a linerless aluminium block produced by the same process as used to create McLaren Racing's 8.1-litre Can Am engine some twenty years earlier.

unexplained tyre blow-outs, the team bounced back to win at the Norisring and Brno.

Over the Mader seasons the key engine developments were the introduction of a Nikasil bore coating, a new lighter crankshaft, improved, higher efficiency turbochargers and a switch to the Motronic MP1.7 engine management system offering more precise control of ignition and injection, plus electronic control of a new wastegate. In addition, a total of 44 lb (20 kg) was saved through lighter internals (including titanium con rods), a lighter flywheel, lighter ancillaries and lighter turbochargers. Even the camshafts were lightened, through a new form of construction.

In terms of performance, the most important developments were the valve timing and the improved turbochargers and engine management system. With

the more precise ignition control of the MP1.7 system the compression ratio could be increased from an initial 8.0:1 to 8.5:1 while power was then officially 700 bhp/7000 rpm on the 1.9 bar absolute race setting. In qualifying almost 800 bhp was extracted.

For 1988 Sauber received official backing from Daimler-Benz and the engines were then supplied direct from Unterturkheim. The race engines were built from production castings which had been taken from the factory and sent to Mahle for a conventional Nikasil coating to be applied to the bores.

The linerless M117 monobloc extended below the crankshaft axis to allow side as well as vertical bolting of the full-width main bearing caps. The four-bolt caps for the five bearings were of cast iron while the race engine's bespoke dry sump (attached via stock studs) was of magnesium and was designed to accept chassis loads. The engine was semi-stressed with loads also fed into the heads. The ported alloy heads were attached by six bolts per cylinder and the valve gear was mounted directly on the head. An aluminium rocker cover was retained from the production engine.

The two-plane crankshaft ran in 2.5 in (64 mm) diameter plain bearings supplied by Glyco and, while lighter than standard, was to the same design with the same balancing webs and journal sizes. An in-house production, it was of forged steel and was only polished, receiving no special treatment. As the production crankshaft, the race crank was fitted with a harmonic dampener but this was of a different design in view of the higher revs sought. It was supplied by Goetze. The flywheel was steel, attached by eight bolts and was sized to match a standard 7.25 in (184 mm) clutch with a starter ring around it. The crankshaft was driven by titanium con rods through 1.8 in (48 mm) diameter plain Glyco bearings.

The fully machined con rods were of I-section and were supplied by Pankel in Austria. At 6.7 in (170.5 mm) eye-to-eye they were a little longer than standard for a shorter, lighter piston. The Mahle piston was attached by a conventional steel gudgeon pin with circlips and was of the oil gallery type, fed by a single jet. The wedge-shaped combustion chamber of the production head was retained, the parallel valves inclined to one side with the plug reaching in on the other. The race engine differed only in that a dish in the piston crown reduced the compression ratio from the stock 10.0:1.

The piston carried three cast iron rings, of which the top was chrome plated. The smaller, lighter piston carried smaller-than-standard rings. American supplier TRW provided the rings at Mahle's recommendation. The special head gasket resembled that of the production car and was supplied by German company Reinz. The head was fitted with Stellite seats for both inlet and exhaust valves which ran in bronze guides. The valves were steel with a Nimonic foot and on the exhaust side were sodium-cooled. Dual steel springs were fitted under a titanium retainer.

The production valve gear was retained, with the finger cam followers reducing side loading compared to direct operation of the parallel valves by the cams. However, for the race engine the hydraulic piston, on top of which the follower's pivot was mounted to provide automatic adjustment, was removed and replaced by a mechanically-adjusted stud. The only other modification was a specially hardened plate which was soldered to the top of the steel follower to form the cam working surface.

The camshaft had journals of large enough diameter to allow it to be inserted through bearing holes in aluminium shaft supports, five of which were bolted to each head. The steel shaft ran directly in its supports and was of a newly devised built-up type produced by a Mahle subsidiary. The method was to produce the cam lobes and the journals separately then to slide them onto the tubular base shaft under a heat process. The resultant shaft was reckoned to be lighter and was less expensive to produce.

The camshafts were driven by a chain off a sprocket at the front of the crank. The double-row chain was a production item and was fitted with a tensioner. Between the front main bearing and the timing drive sprocket was another sprocket, this one to drive the oil pressure pump which was mounted inside the front cover. The scavenge pumps were mounted outside and were driven by a belt from a pulley on the nose of the crank. In fact there were two pulleys, a second belt driving the water pump and alternator.

The water pump was set into the front cover in a central position while the scavenge pumps were to the left of the crankcase, the alternator to the right. Of the five scavenge pumps, three served the engine, two the turbos. Compared to the production engine the dry sump race unit had improved water circulation through enlarged channels – particularly in the head – with twice as much water in circulation.

The alternator was supplied by Bosch, which had developed a distributorless ignition system for the engine. Until mid-1987 it ran with a conventional flywheel-triggered Bosch CD system.

However, with the MP1.7 system, this was replaced by a multi-coil system, the coils triggered by the ECU which took impulses from the flywheel and a camshaft sensor. Rather than having a coil for each plug, one coil jointly served two cylinders and consequently each plug was fired twice per four-stroke cycle. This was not, however, found to affect performance adversely. As for the production engine, the firing order was 1-5-4-8-6-3-7-2.

Fuel was injected into the ports rather than the inlet trumpets. The fuel injectors were screwed into the head, as on the production engine, one injector per cylinder. In spite of this arrangement atomisation was considered adequate, ''with the valve mostly responsible for atomisation, anyhow'', according to Withalm. Earlier the engine had run two injectors per cylinder with the second operating only at full throttle. However, improved injector design and improved control via the switch from MP1.2 to MP1.7 Motronic had allowed one to be dispensed with.

Two throttles were fitted, one just ahead of each entry to the plenum chamber, each turbocharger blowing through its own aftercooler. The inconel turbine turbochargers featured no trickery and had essentially remained unchanged throughout the engine's career. With the MP1.7 system Daimler-Benz produced it own wastegates for electronic control throughout the rev range via the ECU. The driver remained in overall charge of the maximum boost pressure.

The Motronic ECU took readings, apart from those of the crankshaft and camshaft sensors, of charge air pressure as felt in the plenum, air and exhaust gas temperature, water temperature, oil temperature and pressure, fuel temperature and pressure and even turbocharger rpm. However, the system retained a plug-in EPROM, unlike the Zytek system used by Jaguar. It was used in conjunction with a telemetry system on race day, allowing the engineers to monitor temperatures and pressures. The map provided for the engine in 1988 was based on reference points at 500 rpm and 0.1 bar intervals.

By 1988 Daimler-Benz had produced around 30 race engines. Each was reckoned to take two persons one week to strip and rebuild. There were no special qualifying engines but on 2.2 bar absolute qualifying power was rated as ''almost 800 bhp''. Maximum revs were 7000 but the driver was asked to observe a limit of 6500 on race day, aside from overtaking. At the 1.9 bar absolute race setting torque was a massive 800 nm at 4250 rpm and the torque band was spread all the way from 3000 – 6000 rpm: sheer grunt was this unit's great strength.

In the latter half of 1988 the M117 engine took over from the Jaguar V12 as the strongest in Group C and for 1989 performance was strengthened further via a switch to the four valve M119 engine. This was derived from the four valve version of the M117 used to power the marque's 500SL. The four valve M119 version had a block which was a little lower and shorter con rods to suit, this lowering the centre of gravity, an important consideration given the extra weight above the piston.

Tests showed that the four-valve heads offered slightly enhanced fuel consumption, giving Sauber a little more power to the fuel. The M119 engine retained the 8.5:1 compression ratio and had a pent roof combustion chamber with a 37.5° included valve angle surrounded by a squish band. Inside the squish band the piston crown was slightly dished while there were light valve clearance notches. Ignition was via a single central plug. Seven different head and piston designs were tested prior to finalization of the combustion chamber detailing, though the overall chamber architecture was dictated by the production base.

The new head had an integral tappet block and was driven via chain as per the two-valve head. The race camshafts were of the same built-up type running in five plain bearings and driving through steel bucket tappets with the usual shim adjustment. Dual steel springs closed each valve, the valve as usual sodium-cooled and having a Nimonic foot. Valve dimensions and the basic porting were as per the production engine, while each head was based on a production line casting.

The M119 engine was fitted with Motronic MP2.7 with two injectors per cylinder, one pointing into each inlet valve's channel. Otherwise the injection, ignition and wastegate control systems were as per the MP1.7 system, though with finer control. The twin injector arrangement posed a problem of inferior atomisation since each injector only passed half as much fuel. On the other hand volumetric efficiency was improved, though with forced induction this was not a particularly important gain. The same good turbulence as enjoyed by the two-valve engine was maintained while the key gain was improved combustion thanks to a more compact chamber with a central plug, hence the superior fuel efficiency.

Other improvements for the M119 were reduced frictional losses, the means to this undisclosed, and further improved turbochargers. These had a lighter rotor assembly for improved transient behaviour. Normal race boost was 1.8 bar absolute for 700-20 bhp at 7000 rpm with up to 2.0 bar in qualifying when over 800 bhp was seen at 7000 rpm. The engine posed few development problems but its 484 lb (220 kg) weight was a challenge for Sauber, as was its 0.19 in (5 mm) higher centre of gravity. Nevertheless, the increased car minimum weight of 1980 lb (900 kg) helped and the M119-C9 was super-successful, winning Le Mans and the World Championship.

The Le Mans engines "looked like new" when stripped down and a batch was produced to the same specification for 1990 prior to the marque's withdrawal from the race in the face of political considerations. The major change for 1990 was a move to Motronic MP1.8 while the weight of the engine was also reduced for normal races, by 13.2 lb (6 kg). The weight was saved through a titanium flywheel, magnesium cam covers, revised camshafts and new crankshaft damper and turbochargers.

The titanium flywheel was a straight swap for the previous steel item, permitted through the use of a carbon-carbon clutch. The camshaft featured smaller cams in an effort to reduce weight at the top end while the crankshaft damper was titanium rather than steel and the turbocharger had a lighter magnesium compressor housing. The new magnesium cam covers were necessary to allow the provision of a highly advanced detonation sensor.

The MP1.8 system featured one coil per plug for improved ignition control and the in-chamber detonation sensor. This was a cylindrical quartz-based probe with a 0.24 in (6 mm) diameter which reached into the chamber much like a plug. Made by Kistler in Switzerland, it could constantly monitor the pressure within the cylinder, fluctuations within the relevant portion of the normal pressure cycle indicating detonation. Clearly, the MP1.8's ECU could adjust the ignition timing to the individual cylinder accordingly. With the detonation sensor the engine could run closer to the detonation threshold enjoying enhanced fuel consumption as a consequence.

In addition, Daimler-Benz employed an air ratio Lambda sensor in qualifying, mainly to check for misfire. It was difficult to get a good signal given the turbocharging system so the Lambda was not incorporated in the basic MP1.8 control package. The 1990 engine featured revised injectors, still two per cylinder and the MP1.8 system was programmable without the need to physically plug in a new EPROM, like the Zytek system used by Jaguar in the late Eighties.

The other major advance for 1990 was further reduced friction, again the means undisclosed. It involved "a significant mechanical change" and further enhanced fuel consumption. However, race power was still quoted as 720 bhp at 7000 rpm on 1.8 bar. Power in qualifying was up to 850 bhp while 2.4 bar was employed but only to aid the 4000 – 5000 rpm. maximum torque period, being eased off at higher speeds.

Fifty new engines were prepared for the season, matching the number used in 1989. During the course of the season the major activity at Unterturkheim's race engine department concerned the development of a new 3.5-litre atmo engine, this targeted at 13,000 rpm. Likewise designed by Müller and developed by Withalm, it first ran on the bench in June, one year after the memorable Le Mans success.

PART THREE

THE ROLLING CHASSIS

Chapter Twelve

The Right Weave

The key factors influencing Prototype chassis design are aerodynamics, the engine's physical characteristics and the dictates of the regulations. Eighties Group C and GTP regulations were very restrictive in many areas, thus the cars tended to follow a common pattern. For example, Group C chassis regulations dictated a minimum windscreen height of 36 in (920 mm) within a maximum overall height of 40.5 in (1030 mm) while the maximum overall width was 78.7 in (2000 mm). Then there was a limit on overall length of 189 in (4800 mm) and overhang.

That was just the start of it. Bodywork had to cover all the car's mechanicals and two doors (with windows for which a minimum size was specified) were mandatory. So too was nominal passenger space in a cockpit of at least 51 in (1300 mm) width: two seats and two footwells had to be provided, disposed symmetrically either side of the car's centreline. The fuel tankage had to be accommodated within the wheelbase and within 25.5 in (650mm) either side of the car's centreline while the driver's feet had to be kept behind the front wheel axis from 1985 onwards.

Of course, there were many, many prescriptions of a more detailed nature giving the Group C designer plenty to worry about. GTP was just as much a technical nightmare. Given complete chassis freedom aside from the enclosure of all mechanical parts and the Eighties

might have turned up some weird and wonderful fully enclosed racing cars but in the event most Group C and GTP cars tended to follow the pattern of the ground-breaking March M1/C and the Lola T600. There was, however, an important exception in the form of Ford's Mustang GTP car with its front engine.

It had long been established that the ideal location for the engine was between the driver and the rear wheels, this position offering a better weight distribution, less weight (due to the proximity of the driven wheels to the clutch) and less frontal area. Although a front-engined car could achieve a well balanced 40-60 front-rear weight allocation, it tended to have a higher moment of polar inertia and was thus less responsive. Further, dynamic weight distribution saw less weight move rearwards under acceleration, hence traction was inferior.

In the case of a fully enclosed car, there was not such a frontal area problem posed by a front-engined layout while the advent of the underwing made the layout look attractive from an aerodynamic point of view. The 1984 Ford featured an advanced composite chassis: only its layout was old-fashioned. It proved fast on certain circuits but the unusual engine position caused a number of problems, not least heat intruding in the cockpit.

The Ford was intended to run a new

aluminium alloy turbo engine but had to rely on an older iron block which put too much weight up front: the distribution was 48-52 front-rear. As well as poor traction, this tended to lead to overloaded front brakes. Further, the available tyres did not suit the machine's characteristics. By mid-1984 Ford had committed itself to the mid-engined Probe GTP car.

Thus, all successful Eighties Prototype had mid-engines, generally with the gearbox outrigged behind the c.w.p. though there were a few instances of an inboard gearbox. For example, the Nissan GTP car at first ran the Weismann inboard transverse gearbox used in early Eighties Indy Car racing and the BMW-Brabham BT55 Formula One car of 1986 while the 1989 Aston Martin Group C car had an inboard Hewland-based transmission following the Cosworth Ford-Benetton Formula One car. The inboard gearbox in theory further reduced the polar moment of inertia but in practice Electramotive Nissan could not detect any such effect from it and switched to an outboard gearbox.

The Porsche 956/962 had a very short, light engine which was positioned well ahead of the c.w.p. leaving a long bellhousing-cum-spacer in between, empty as the gearbox was in the time-honoured location. It was important not to have an engine too close to the rear wheels to avoid an excessive rearward weight bias. One key difference between the Group 44 Jaguar XJR-5 and the TWR XJR-6 was in the length of the bellhousing. The Jaguar V12 engine was very long and heavy and to put it a reasonable distance ahead of the rear axle TWR had to sink it into a recess in the rear bulkhead, then wrapping the fuel cell around the front of it. This was made possible through a complex advanced composite moulding, whereas Group 44's older car had employed a traditional aluminium tub.

The Coventry V12 was perhaps the most difficult of all Prototype engines to package due to its high centre of gravity as well as its length. As XJR-6 chassis designer Southgate remarked to the author: ''it was obvious that the engine would dominate the car in terms of performance due to its weight, the position of its centre of gravity and its

Group 44 Jaguar XJR-5 uncloaked. Note how the V12 engine is a stressed member of the chassis, the transaxle carrying the rear suspension. The monocoque is conventional aluminium with a steel roll cage.

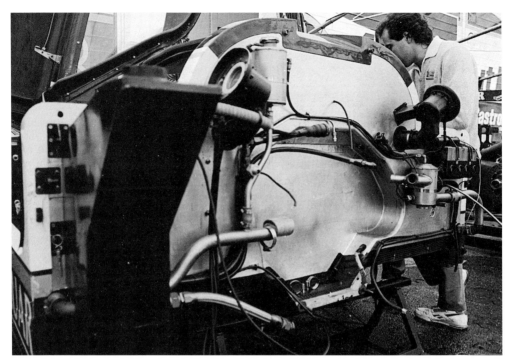

Recess in the rear of the TWR Jaguar XJR-6 monocoque allowed the engine and fuel tank to overlap, thus the long V12 engine sat further forward. This made for an improved weight distribution.

length. The position of the fuel was less important than the position of the engine, so the engine was put as close as possible to the driver.''

Southgate's complex moulding slotted the engine into a 4 in (100 mm) deep recess in the rear bulkhead. The tank was then formed around the engine, flanking it and extending forwards to form the sloping back of the driver's seat and that of the hypothetical passenger. The extent of engine/monocoque overlap allowed Southgate to keep the engine far enough ahead of the rear axle without compromising the length of the wheelbase. Group C regulations demanded a maximum front and rear overhang of 80 per cent of the wheelbase and, restricted to an overall maximum length of 189 in (4800 mm). Southgate wanted all the overhang he could get for aerodynamic reasons.

By this stage Group C regulations demanded that the pedals be set within the wheelbase so Southgate had to get driver, central 100 litre fuel tank, engine and bellhousing all within the shortest possible wheelbase. The central fuel tank location was dictated by the regulations and in any case a central location was advantageous compared to the alternative of setting fuel in the sponsons. The single central tank is lighter, easier to protect, helps make the entire structure more rigid and does not upset the weight distribution as the fuel load lightens. In theory a wheelbase should be 105 in (2666 mm) for a maximum possible overhang of 80 in (2134mm) but Southgate settled for 109.5 in (2780 mm) in view of the packaging problem and given consideration of handling: a longer wheelbase tends to make a car more forgiving, easier to drive.

In terms of weight distribution, the XJR-6 was further influenced by the choice of a front radiator location. The oil tank was set in the front of the engine bay rather than the bellhousing and the car ran out with a 40-60 front-rear weight distribution. In view of the high centre of gravity of the V12, all chassis components were mounted as low as possible and the fuel load was kept low. Overall, a low centre of gravity is always to be desired since the lower the centre of gravity, the higher the cornering force that can be obtained, all other things being equal. However, if it is extremely low this can be at the expense of weight transfer from front to rear, hence at the expense of traction.

The centre of gravity of the Jaguar V12 prototypes was always too high for comfort due to the architecture of the engine. Whenever the XJR-6 (or one of its sisters) was thrown into a corner the high centre of gravity caused a severe diagonal pitch across its weighty Prototype chassis. Given the download generated by a Prototype underwing, the car could be thrown into the corner with aplomb: squashed into the ground, it did not roll into the bushes. However, weight vaulted alarmingly from inner rear to outer front tyre, heavily loading the hard worked front. Cars equipped with an effective underwing tend to run stiff springs at the front: the XJR-6 also had to have an extremely stiff front anti-roll bar.

The anti-roll bar resists roll and also acts like an extra spring added to the existing ones, particularly at the outer wheel. It can provide effects far more powerful than fitting harder springs. In crude terms, as the XJR-6 was dialled in it had to have an extremely stiff front anti-roll bar as a prop, to stop it burying itself in the ground. In this respect it was important that its advanced composite chassis was stiff enough to handle the bar loadings. Significantly, when TWR moved to a purpose-designed turbo engine it was a V6 with a low centre of gravity: it even had the smallest possible flywheel to which was attached a 5.5 in diameter clutch rather than the regular 7.25 in diameter item.

The XJR-6 was the first front-running Sports Prototype to have an advanced composite chassis. Sixties Prototypes had featured multi-tubular frame, aluminium monocoque and aluminium honeycomb monocoque chassis construction. The honeycomb monocoque was common in Formula One in the late Seventies and it

Front radiator location for the Jaguar XJR-6 puts additional weight ahead of the front wheel axis. This further helps the overall weight distribution and ensures good engine cooling.

The XJR-6 required a massively stiff front anti-roll bar to help counteract the effect of the top-heavy V12 engine wallowing around in the back of the chassis. The bar was of Kevlar.

was years since a Grand Prix had been won by a tube-frame car. Nevertheless, the 1980 and 1981 Le Mans races were won by tube-framed Cosworth-Rondeau and Porsche respectively.

A chassis exists primarily to carry the other elements of the car – engine, transmission, suspension, bodywork and so forth. It must hold all the elements in proper relationship to one another in the face of the loading from the suspension and aerodynamic forces and any lack of rigidity will manifest itself as poor suspension performance. In theory, since the main loads are the suspension loads which are point loadings a tubular frame should be well capable of handling them. However, for maximum rigidity it must be properly triangulated.

The ideal is the pure spaceframe in which all tubes are arranged so as to be free from bending loads. To achieve this within the constraints of a race car chassis would require such complex and complete triangulation of the frame that none of the resultant apertures could be large enough to allow driver access.

Provide a cockpit aperture and stiffness deteriorates markedly: the rigidity of the whole is that of the weakest area.

Nevertheless, it is possible to design a multi-tubular race car frame that offers good rigidity with the benefits of ease of construction and excellent service access. In the early Sixties the monocoque Lotus 25 set a new standard in Formula One, primarily through improved packaging. With a combination of twin fuel-carrying full-length torsion boxes linked via bulkheads, a stressed floor and the engine it was possible to achieve good rigidity while keeping the fuel load low and minimizing the frontal area.

The Lotus introduced the concept of the monocoque tub as opposed to the pure monocoque fuselage. A single-shell aircraft-style monocoque would, in theory, offer higher rigidity since the rigidity of a tube not only increases with any increase in diameter, but at a greater rate. However, a single shell would have been weakened by the cockpit aperture: the Lotus twin tube tub was a more practical proposition for a

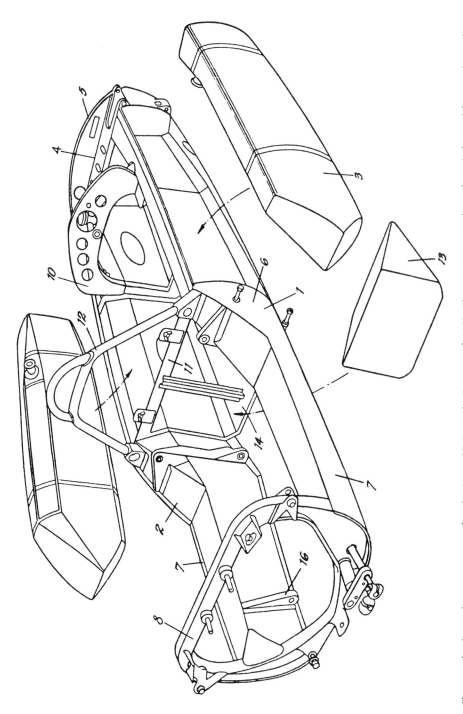

Colin Chapman's pioneering monocoque for the Lotus 25 Formula One car of 1962. The concept was that of a tub formed from twin torsion boxes linked by various crossmembers and the engine.

single-seater racing car, offering good rigidity with reasonable service access. The torsional rigidity of the revolutionary Lotus 25 was 2400 lb/ft per degree with the stressed engine bolted firmly in place, compared to 700 lb ft per degree for the preceding Lotus 24 tube frame car.

The 1962 Lotus 25 inspired the monocoque Ford-Lola GT of 1963 which was followed by the Ford GT40 of 1964. Packaging was less of a consideration given a fully enveloping body but Eric Broadley was attracted by the rigidity of a monocoque tub compared to that of a spaceframe. Like Colin Chapman he used the torsion boxes to house fuel and at first he dispensed with the aircraft-style fuel bags employed by Lotus, sealing the box instead. However, fuel bags proved a more practical proposition. Whereas his Lola GT had an aluminium tub like the pioneering Lotus, the GT40 had a heavy steel monocoque.

The GT40 tub had torsion box sponsons running from directly behind the front wheels to the rear wheels and linked via bulkheads including a front bridge section carrying the suspension and a boxed rear sub-assembly supporting the transmission and suspension. The engine was unstressed but the roof was integral and with the use of 0.024 in (0.6 mm) and 0.028 in (0.7 mm) thick steel panels a claimed torsional rigidity of 12,500 lb ft per degree was attained.

A couple of years later Ford produced a honeycomb monocoque for the MkIV 7.0-litre version of the GT40 with a weight reduced from 300 to 110 lb (136-50 kg) for a similar torsional rigidity. The MkIV employed a sandwich of aluminium honeycomb 0.5 in or 1.0 in (12.7 mm or 25.4 mm) thick between aluminium sheets only 0.016 in (0.4 mm) thick – so flimsy alone that they were in danger of damage from tools placed on them. The honeycomb-form aluminium foil acted as a continuous sheer web, dramatically improving the strength to weight ratio. Adhesives held the sandwich together, and held carefully shaped and cut honeycomb panels together to form the tub. Even the suspension and engine pick-up brackets were bonded in place. The brackets spread the point loading over an area of

honeycomb panel.

Later versions of the honeycomb tub had L-section strips of aluminium riveted on the outside of the bonded panel joints and some reinforcement inside of key joints. These added little to rigidity but ensured structural integrity in the event of a shunt. A steel roll cage was also added to all later versions of the GT40 in view of safety. Meanwhile, arch-rival Ferrari persevered with tubular frame construction throughout the Sixties, although with increasing use of stressed-skin reinforcement in the form of sponson boxes and the like. Those boxes wrapped around the frame, not replacing it.

Ferrari's reinforced frame "offered a good stiffness to weight ratio at a very reasonable price" according to Forghieri, who also points to its ease of repair and maintenance. It was a feature of the P4 and the 512S/M, while the rival Porsche 917 retained a pure tubular frame. The Porsche frame was in aluminium, the company having moved on from steel to the lighter, more rigid but harder to weld alternative. The aluminium tube had to be arc welded in an inert atmosphere which was provided by a shield of argon gas. Retaining an old-fashioned tube frame, the 917 chassis was notorious for its lack of rigidity but this did not stop the car's success. The 1971 Le Mans race was won by a titanium frame car.

In the Seventies Porsche added a roll cage to its 911 production shell, one which took the form of a quasi-frame and thereby achieved a higher torsional rigidity than for the 917 frame. Nevertheless, the regular 917 aluminium frame formed the basis of the 936 spyder frame that was still in service in 1981. Meanwhile, Porsche was developing the 956 with its first-ever monocoque chassis. This was of aluminium sheet and ran from the front of the pedal box to the back of the central fuel tank in conventional fashion. While it was good in torsion there was a question mark over its strength in bending. For this reason, Richard Lloyd Racing introduced its own honeycomb monocoque in 1984.

The team created a replacement tub incorporating honeycomb panels and additional crossmembers for increased stiffness. Basing this on standard dimensions was a headache for designer Nigel Stroud. For example, the radiators were so close to the fuel tank that honeycomb could not be used at the back of the tub and the construction had to carefully blend from honeycomb to single-skin aluminium. The Stroud monocoque had a honeycomb floor back to the dash hoop and honeycomb inner panels extending back to the fuel tank area. It also had additional strengthening diaphragms while having a standard design roll cage for Group C admission.

The overall effect was an increase in weight of a couple of kilos and greater stiffness in bending, though only a small gain in torsional rigidity since that relies largely on the sectional dimensions which had remained unchanged. With the improved strength in bending Stroud considered his tub significantly safer than the standard item it replaced. In 1987 the team had to replace its modified 956 by a version of the 962C since it was no longer legal to run with the pedals ahead of the front wheel axis. Stroud drew a similarly modified 962C tub, which added length in the front section, pushing the front wheels further forward relative to the pedal box.

Although the pedal position ruling was

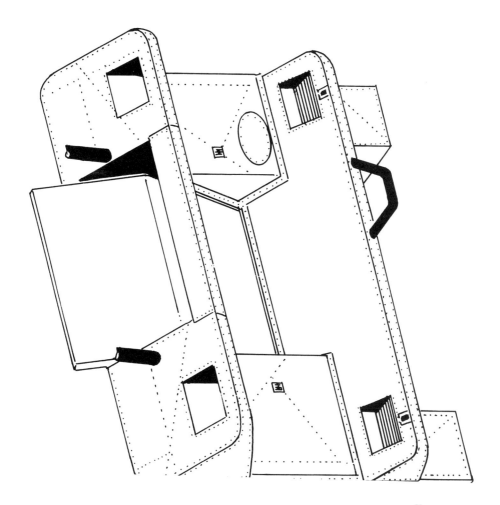

The Ferrari 312P of 1968 had a practical alternative to the monocoque tub – a spaceframe chassis with its centre section reinforced via aluminium panelling. The 512S/M was based on similar technology.

Cockpit of an Eighties Group C car had to have enough space to accommodate a theoretical passenger. This is the Lloyd honeycomb monocoque for the Porsche 962C.

intended to make a chassis safer, in the case of the move from 956 to 962C it added tub length in the weakest area, which was hardly in the interest of safety. Stroud had to follow this route for his standard dimension replacement tub: "Porsche had put four inches into the weakest area: I hated doing that but I had to if the standard body was going to fit."

By the late Eighties other Porsche teams had followed the aluminium replacement tub route and there was even a move to an advanced composite monocoque, though the factory stuck with the aluminium sheet original. The first advanced resin/fibre composite Group C1 car was the Aston Martin-Cheetah, followed soon after by the XJR-6. The original resin/fibre monocoque was the fibreglass Chaparral

chassis which set fibres of glass in a polyester resin. This low technology material was worked at atmospheric pressure and was cold rather than hot cured which made it easy to handle.

The breakthrough that paved the way for higher performance, hi-tech plastic composites was hot cured epoxy resin which could be combined with fibres of glass, carbon or Kevlar. Glass was only a fraction of the price of the more exotic materials but offered far less strength while imposing much more weight. Pressure bonded carbon and Kevlar based resin/fibre materials were a major advance. They were more tear-resistant than aluminium honeycomb, the product could be moulded into complex forms and the finished article had less weight and far greater torsional rigidity.

The strength of a resin/fibre composite

Richard Lloyd Racing honeycomb chassis for the Porsche 962C was a straight swap for the standard factory item. It was claimed to be more rigid, particularly in bending, hence safer.

is in the fibre. These materials incorporate fibres perhaps only 0.005 in (0.127 mm) thick spun from carbon or the DuPont Corporation's Kevlar aramid. While carbon and Kevlar fibres offer truly exceptional tensile strength and stiffness, they do so in only one direction: axially. Loads have to be fed along the axes of the fibres. The epoxy resin is used to envelope the fibres, after they have been woven into a cloth. The resin forms a plastic matrix which secures the fibres in the proper relationship to one another and bonds several layers together to a required thickness.

Weaves can be anything from a right angle lattice (50/50) to unidirectional and there is also the choice of fibre weight and stiffness for a given fibre type. The resin matrix offers no significant strength in its own right yet accounts for a high proportion of the total weight of a composite material. But it plays an indispensable role since, while it transmits loads to the fibres, it will not transmit cracks, and individual fibres can

fracture without causing significant reduction in component strength as neighbouring fibres will consequently not be affected and will bridge the gap.

Generally a resin/fibre composite is supplied as pre-preg sheets which means that it is already impregnated with heat curing resin and only needs baking under pressure once it has been worked into the shape of the component. This can be achieved by wrapping the unprocessed component in a vacuum bag and placing the bag in an oven or by using a special high pressure oven known as an autoclave, in which case higher pressures can be achieved.

Clearly there is an almost infinite choice of combinations of fibre, weave and resin that can be supplied as pre-preg material and thus it is produced to order. The key differences between carbon fibre and Kevlar are stiffness, impact resistance and cost. Carbon fibre is stiffer while Kevlar is less expensive and absorbs kinetic energy better. The combination of carbon fibre and Kevlar

The Aston Martin-Cheetah was the first Group C1 car to sport an advanced composite monocoque. The car was produced in Switzerland and made its début at Francorchamps in 1984.

offers a good compromise between stiffness and impact resistance.

In 1981 McLaren International unveiled the first advanced composite monocoque car, the McLaren MP4 which employed carbon fibre skins. One week later Lotus unveiled the first carbon fibre/Kevlar car, and it was the latter combination that became the most widely employed in the early Eighties. However, McLaren bonded together five sections (including bulkheads) moulded to shape by American rocket maker Hercules, while Lotus formed its composite tub by folding up two panels to form a shell into which aluminium bulkheads were inserted. Moulding to shape then bonding became the norm, the tub usually split into two main shell halves – either upper and lower or two sides – with bulkheads added, often of aluminium.

The crash resistance of composite tubs worried a number of designers while the technology was young. The traditional aluminium sheet monocoque deformed progressively and if properly designed would absorb a great deal of energy in the process. Advanced composites were acknowledged as stiff but it was feared that they would prove dangerously fragile upon secondary impact. A number of early Eighties tubs were designed with all or some of the outer skin aluminium though with greater experience of the materials this practice died out.

Experience of the materials themselves and of the possibilities associated with them saw Formula One designers achieve ever higher degrees of torsional rigidity. By the mid-Eighties, with the use of advanced composites Formula One designers were able to achieve a figure in excess of 15,000 lb ft per degree in spite of the narrow cross-sectional area of a single-seater monocoque.

McLaren's trend setting MP4 design started the fashion not only for an advanced composite tub but also for the use of such materials as body panels, undertray, wings, brake ducts and so forth. For example, the radiators were

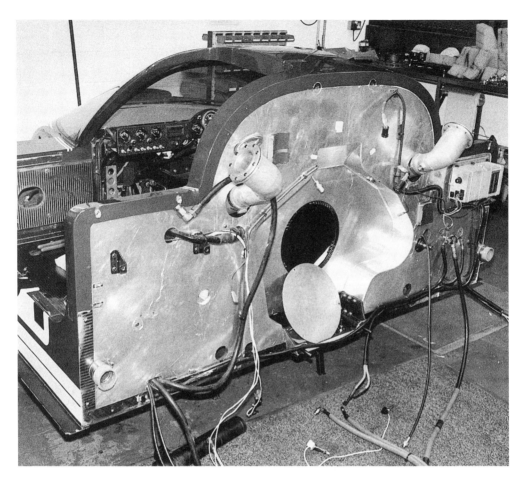

Above and facing page: The first successful Group C1 car to have an advanced composite monocoque was the Jaguar XJR-6 which emerged in 1985. The tub was assembled from a number of panels like a giant Airfix kit.

carried in carbon fibre boxes strong enough to act both as mounts and ducting, replacing conventional metal subframes plus fibreglass ducts. Ahead of the engine was less metal, less weight. The advanced composite monocoque Formula One car was stiff yet as light as the regulations permitted even when burdened with the weight of turbocharged engine ancillaries.

For Southgate and TWR, in 1985 the XJR-6 Formula One style tub was a step into the unknown. How strong would it be with such a large floor area? Essentially it was a big carbon fibre box, of which the large cross-sectional area compared to a Formula One tub allowed Southgate to achieve exceptional stiffness. It was, however, somewhat

over-engineered since it represented a venture into virgin territory. ''With the first car I could not be sure of the strength-to-weight ratio – if in doubt I made it too strong,'' Southgate admits. ''It was therefore too heavy; I could chop the weight down without significant loss of structural rigidity.''

Primarily the XJR-6 tub set carbon fibre skins over Nomex honeycomb. Naturally the number of layers and the weaves employed in the pre-preg skins varied according to application. The actual moulding process was not particularly involved since the tub was formed as a system of relatively flat sections, mostly in female tooling and each piece was small enough to slot inside the autoclave. The vacuum pressure-bonded, heat-cured

pieces were then cold-bonded together with a two-part adhesive. Around 20 major sections were assembled like a giant Airfix kit, the number of parts reflecting the extent and complexity of a prototype tub compared to a single-seater tub.

The thickest, strongest part was the rear bulkhead which was carbon fibre over aluminium honeycomb. It had a forward projecting rim around its periphery, this flange adding significantly to rigidity while it also incorporated carbon blocks at stress points and Kevlar rods to spread the vertical loads. However, the structure was, Southgate says, strong enough without the rods. It contained no metal yet, in a press, recorded twice the FISA strength requirement for a roll hoop – without the Kevlar rods in place.

The only steel roll-cage elements were a windscreen hoop (bonded to the pillars) and two tubes running back from that hoop across the roof to the top of the rear bulkhead. When the engine was in place, the roof tubes were linked to the cam covers via bolt-in engine bracing struts which located mid-way along the respective cam cover. At the front, since the engine slotted into a recess it was possible to bolt directly into each cam cover from above, down through the roof of the recess. Two lower longitudinal, horizontal bolts attached the sump.

The rear bulkhead had a separate carbon fibre over Nomex fuel tank/seat back moulding bonded to it. Underneath, the wide floor panel was a 50/50 carbon fibre/Kevlar skinned moulding which extended under the side boxes, the Kevlar weave offering tear and impact resistance. Kevlar was also used at the front of the side boxes, the portion facing the front wheels, for its resistance to stone damage. The side boxes were structural items, as were bulkheads at the dash and the front end. Other important structural items included the roof, an under-knee leg support panel which linked the side boxes across the cockpit floor, and a long panel extending from the dash to the front of the monocoque, forming the scuttle and enclosing the front suspension support assembly.

The front suspension was partially carried by a double bulkhead formed as two aluminium plates which were bolted into the advanced composite structure – the only major parts of the tub in metal. This bulkhead assembly straddled the front wheel axis and the pedals were fixed inside so the driver's feet reached just as far as it, staying within the wheelbase. Ahead, the master cylinders were enclosed by the composite front bulkhead, to which a composite nose box was bonded. Small magnesium castings were bolted inside the front corners of the monocoque to accept the leading front suspension pick-ups and spread the load. Use of magnesium rather than carbon for these pick-ups eased manufacture.

Overall, TWR's composite tub was reckoned to be at least 15 times stiffer than the Porsche's traditional sheet aluminium tub. Indeed, its torsional rigidity was so great that available measuring equipment was not man enough to deflect it. Advanced composites were not only used for the tub. The rear wing and diffuser tunners were carbon fibre over Nomex honeycomb. Each wing element contained two transverse cross beams and four longitudinal formers, all in

Below and facing page: Components of the Spice Group C car showing monocoque elements, and front and rear suspension parts. Seen in C2 and Camel Lights, the Spice car had an aluminium honeycomb monocoque.

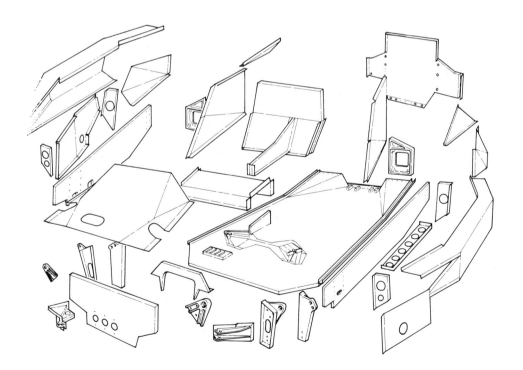

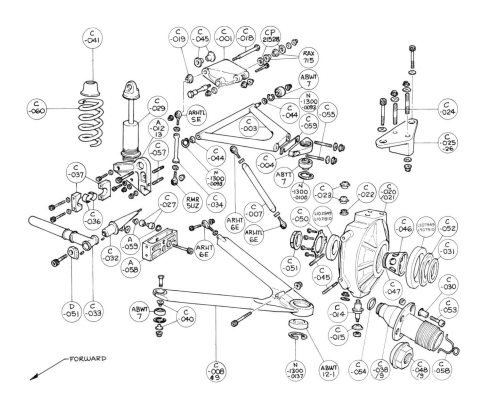

FORWARD

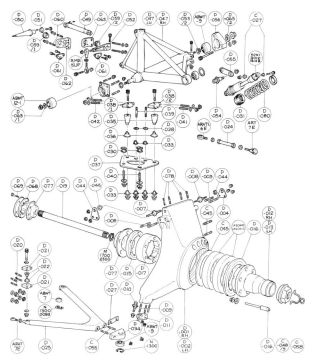

carbon fibre under a carbon fibre outer skin. The tunnels needed to be rigid enough to hold shape in the face of strong aerodynamic forces and were in fact structural members, tying an aluminium rear suspension crossbeam to the rear of the monocoque. Additionally, the engine was stressed while the transaxle case formed the rest of the rear part of the chassis.

Up front, the radiator was outrigged from the nose box, where it was encased by the nose and splitter. With scuttle, side box and roof shapes formed by the monocoque's outer surface, the nose, doors and tail were the only major body panels and these were not of fibreglass. The bodywork was formed of carbon fibre skins over Nomex honeycomb using pre-preg woven glass bonded under vacuum pressure and cured under elevated temperature using a vacuum bag and large oven. Kevlar was again used for wear resistance inside the wheel arches.

This, then, was the state of the art in mid-Eighties Prototype chassis technology, ousting the familiar combination of metal and fibreglass for a far stronger yet lighter structure. However, many cars continued to employ fibreglass bodywork (aside from wings and underwing) since the cost saving was significant, the weight saving on bodywork alone slight.

Whatever the materials used for the chassis, the Eighties Prototype had conventional race car suspension with wishbone linkages and coils as the springing medium. Generally conventional anti-roll bars were fitted front and rear and always rack and pinion steering was employed. Uprights were cast magnesium or aluminium while the wishbones were typically steel fabrications.

Tyre technology tended to govern the location of suspension pick-up points on the monocoque. Often the rear coils were inboard over the transaxle to clear the diffuser tunnels while Southgate put them inside the wheel wells. Inboard coils were operated via rockers actuated by the upper wishbone or via pushrods. Sometimes pushrod front suspension was employed but there was no major gain to be found from mounting the coils inboard.

On the 956, the springs were titanium while the dampers were Bilstein gas units. The coils wrapping the front Bilsteins were of taper wire and varying wind to provide a measure of progressive rate, a trick long used by Porsche. On the XJR-6 a pushrod front suspension system offered a degree of progressive rate, though with higher downforce this was less significant. A Koni gas/fluid adjustable damper was run inside a titanium fixed rate spring: TWR found the Koni was faster-reacting than the Bilstein and it offered harder settings, if less ride comfort.

Eighties Prototype wheel rim sizes ranged from 16 in to 19 in (406 mm to 482 mm) diameter, the latter capable of accommodating Southgate's upright rear spring/damper unit and the largest, 14.8 in (375.9 mm) diameter brake disc. GTP rim sizes had to be the same front and rear and thus tended to be 16 in or 17 in (406 mm or 413.8 mm) diameter. A 16 in (406 mm) rim was large enough to accommodate a 13 in (330 mm) diameter disc which was the smallest considered adequate for the job. In general, the larger the rim, the larger the tyre circumference hence the less revolutions for a given speed and less G-force trying to throw the tread off.

Both Porsche and TWR employed Dunlop Denloc tyres. Denloc is a system to keep the bead in place in the event of a puncture: it is when the bead collapses into the well that the driver finds it hardest to control the car. The 956 ran on Denloc shod BBS modular (magnesium centre/aluminium inner and outer section) rims, 16 in (406 mm) both front and rear and incorporating extractor fans to draw hot air from the brakes. The XJR-6, with its bigger, 17 in (413.8 mm) front, 19 in (482 mm) rear rims had specially commissioned one-piece magnesium wheels from Speedline in Italy.

Chapter Thirteen

Stop and Go
(Transmission and Brakes)

The only Eighties Sports Prototype manufacturer to produce its own transmission and brakes was Porsche. Porsche had a long tradition of gearbox manufacture and moved into brakes in the Seventies, in response to the demands of its 1000 bhp Can Am cars. The massive torque of its ground-shaking 5.0-litre turbocharged spyders called for a stronger transmission while the strain on the brakes as the driver accelerated with his foot still on the brake pedal in an effort to combat turbo lag overheated pads and fluid. Thus, the Can Am car was equipped with a new beefy four-speed gearbox and Porsche's own four-pot caliper brakes with special finned aluminium alloy caliper bodies to better dissipate the heat generated.

As usual the Can Am transmission was to the conventional mid-engined racing car pattern with the gearbox outboard of the c.w.p., the clutch shaft running under the crown wheel to form the lower of two gearbox shafts, the upper shaft feeding direct to the pinion. The clutch was a quadruple plate Borg and Beck item while no differential was employed, the inboard cv joints linked by a titanium tube bolted to the crown wheel. This so-called spool was favoured by American oval racers who did not require normal differential action, having tyre stagger to compensate.

Elsewhere, limited slip differentials were standard wear. Ironically, it was the Porsche company that had introduced the limited slip differential to racing, back in the Thirties. At first the Porsche-designed Auto Union V16 supercharged Grand Prix racer fed its formidable 400 bhp plus through a conventional open differential but it was found that there was a pronounced tendency for the inside rear wheel to spin if power was applied while the car was under a cornering load. Torque takes the path of least resistance and it would go up in inside wheel tyre smoke whenever weight transfer loaded the outer wheel. The ZF differential introduced by Porsche permitted one rear wheel to spin at a speed no more than 15 per cent greater than the other before a system of wedge-shaped cams running freely between two rotating sleeves jammed solid, locking the differential action.

The ZF cam and pawl differential became standard wear for Grand Prix cars and Sports Prototypes after the war, then in the Seventies the Salisbury-type clutch pack differential arrived and did the job much better, its multi-plate clutches locking the differential action in a smooth, progressive and easily adjusted manner. Meantime, Porsche had tried progressively reducing the permitted ZF differential action on its Can Am car and on the skid pan it had kept cornering faster. Reducing the differential action promoted understeer which countered the car's inherent oversteer. To run a spool was the logical conclusion of this investigation.

Porsche's 1000 bhp Can Am car of 1972 stressed brakes like never before. Porsche devised these four-pot caliper brakes with aluminium bodies which were often finned to better dissipate heat.

The other unusual feature of the Porsche Can Am transmission was synchromesh for the gearbox. Synchromesh adds weight, creates heat and slows changes. However, Porsche had its own patent system which it licensed throughout the world and liked to promote as used in racing. The Can Am brakes featured 11.8 in (300 mm) diameter radially ventilated cast iron discs which were cross-drilled for lightness. The straight-walled radial vents centrifuged the air out of the disc, providing very effective cooling. The finned four-pot calipers were three-piece aluminium items which were run with Textar linings.

Subsequent Seventies developments saw Porsche switch to Fitchel and Sachs clutches and Raybestos pads. The three-piece calipers were replaced by one-piece aluminium items which were stiffer and lighter while 13 in (330 mm) diameter curved vane discs were introduced. The spool was retained since it created a comfortable amount of understeer. This established transmission and brake equipment formed the basis of the 956 package.

Changes included a switch to twin two-pot calipers, one either side of the disc. The five-speed gearbox was new for the 956 and was designed to run upside down, with the input shaft running above the c.w.p. to suit chassis packaging requirements. Since the 956 boxer engine was very short a long bellhousing-cum-spacer was required ahead of the gearbox and this was initially of magnesium, like the c.w.p. housing and the gear case. However, it was subsequently replaced by an aluminium casting adding 8.8 lb (4 kg) but also stiffness which increased the car's axle to axle torsional rigidity. A hatch in the casting provided clutch access.

Porsche ran 1.3 in (33mm) thick cast iron curved rather than straight vane discs throughout the Eighties, drilled

External view and internal components of the Porsche 956/962C transaxle. Porsche employed a synchromesh gearbox and a spool rather than a differential, though this customer car has a differential.

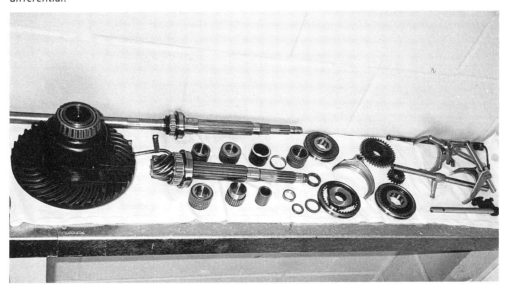

through the vanes for lightness. However, for 24 hours at Le Mans, undrilled discs with slightly thicker plates were employed. This provided more mass to retain heat as the disc ran free on the Mulsanne. The temperature differential created by running the long straight and then banging the brakes on hard for the Mulsanne corner had been known to lead to disc cracking.

In 1984 Richard Lloyd Racing introduced its honeycomb monocoque 956 with AP Racing brakes, these having similar size curved vane discs and single four-pot calipers. They were run with Ferodo DS11 pads. In 1987 Lloyd switched to Brembo brakes, these offering a similar four-pot caliper which the team considered stiffer. The Italian company also had an interesting Pioli cast iron disc, which it introduced to Group C the following year in a 14 in (356 mm) diameter size. The 1.25 in (32 mm) thick Pioli disc set rods rather than curved vanes between the disc plates, the rods arranged so as to have a similar aerodynamic effect to curved vanes.

The staggered rods were an elegant means of flinging air out of the periphery of the disc. Brembo claimed the cross-drilled Pioli disc was lighter and that it ran with a more even distribution of temperature over the surface of the plates. Each disc was claimed to weigh only 13.6 lb (6.2 kg) while the attendant two piece, differential bore aluminium caliper weighed 7.04 lb (3.2 kg). The differential bore followed AP Racing practice, helping combat taper wear of the pad. Brembo supplied Lloyd with asbestos free pads produced by the Pagid company in Essen, Germany rather than the usual copper-asbestos Ferodo DS11 pads. The RS9 Pagid pad had a claimed Mu value of 0.37 compared to 0.30 for the familiar DS11.

Aside from Brembo brakes and Pagid pads, the Lloyd Porsche was also unusual in its use of a Salisbury-type differential in 1987. This was found in particular to improve turn in to slower corners. However, the spool was re-fitted for Le Mans since it ran cooler and ensured that failure of one of the driveshafts did not strand the car out on the circuit. In 1988 the factory started deploying a Salisbury

for certain races, finding its reduction of understeer made the 962C more stable in fast corners.

The factory had an interesting clutchless, push-button gear selection transmission which it ran in certain of its cars on an experimental basis. Known as PDK – Porsche Doppel-Kupplung – this system was primarily for the road since it was somewhat overweight for serious racing. It retained a conventional clutch purely for starting, while employing two small clutches in the process of gear shifting, these electro-hydraulic under the control of an ECU. The two selector clutches sat at the front of the gearbox and drove concentric input shafts, these carrying positively-driven gears in constant mesh with the respective gear on the output shaft. The gears on the output shaft were free to rotate until selected by a dog clutch.

The basic principles of operation were straightforward. Consider a change from first to second. As the gearbox was in first, the clutch driving the second gear input shaft would be free. Thus, second gear could be safely selected before the first gear dog was released. Second gear having been selected, the second gear clutch was progressively taken up while the first gear clutch was released. Finally, the first gear dog was released.

Clearly the PDK transmission allowed gear changing under full load. Since the selector clutches and dogs were under electro-hydraulic activation, the push button gear changes were as good as instant. The hydraulic pump sapped a little power but otherwise the system was just as efficient as a conventional gearbox, if somewhat heavier. It allowed the flexibility of gear ratio changes at the track, essential for professional racing.

The control system was designed to actuate the twin clutches only at matching engine and road speeds, allowing the driver to pre-select gears via the steering wheel push button. Changing gear under load opened up the possibility of changing gear in mid-corner without unsettling the car. Further, the electronic control removed the danger of damaging the engine through premature downshifting.

For its PDK-equipped 962C, Porsche

Richard Lloyd Racing was a pioneer of Brembo brakes in Group C1, switching its Porsche from AP having in turn moved from the regular Porsche issue.

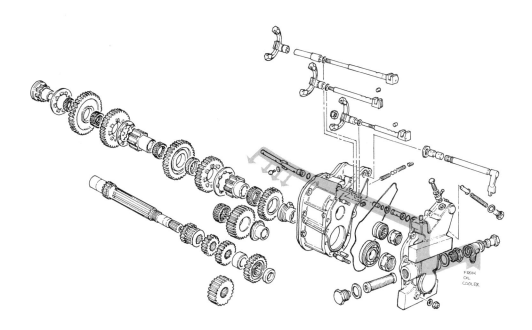

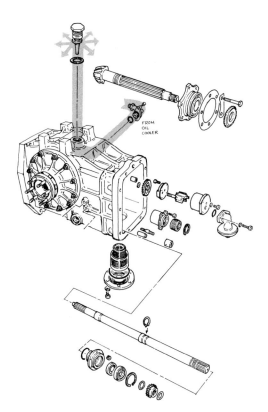

Exploded drawing of the Hewland DGB gearbox, used for lower power Eighties prototypes. High power cars used the beefier, heavier VGC version, essentially to the same layout.

provided two steering wheel push buttons, one for up shifts, the other for down shifts. A digital display on the dashboard told the driver which gear was engaged and the next gear selected. Flat out in fifth, the driver could punch the down button three times for a change into second which would occur as the road speed fell appropriately under braking for the next corner. PDK gear changing was foolproof and effortless. However, aside from the weight of the system, drawbacks included increased fuel consumption and the fact that there was more to go wrong.

The factory team introduced PDK in the mid-Eighties, generally for a third string entry. After a lightening programme shed 33 lb (15 kg) Hans Stuck used PDK en route to the 1987 German Supercup series title. PDK did not find such success in the World Championship, which was the preserve of the conventional gearbox.

The most conventional of all was the Hewland DGB five-speed gearbox as illustrated in the accompanying exploded diagram. This had a combined c.w.p. housing and main case (with detachable sideplates for differential access) to which was bolted the bearing carrier and end plate, as illustrated. Hewland offered DG and heftier VG gearboxes for Eighties Prototypes, the most substantial of all the VGC introduced in 1985 in response to the massive torque of mid-Eighties Group C and GTP cars. This had a larger c.w.p. housing to accommodate a larger, stronger c.w.p.

The VGC was run with great success by the Electramotive Nissan GTP team but was not found strong enough in its standard guise by the Sauber team. Sauber ordered its own c.w.p. from ATE in Finland and gears from the Staffs Silent Gear Co and found it necessary to change the c.w.p. and gears prior to each race. The Group C Nissan-Lola had a VGC with a semi-dry sump modification by Lola which saved oil drag and weight.

TWR looked to the alternative to the Hewland VGC produced by March Engineering, the 85/88T. This followed the general pattern of a Hewland but its magnesium main case (carrying the gears and the c.w.p.) split transversely at the rear axle line to allow installation of a

larger, stronger c.w.p. Additionally, between the main case and the bearing carrier was a so-called strap to provide additional shaft support, again in the interest of strength. The strap piece set an additional bearing on each shaft run and four gears lay ahead of it, two behind.

Porsche, Hewland and March five-speed gearboxes were used by all serious Eighties Prototypes, generally fed via a Salisbury-type clutch pack differential. Seasoned Le Mans runners employed the spool for its help in getting a car home but elsewhere the spool was inappropriate since it tended to create excessive understeer in high speed corners and poor turn in to slower bends.

Salisbury Transmission Ltd's Powr-Lok Mk11 differential is illustrated in the accompanying exploded diagram. The basic principle of the Salisbury-type differential is that inner and outer clutch plates are splined respectively to the side gear and the case. Since bevel gears are employed an axial thrust is developed which is proportional to the torque applied by the crown wheel to the differential. Under low torque conditions the differential functions normally but if the torque is increased the clutch pack will be loaded and this will resist the side gear from rotating at a different speed from the case.

The drive is transmitted from the differential case to the side ring gears thence through the pinion mates to the side gears. Cam action is exerted between the ramp-like cam surfaces on the shoulder of each side ring gear and the mating abutment shoulder of each pinion mate. Cam forces on the cross pin further load the clutches which inhibit the differential action. The clutches may be pre-loaded via the use of optional belleville spring plates.

Re-arrangement of the stacking order of the plates and the addition or deletion of belleville plates varies the performance of the differential, as does the ramp configuration chosen. Three different ramp configurations are possible through changing the ring side gears. Those gears with equal 45° ramps provide an equal amount of differential action under acceleration and braking.

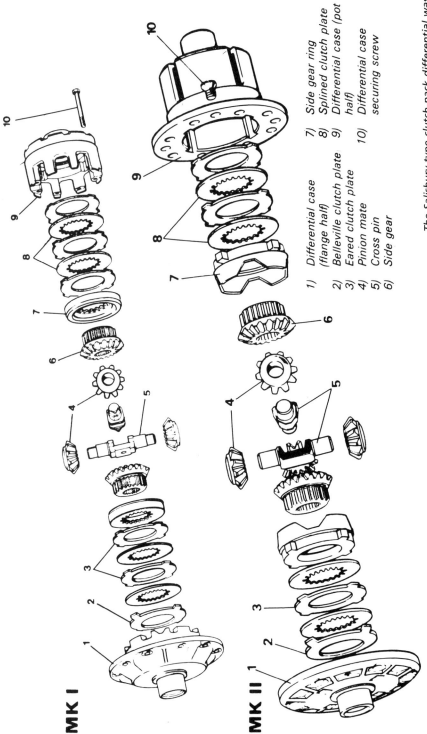

MK I

MK II

1) Differential case
   (flange half)
2) Belleville clutch plate
3) Eared clutch plate
4) Pinion mate
5) Cross pin
6) Side gear

7) Side gear ring
8) Splined clutch plate
9) Differential case (pot
   half)
10) Differential case
    securing screw

The Salisbury-type clutch-pack differential was favoured by Eighties Group C and GTP cars, other than for 24 hour racing. The disadvantage was an inability to limp to the pits in the event of cv failure.

When ramps are 30° and 60°, differential action is greater under braking. A 45° and 90° set of ramps yields a free differential under braking.

The Prototype transaxle typically incorporated Lobro steel driveshafts with conventional inner and outer cv joints and driving through a steel hub with half a dozen pegs to drive the disc bell and wheel. In the case of the Sauber C9 the wheel drive pegs were formed with the wheel so there were fresh pegs with each change of wheel. The transaxle was typically fed via a conventional triple plate clutch. The most common clutch was the AP Racing 7.25 in (184 mm) gear driven unit, as used almost universally in twin plate guise by 3.0-litre Cosworth Formula One cars. This was a diaphragm spring unit with gear-driven pressure plates.

Sandwiched between the flywheel and the dished end cover carrying the diaphragm spring was a steel adapter ring with gear teeth cut into its inner surface. Those teeth meshed with teeth around the circumference of each steel pressure plate. The end cover and adapter ring were attached to a steel flywheel, by either six or twelve bolts, the latter arrangement used where an engine had harsh power characteristics. The steel flywheel and pressure plates worked in conjunction with steel driven plates onto which a bronze-based friction material was sintered. In the twin plate Formula One version the driven plates were rigidly attached to hubs splined to the gearbox input shaft.

In 1986 AP Racing was honoured with a British Design Council Award in recognition of the excellence of its classic clutch. The triple plate version most commonly used for Group C1 had only one driven plate attached directly to a hub splined to the gearbox input shaft. This hub also carried external teeth which married with internal teeth on the two other drive plates, which could therefore float. It was available with steel or lightweight aluminium cover. Compared to the twin plate Formula One clutch, it had more surfaces to take up heat and spread the load and thus had a longer life. The 12-bolt version tended to be standard for Le Mans.

In the late Eighties the carbon-carbon clutch started to make inroads into Prototype racing following its successful exploitation in Formula One. The material in question was essentially the same as used for carbon-carbon brakes and was manufactured by either Hitco in the USA or Carbone Industrie (CI) in France, primarily for military applications. For example, Hitco, a division of Armoc Steel, produced carbon-carbon disc brakes for fighter aircraft. The material was difficult and expensive to produce.

Essentially, carbon-carbon consists of a matrix of carbon/graphite material reinforced with carbon/graphite structural fibres. Production entails putting a woven web of carbonised rayon or similar fibre in a methane gas filled furnace where, red hot, carbon atoms form on it in a top secret process known as carbon vapour deposition. Densification is accomplished by impregnating fibres with carbon during repeated steps at high temperature and the entire process can take many weeks. The product has to be machine-finished using diamond tooling.

AP Racing first played with carbon-carbon as a clutch friction material in the early Eighties but expense was a major concern and the available material from Hitco did not work very well due to a poor low-temperature co-efficient of friction. When cold the clutch slipped badly. In the mid-Eighties AP Racing engineer John Lindo moved to Tilton Engineering Inc., the California-based racing equipment supply company run by McLane "Mac" Tilton which was AP's West Coast distributor. Here Lindo was able to continue development of the carbon-carbon clutch away from the day to day pressures of Formula One supply.

Hitco improved the low-temperature co-efficient of its material and Lindo discovered that only a small input of heat was sufficient to double the Mu value. A conventional clutch had a Mu value in the region of 0.30. The Tilton/Hitco clutch had a static value of 0.20 which rose rapidly to 0.40. By 1987 Tilton 7.25 in (184 mm) carbon-carbon clutches were running in a wide variety of American racing cars, including some Camel Lights. That year Lotus and Ferrari tried a 5.5 in (140 mm) lug-driven version in Formula One and, stirred by Tilton's

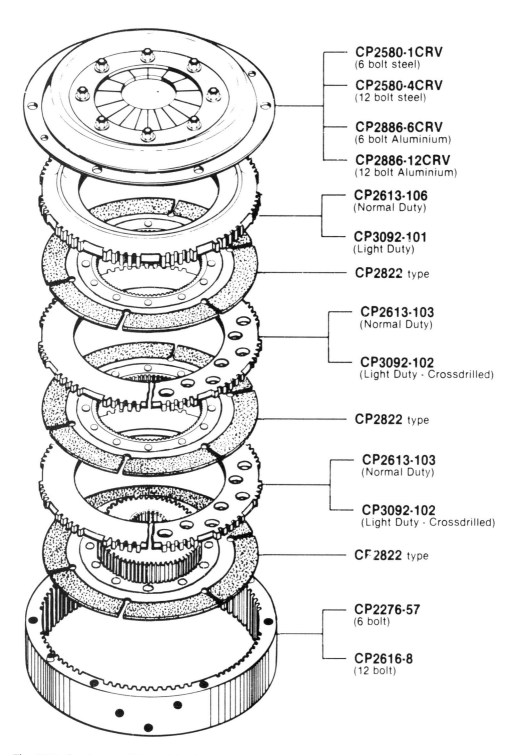

CP2580-1CRV
(6 bolt steel)

CP2580-4CRV
(12 bolt steel)

CP2886-6CRV
(6 bolt Aluminium)

CP2886-12CRV
(12 bolt Aluminium)

CP2613-106
(Normal Duty)

CP3092-101
(Light Duty)

CP2822 type

CP2613-103
(Normal Duty)

CP3092-102
(Light Duty - Crossdrilled)

CP2822 type

CP2613-103
(Normal Duty)

CP3092-102
(Light Duty - Crossdrilled)

CP2822 type

CP2276-57
(6 bolt)

CP2616-8
(12 bolt)

The AP Racing Borg and Beck triple plate 7.25 in (184 mm) clutch was standard prototype issue in the Eighties. It was gear-driven as is made clear in this exploded drawing.

progress, AP Racing came in with its own carbon-carbon Formula One clutch.

AP Racing used material supplied by CI, initially for a four-plate 5.5 in (140 mm) Formula One clutch. The 5.5 in (184 mm) conventional lug-driven clutch was in the process of replacing the 7.25 in (184 mm) gear-driven clutch as engine manufacturers sought a lower crankshaft axis and the AP carbon-carbon clutch was virtually a regular clutch with carbon-carbon replacement plates. Tilton won Detroit with Honda-Lotus, then AP Racing won Monza with Honda-Williams.

AP soon found that it could take the fourth plate out and in 1988 it took over the entire Formula One carbon-carbon clutch market. For C1 Prototypes it devised a triple plate 7.25 in (184 mm) carbon-carbon clutch. The larger diameter offered a higher torque capacity, although the clamp load was another factor affecting torque capacity. The 7.25 in (184 mm) unit was tried by TWR in 1988 but the wear rate was found unacceptable. However, following development work this clutch was used very successfully by Daimler-Benz in 1989 (other than at Le Mans).

The AP Racing 7.25 in (184 mm) carbon-carbon clutch was lug-driven. The pressure plates were driven by a dozen lugs projecting from the end cover and bolting through to the flywheel. In turn, the drive plates slotted over lugs on a single hub splined to the gearbox input shaft.

Compared to a gear drive, the lug drive was a little lighter, ran cooler and did not trap dust and debris as the clutch wore. A further consideration was easier machining of the plates, important since carbon-carbon is hard to work. None of the plates was metallic. The carbon-carbon plates were thicker than conventional plates, hence the triple plate carbon-carbon clutch was as wide as a quadruple plate conventional clutch. However, it was significantly lighter than a conventional triple plate 7.25 in (184 mm) gear-driven clutch.

The advantages of the carbon-carbon clutch were many. The clutch could be

Towards the end of the Eighties AP Racing introduced a carbon fibre-reinforced carbon clutch for Prototype use. It was lug rather than gear-driven, as is evident here.

run with a lighter flywheel and the combination of lighter clutch and lighter flywheel offered reduced inertia which allowed some engines to run higher revs. In theory it should improve engine response and acceleration. Further, the carbon-carbon clutch plates did not warp and thus released more cleanly while this and the lower plate inertia was kind on the gearbox. Additionally, the wear rate was low and the clutch was resistant to

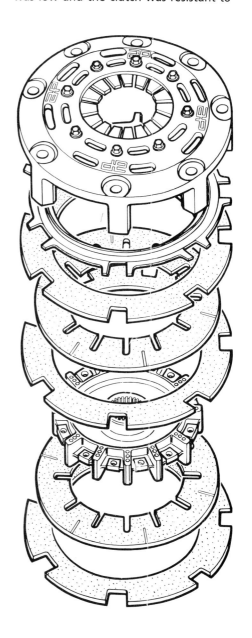

abuse. The effect of any clutch slip was not to induce further slip, as in the case of a conventional clutch but was to produce more heat, increasing friction.

Even more advantageous was the use of carbon-carbon as brake friction material. The carbon-carbon brake disc was extremely light and a carbon-carbon brake stopped a car much faster than a conventional brake. The combination of carbon-carbon disc and pad offered a Mu value in the region of 0.60. The disadvantage was a far higher operating temperature – as high as 600° centigrade. Carbon-carbon radiates heat: everything around it gets very, very hot. This heat was hard to dissipate and that affected the wear rate, the fluid – which could boil – and sometimes even the caliper body: magnesium started to fail at that temperature.

Carbon-carbon brakes were developed for Formula One in the early Eighties, Brabham with Hitco and then McLaren with CI leading the way. In the mid-Eighties AP Racing joined forces with Hitco as CI went its own way, embracing teams other than McLaren. Indeed, in 1985 CI had a virtual monopoly since

Hitco was slow to develop a radially ventilated carbon-carbon disc, the pioneering discs having been solid. Hitco ventilated discs were widely used by atmo cars in 1987 while the turbo runners tended to prefer CI discs. The CI disc had a lower co-efficient of friction when cold and increased its co-efficient more violently, albeit reaching a marginally higher value. Significantly, the turbo car had plenty of performance to put heat into the disc.

For Prototype racing, both AP and Brembo came to agreement with CI for the supply of suitable 14 in (356 mm) discs. Running these the overall weight saving was in the region of 55 lb (25 kg), and unsprung weight at that. Since this was a saving of rotating mass, in theory there was a slight fuel saving. More significant was the sheer stopping power of the carbon-carbon brake and for this reason it was raced in the cut and thrust of GTP before Group C.

TWR first tried 13 in (330 mm) diameter disc carbon-carbon brakes during a mid-1987 test at Silverstone. The driver initially found poor braking performance and consequently started playing with

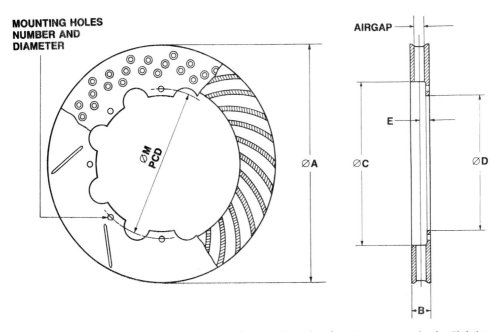

Conventional cast-iron curved-vane disc as supplied by AP Racing for Prototype use in the Eighties. It was typically 14.0 in (355.6 mm) in diameter and 1.1 in (28 mm) thick and was cross-drilled to save weight.

the brake balance control. Suddenly the brakes hit the crucial operating temperature range and came in with a bang, locking the wheels at the chicane. The car shunted. In 1988 the team started using AP carbon-carbon brakes for qualifying, carefully exploiting their stopping power. No lap time could be found in the reduced unsprung weight. Meanwhile, the new TWR GTP team race-débuted the new brakes.

Since Group C was endurance racing to a given fuel allowance, harsh braking tended to be avoided – the cars glided into the corners. Sprint-orientated GTP tended to call for the need to be able to dive inside and outbrake other cars. Carbon-carbon brakes were raced for the first time on the XJR-9 at Sears Point in 1988. Keeping the brakes within their high and narrow working temperature band was a major headache given the full enclosure of the wheels. The radiated heat could be enough to set brake ducts alight! Modified calipers had already been developed for Formula One, typically machined from solid one-piece items with heat insulation inserts.

Compared to Formula One, Prototype racing was very late in the exploitation of carbon-carbon brakes. The heat dissipation problem was greater, there was less finance to throw at the challenge since the teams tended to be poorer while with greater overall car weight the weight saving was less significant. Further, given the endurance factor, the teams were not looking as hard for the ultimate technical solution. The new brakes were used widely in 1989, though not on all circuits. No team ran carbon-carbon in the 1989 Le Mans race while only Nissan raced carbon-carbon at Brands Hatch, the most difficult circuit for the new technology. Its car had Formula One uprights which over-cooled conventional brakes.

Prototypes tended to run 14 in (356 mm) carbon-carbon discs, bigger than Formula One discs in view of the greater weight to be stopped. Indeed, throughout the Eighties, Prototype cast iron disc diameters had tended to grow with increasing performance. The size range was from 11 in (279 mm) diameter discs for 13 in (330 mm) wheels, eventually to 14.8 in (376 mm) diameter,

the largest that could be squeezed into a 17 in (432 mm) diameter rim. The bigger the disc, the more braking torque that could be produced since the pads operated on a larger radius. In general terms, brake torque ought just – and only just – be sufficient to enable the driver to lock the wheels.

Increasing downforce allowed cars to be able to handle higher brake torque. The bigger disc pumped more air and hence ran cooler; while for a given wheel speed the pad rubbing speed was higher, hence pad wear was higher, but disc wear was lower while heat was put into the disc more rapidly. This was an important consideration with regard to carbon-carbon discs. The 14.8 in (376 mm) diameter disc was introduced by AP Racing in 1990 to assist Nissan's quest to race Le Mans on carbon-carbon discs, as described in Section Four.

The conventional AP Racing cast iron disc was the curved vane type, this being more rigid than the straight vane, the curves running in the direction of the airflow and helping centrifuge the air out. In the early Eighties AP had a so-called Sphericone disc which set pillars of iron in the gaps between the curved vanes. These increased the surface area, assisting cooling but the Sphericone cooled too well, extremes of temperature leading to cracking. The same problem saw thicker and heavier discs run at Le Mans, the better to retain heat on the Mulsanne.

By the mid-Eighties the AP Racing curved vane disc was standard for non-Porsche users, then along came the Brembo Pioli disc. The Pioli disc by its construction offered less structural rigidity than the curved vane and this became a problem following the introduction of carbon-metallic pads in 1989. Produced by Performance Friction in the USA, the new pad consisted essentially of a block of carbon impregnated with metal particles, the latter around 45 per cent of the total content. It had to be very carefully bedded in to coat the conventional cast iron disc with the residue of it, then offered an extremely high Mu valve – around 0.55 – and thus comparable stopping power to carbon-carbon.

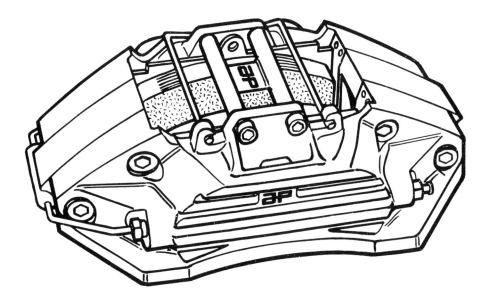

The typical non-Porsche Eighties Prototype caliper was the AP Racing four-pot caliper with open back as shown here. It was of aluminium alloy and had differential bores to combat taper wear.

As with carbon-carbon, torque rose at a crucial high temperature and some drivers found it hard to control. AP found it the first serious threat to DS11, recommending it unlike Brembo. For Brembo carbon-metallic pads brought problems of its use in conjunction with its elegant Pioli disc which was less able to withstand the increased load. The carbon-metallic pad was hard on a disc, as was to be expected: stopping faster generates more heat.

The traditional DS11 pad was asbestos based with a high copper content and was used by AP and its rivals for much of the decade of the Eighties. Its friction characteristics were not high but were stable and the wear rate was reasonable. The typical non-Porsche Prototype brake was an AP four-pot caliper running DS11 pads on a curved vane cast iron disc. In the early Eighties AP offered a closed-back aluminium four-pot caliper but most serious runners were Porsche customers and the twin two-pot Porsche arrangement was the leading brake. The balanced two-pot arrangement put less stress on the wheel bearing.

In the mid-Eighties AP came to prominence with TWR and moved to an open back four-pot caliper, the easier to keep pads cool as car performance rose. The initial open-back design was four-piece with a bridge at each end and two side pieces, then AP moved to a two-piece version which lasted the rest of the decade. Expense kept out the machined-from-solid Formula One caliper for cast iron applications. Machining from solid offered a slightly better grade of material than could be employed with casting. This improved strength at high temperature – a vital consideration given carbon-carbon brakes.

An interesting AP development was a twin disc system, introduced first to Formula One in 1986, in carbon-carbon, partly to offset the disadvantage of Hitco versus CI discs in terms of ultimate performance. Two floating discs were operated by a single piston on the inside of the caliper so there was no fluid on the outside, helping reduce the problem of heat transfer to the fluid. An altered ratio between master cylinder and piston provided much reduced pedal travel while less pedal effort was another advantage.

The performance of the twin disc brake was superior but cooling the outer disc was a problem. Thus, the system tended only to be used in qualifying and it faded away with the passing of the turbo era. Meantime, a spin-off twin cast-iron disc version had been evaluated by TWR in 1986. Again, two fully floating discs were squeezed by a single piston on the inside of the caliper, but knock-off was a problem until the single caliper was replaced by twin balanced calipers. That added weight and complexity and did not overcome the problem of cooling the outer disc. Problems mounted and when one driver was testing the system an inner disc exploded and cut through the wheel and tub to land inside the cockpit as the wheel fell off!

PART FOUR

JAPANESE ADVANCE

Chapter Fourteen

Nissan VG30

Nissan got serious about Prototype racing in 1984, in which year it formed its so called NISMO competition wing. Prior to that it had supplied a couple of Japanese teams with 2.1-litre in-line four Group C turbo engines but was much better known for its production car based race and rally efforts. The L-series in-line four and in-line six cylinder engines were familiar in North American road racing circles and six cylinder Z cars had regularly beaten Porsches in SCCA racing.

Bob Sharp was one of America's leading Nissan entrants. Following the arrival of the new VG series 2960 cc 60° vee-six engine in 1983 he had planned an ambitious Trans Am effort with it. Meanwhile, that year Nissan took a total of 600 race wins in the USA, mainly with L-series engines. In 1984 Sharp duly wheeled out a 300ZX turbo for Paul Newman, the only turbo car in the title chase. Alas, the effort was bugged by the problem of properly re-programming the VG30's sophisticated brain.

The VG30 production engine had been conceived from the outset with 16-bit micro processor control of its injection and ignition systems: Nissan called it the ECCS – Electronic Concentrated (Engine) Control System. Engine management systems were new in racing – few 1983 Grand Prix cars had run them, for example. However, Sharp found help close at hand in the form of El Segundo, California-based Electramotive Inc a company run by IMSA GTO Nissan racer

and aerospace engineer Don Devendorf and computer boffin John Knepp.

Devendorf had raced Nissans since 1973 and Electramotive had devised its own fully electronic injection system for the in-line six engine as early as 1981, before the technology entered Formula One. Electramotive's success in making a racing version of the ECCS for the V6 came to the attention of the factory and talks led to a joint project between NISMO and Electramotive to develop the V6 turbo for Group C and GTP application.

Electramotive's electronic in-line six GTO engines had shown the power potential. Further, Nissan appreciated that successful development of a turbocharged racing engine was heavily dependent upon engine management: Bosch Motronic had been the secret of both Porsche and BMW's success in 1983 (Porsche winning the World Endurance Championship, BMW the World Championship with Brabham and Nelson Piquet). Porsche had worked with fully electronic injection (like Electramotive before it), BMW electro-mechanical injection, the former offering more sophisticated control, the latter a higher injection pressure for improved atomisation.

For the Nissan V6 turbo Electramotive was to develop an engine management system utilizing Bosch solenoid injectors – as Porsche and its own earlier in-line six system – and its own control

package based on the ECCS. It was also to undertake development of the mechanical side of the engine with the assistance of factory engineers.

The VG30 was an over-square engine, displacing 3.4 x 3.3 in (87 x 83 mm) for 2958.9 cc and it had a short, stiff six-pin, four-bearing crankshaft in a rugged iron block. The unit was no longer than the L-series in-line four and its monobloc's 60° vee configuration offered strength as well as compactness. The six-pin crankshaft had throws spaced at 60° to each other and firing intervals were equal at 120°. The engine was run as three vee-twins, each pair of cylinders firing in turn, hence there were alternate power strokes from each bank.

The three pairs of reciprocating components cancelled out to give both primary and secondary balance for smooth operation, to the obvious benefit of endurance running. Further, the spacing of exhaust pulses offered full tuning potential from a straightforward

three-into-one system on each bank. Given the need for turbocharging, it ensured a good feed to the turbine at low engine speed. The base of the engine was a linerless thinwall iron casting which was run in conjunction with a saddle-type integral main bearing cap casting for bottom end strength together with aluminium heads to save weight higher up.

The heads provided two valves per cylinder with crossflow hemispherical combustion chambers, the inclined valves operated through shaft-mounted aluminium rockers via a single cog-belt driven overhead camshaft per bank. The camshaft ran in the centre of the aluminium head, under the rockers which were operated through hydraulic, automatic adjustment lifters. The plug was inserted into the inlet side of the chamber, the inlet manifolding sitting within the vee. The inlet porting was semi-downdraught without sharp turns, thus offering the potential for high volumetric efficiency.

Of the two turbocharged Prototype race engines under development for 1985, the GTP version was restricted by

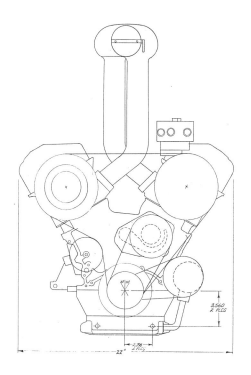

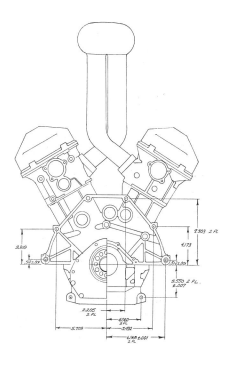

IMSA regulations to a single turbo. Both retained the stock displacement. The aim was to uprate the engine to three times and more its production power level – 220 bhp for the street turbo version – retaining the basic structure. In this respect, the engine management system and generous car cooling provision were considered vital. An iron block does not reject heat as well as an aluminium block and uncompromised water and charge cooling were stipulated by Electramotive from the outset.

The basic architecture of the engine was strong enough to handle the power, though a strengthened saddle was specified to stiffen the block, while weight was saved wherever possible to help keep the various Prototypes to the permitted minimum weight. It was possible to lighten certain castings while some new magnesium parts – cam covers and sump in particular – and titanium fasteners helped. The basic race engine specification included the strengthened saddle, larger main bearing journals on a stiffer crank, alloy pistons, Inconel exhaust valves, Stellite valve seats, roller rockers and an uprated water pump.

The twin turbo Group C installation called for twin aftercoolers but the provision of a separate turbo system for each bank kept pipe runs short. Each turbo could harness the three well-spaced exhaust pulses while the short charge plumbing was to the benefit of response, enhancing the effect of the smaller turbos. Watercooled turbos were employed, the main benefit of this seen when the car sat in the pits: it saved the Formula One technique of blowing cool air onto each stationary unit. Indy Car style Garrett AiResearch T03 turbos were utilized, Electramotive benefiting from Garrett's heavily funded development programme for Formula One.

Compared to the GTP engine, initially the Group C unit required a more complex engine management programme: thanks to its strict ration of low octane fuel it lived closer to the ragged edge. The GTP engine benefited from IMSA's higher permitted octane level which lifted the detonation threshold while the vaporisation of excess fuel within the combustion chamber was feasible as an additional

cooling ploy given the unlimited supply.

Both engines were given a 9.0:1 compression ratio and were pressurized to around 2.2-2.3 atmospheres in the normal course of duty and ran up to 8000 rpm for maximum power. Power was a respectable 12.9 bhp per litre per bar boost per 1000 rpm: race power was in the region of 680 bhp at 8000 rpm pumping 2.2 bar absolute. However, Nissan was prepared to crank special Group C qualifying engines up by as much as an extra atmosphere to extract the best part of 1000 bhp for qualifying glory runs.

The race power level achieved by the 3.0-litre V6 was comparable to that of the 2.65-litre Porsche Group C engine (which was not run beyond 2.4 bar absolute in qualifying). However, for GTP competition 720 bhp was the going rate for the 3.2-litre Porsche. That output took 2.4 bar in the plenum of the 962, the engine running only to 7300 rpm while producing a comparable 12.9 bhp per litre per bar boost per 1000 rpm. The sister Porsche Group C engine ran to over 8000 rpm for its race power and the lower speed, single turbo Stuttgart GTP contender was noted for a strong power band.

To run the new VG30 engines NISMO ordered chassis from both Lola and March. Lola devised bespoke Group C and GTP cars based on its familiar T600/T700 models while March supplied a Group C-legal version of its G series GTP project. The Group C Lola and March challengers were run by Japanese teams while the GTP Lola was run by Electramotive as part of its overall deal. A spin-off company Electramotive Engineering Inc in which Knepp was a minor associate, ran the IMSA programme. The Electramotive Nissan prototype came out first, the VG30-T810 débuting at the IMSA Charlotte event in May 1985 while the Japanese cars first undertook a National series Group C race at Fuji in July.

The Hoshino Racing VG30-85G was dubbed the Nissan Silva, Hasemi Motorsports' similar car was the Nissan Skyline while the Central 20 team VG30-T810 was the Nissan Fairlady 2. The Silva and Fairlady ran on Bridgestone tyres like the American entry while the

Skyline was Dunlop shod. Second time out at Suzuka, the Silva took pole and led until it retired, then in October the same car won the Fuji World Endurance Championship event from which the European teams withdrew in the face of a flooded track. In spite of the reduced competition, it was an uplifting triumph.

Spurred by its Fuji success, NISMO ordered a brand new bespoke March chassis for Group C racing 1986 and this 220 lb (100 kg) lighter machine was shipped to Le Mans. It was a heavily revised version of the 85G with mid-mounted radiators, hence an unfamiliar wedge nose. As usual the March was running the VG30 semi-stressed, supported by titanium A-frames. The lightweight chassis featured extensive use of aluminium honeycomb in the tub and magnesium bulkheads while carbon fibre and Kevlar-based composite bodywork saved a lot more weight.

At Le Mans the engine management system caused headaches, as did cultural differences with NISMO, March Engineering and Electramotive. The 86S

retired in the eighth hour while a back up 85G made it home in 17th position overcoming its engine maladies. At the Fuji WEC counter the two cars qualified fourth and fifth but they weren't as competitive as that in the race.

In 1987 the 86S returned to Le Mans as a private entry, the factory now running a bespoke V8 turbo Group C engine. Electramotive continued to service this back up car run by Tom Hanawa's Italya Sports and supplied a new 3.2-litre aluminium block version of the VG30 for qualifying. The block was a made in America replacement for the stock item carrying wet iron liners and having a 3.5-litre displacement potential. To allow the full 3.5 litres, Electramotive was co-operating with NISMO in the development of a big bore head. The enlarged bore 3.2-litre displacement was 3.6 x 3.3 in (90.8 x 83.0 mm) for 3223.1 cc.

Developed by Electramotive Engineering, the alloy block was cast in California and was reckoned to save 70.4 lb (32 kg) over the standard race engine, the weight of which was around 330 lb (150 kg). It was essentially to the pattern of the stock block but was deep skirted and individual sandwiched main bearing caps were side bolted. The alloy block saw the VG30 extend its range of activities as a race engine and it was even developed as an aero engine. ''Our alloy V6 is one of the most effective race engines available for size, weight and cost,'' reasoned John Knepp.

At the 1987 test weekend the 3.2-litre Italya Sports entry lapped quicker than the new V8 factory cars but qualifying for the race was interrupted by a shunt. Sadly, the car crashed again on Saturday night after running strongly. However, at Fuji's WEC counter in September the 3.2-litre American engine put the uprated, 1987 tub version of the same car on pole in the hands of Takao Wada, though the machine did not feature in the race.

Knepp was back again in France in 1988 servicing alloy qualifying and alloy race engines, the drivers having much preferred the 3.2-litre unit in 1987. This year Hanawa had the uprated 86S backed by a new 88S, but again failed to find success. In 1989 Knepp's engine was married to Cougar aerodynamics but at the heart of the Nissan-Cougar was the old Fuji pole-winning chassis. The glory days were long gone for the Electramotive V6 turbo in Group C but late-Eighties IMSA GTP was a very different story.

The Camel GT programme had made a false start at Charlotte back in 1985, the T810 hitting the wall as it entered the banking. The suspension had broken, reported a shaken Don Devendorf. The chassis was badly damaged but the car came out again in July at Portland where it retired from the top ten with transmission problems. However, it finished ninth at Sears Point, its next race, then was crashed again at Elkhart Lake following a tangle with another car, ending its season prematurely.

Mixed fortunes had likewise characterized the 1986 season and the team continued to concentrate on sprint racing. Thus, it had first been seen at Miami in 1987, then at Riverside, where at last it benefited from extensive testing. At Riverside the Nissan was

fastest through the speed trap at 207 mph and made a serious challenge for pole. The car was now a major force and took its first GTP win during the season. Then had come the move to a stiffer American-produced chassis, with which there was a switch to Goodyear tyres. With that Electramotive's GTP programme got into top gear, the team dominating the Camel GT Championship in 1988 and 1989.

IMSA had banned cockpit boost control for 1986 and mid-way through that season permitted alloy replacements for iron production blocks, though the Nissan GTP continued to carry the proven iron engine until the 1987 season when stock block turbos were restricted to 3.0 litres rather than 3.5 litres so the larger displacement potential of the aluminium block was not a factor. However, early problems with the alloy engine having been overcome, Devendorf reckoned it was ''55 lb (25 kg) lighter than the iron engine and twice as strong''.

The 1987 3.0-litre aluminium GTP engine was developed to produce over 1100 bhp for qualifying, pumping 3.2 bar absolute and running to 8500 rpm all on IMSA high octane fuel, with some use of toluene as in Formula One to keep combustion chamber temperatures under control. Electramotive's fuel was brewed by the Engine Research Company (ERS) on the West Coast and was rated around 110 octane. Come 1988 and all turbos had to pull 2046 lb (930 kg) and be fitted with a 2.25 in (57 mm) air restrictor.

That ended the days of outrageous power, physically limiting the amount of air it was possible to cram into the engine. Airflow through a given orifice cannot be allowed to go supersonic while the speed of a given flow is directly related to its pressure and to the size of orifice through which it is flowing. As the speed of a given flow increases through an orifice to match increasing engine speed, for a given pressure there comes a point at which the flow will reach supersonic and will surge, in other words reverse direction.

In practice, under the 2.25 in (57 mm) engine restrictor, for any given engine speed there was a maximum level of charge pressure that it was possible to run. Clearly, for top-end power, there was in theory a choice between engine speed and boost, trading one for the other. Running to a lower peak power speed had the advantage of reduced frictional loss, although higher boost implied higher exhaust backpressure. Electramotive found that it was necessary to run to 9000 rpm to be competitive in 1988.

Of course, the restrictor put all the emphasis upon tuning for a wide power band rather than the search for ever increasing top-end power. In 1988 top-end power was in the region of 680 bhp since it was not possible to pump more than 2.0 bar through the restrictor given the airflow required at the 9000 rpm peak power engine speed. Since it was possible to pump higher pressures at lower engine speed the electronic wastegate control developed by Electramotive since the early Eighties came into its own. Matching boost to engine speed via the engine management system made the most of the potential of the engine running under the restrictor.

In mid-1988 IMSA juggled again with weights: the Nissan GTP had now to run at 2090 lb (950 kg) but that did not interrupt its winning run. Rival Porsche teams had to rig up improvised wastegate control systems to try to get on terms with the super-competitive Electramotive Engineering engine package. Development of the Nissan engine under the restrictor was concerned with maximum efficiency, getting the most out of the amount of air it was possible to cram into the engine. Peak power speed came down with development, reducing frictional loss and valve train inertia problems.

At this stage Devendorf bought out Knepp who concentrated on Electramotive Inc supplying the V6 turbo for numerous competition and related activities. Electramotive Engineering Inc subsequently became Nissan Performance Technology Inc (NPTI). At that stage Devendorf left his long-standing position as chief scientist at the Hughes Aircraft Corporation. "Racing demands the same logical techniques," explained Devendorf, whose NPTI operation was seen at Le Mans in 1990 as part of the massive Nissan V8 turbo Group C effort.

For 1990 the GTP V6 engine had to run a 2.12 in (54 mm) restrictor with an alternative of twin turbos and two 1.5 in (38 mm) restrictors. That route was taken for a new GTP chassis, "more for packaging reasons than for response", according to Devendorf. Indeed, if anything response was worse although low-speed torque was stronger. Overall, the GTP engine was outwardly little changed from the unit first seen back in 1985 but was far more efficient.

Both iron and alloy versions were extremely rugged with a pair of vertical bolts flanking each main bearing. Both versions had the same heads and essentially the same guts; otherwise key differences were in engine plates to suit a specific chassis and in turbo installations. However, the 3.2-litre Group C engine was run with flat-top pistons (having small valve clearance notches) while the GTP unit had shorter con rods and taller pistons for the same stroke, its pistons having a slightly domed crown to maintain the desired 8.5:1 compression ratio.

The aluminium head was based on a stock casting supplied by Nissan. The head sealing incorporated a Cooper ring atop the liner flange, retained by an aluminium gasket, with Vitron O-rings for water passages. O-rings were used throughout the engine, there being no conventional gaskets. O-rings sealed the bottom of the liner, which was left free to expand. The head was closed by a magnesium cam cover cast in the UK by Kent Aerospace, while magnesium sumps were produced locally.

Electramotive ordered high strength iron liners for the alloy engine from various US suppliers and these were run uncoated. The three iron piston rings were, however, molybdenum faced. While Sealed Power rings were generally used, others were supplied by Riken, a Japanese company. The pistons, forged in California by the Ross Racing Piston company were run without oil gallery or even a spray. Knepp reckoned oil gallery pistons to be notoriously unreliable, and in any case considered a spray to be "unnecessary"; indeed, a waste of power.

The four (plain) bearing, six-pin crankshaft was machined from a solid billet of steel and featured wider journals and different webs compared to the stock item. By mid-1988 it had been redesigned a number of times, saving a total of almost 4.4 lb (2 kg). The main bearing journals were of 2.5 in (63.5 mm) diameter while the big end journals measured 2.1 in (53.3 mm). A six-bolt steel flywheel (with integral starter ring) was supplied by Quartermaster. Sometimes a Quartermaster clutch was run but more often the 7.25 in (184 mm) item was from AP. At the nose of the 9000 rpm crankshaft, a hydraulic vibration damper was fitted in respect of crankshaft harmonics. This was supplied by Hudi, an American company, and was one designed for truck camshaft applications.

The crank ran in plain Sealed Power bearings and was turned by Crower Cams produced I-section rods. These were to Electramotive's design and specifications. Iron rods were run until 1988 when the aluminium engine was first fitted with steel rods machined from a solid billet: a stronger yet lighter solution. The gudgeon pins were also devised by Electramotive and were 1.0 in (25.4 mm) diameter steel pins retained not by circlips but by Teflon buttons. The buttons were a push fit and were free to rub the cylinder wall.

Retained by 13 larger-than-standard studs, each head was of a regular (production) combustion chamber layout, accommodating two large valves. Electramotive ported and polished the stock heads, lightly machining the intake side and fitting new valves, seats and guides. Valves were solid, of titanium on the intake side, Inconel for the exhaust, on which side Stellite seats were fitted. Dual steel springs were used, with a titanium retainer. Valve sizes were 1.74 in (44.07 mm) intake and 1.38 in (35.05 mm) exhaust.

The valves were activated by forged aluminium roller rockers designed by Electramotive and reckoned to be five times stronger than the production item. The production car hydraulic lifter was replaced by a plain steel lifter running in the stock lifter guide – the only production part left above the camshaft. While the camshaft ran directly in the head, a needle bearing was fitted at the front of the right hand head, ahead of which was taken the alternator and fuel pump drive. As standard, there were four bearing bosses for the shaft which was machined to Electramotive specifications from a steel billet supplied by Nissan. The two camshafts were turned by a Uniroyal belt direct from a cog mounted at the front of the crank.

While the right-hand shaft drove the alternator and fuel pump the left-hand shaft drove the distributor. Ahead of the timing pulley on the nose of the crank was a magnetic trigger, then the damper, then an oil pump drive pulley then the water pump pulley. Located alongside the block, the oil pump was of sandwich construction, incorporating three engine-scavenge, one turbo-scavenge and the pressure pump.

On the front of the block, the water pump was Electramotive's own design with a special impeller: "to flow a tremendous amount of water. We use a high water pressure – 45 psi – mainly to eliminate hot spots. This enables us to run more boost," John Knepp explained.

The turbocharger installation variations between Group C and single turbo GTP engines saw the former having a conventional overhead plenum while the latter had it offset and fed from a single aftercooler. In each case the plenum was of magnesium with a single butterfly throttle at its entrance and an individual outlet pipe for each cylinder. The turbocharger was of conventional design, based on T31 parts with Inconel turbine wheel and aluminium compressor wheel. Electramotive developed bespoke wheel profiles in conjunction with Garrett.

The wastegate was Electramotive's own product and with the use of titanium, aluminium, stainless steel and Inconel it was reckoned to be the lightest in racing. It featured an electro-pneumatic boost control capable of continual adjustment by the ECU. The Electramotive engine control system ran the wastegate, the fuel injectors and the ignition timing. Control of the wastegate was one of the key factors in the engine's 1988-9 success.

The fuel injection system still utilized Bosch solenoid injectors, two per cylinder. Injector position varied according to the specific application, being regularly used as a tuning tool. The ignition system supplied by MSD was modified by Electramotive. It was a conventional CD racing system triggered by the magnetic pick-up on the crank and with advance/retard set by the ECU. It fired a single Bosch 0.55 in (14 mm) platinum plug per cylinder. The distributor was a stock Nissan part with its internals ripped out. In addition to a new ignition rotor it was equipped with another magnetic trigger, this one for injector sequencing.

The ECU and its attendant parts was designed by Electramotive specifically for the V6. Knepp reckoned Electramotive's system was ''eight times as powerful as Motronic (MP1.2)'', offering greater precision and flexibility. The ECU recalculated between each firing. Readings were taken of crank position (speed), manifold pressure and throttle position (load), boost control pressure, fuel pressure and air and water temperatures and either one or both injectors were driven, according to the given map. The production detonation sensor (screwed into the side of the block) was retained and apart from injection, ignition and wastegate control the ECU activated warning lights on the dashboard and provided a data logging facility.

Chapter Fifteen

Nissan GTP

As we have noted, engine control and cooling were central to the successful Nissan GTP engine concept. A turbo race engine flirts with detonation, excessive heat its main enemy. Electramotive chose the Lola chassis route partly since the Huntingdon manufacturer was willing to work closely with it to ensure high cooling efficiency. Indeed, at first the car was purposely over-cooled to avoid any potential problem. As described in Chapter Eight, the T810's aerodynamics were developed by Lola in conjunction with Suzuka who carried on the work in Electramotive's own rolling road wind tunnel. Meanwhile, Trevor Harris was brought in as chassis consultant while the Electramotive Engineering team's Crew Chief was Ashley Page.

The car supplied by Lola at the outset had a monocoque chassis with aluminium honeycomb for the inner walls and an advanced composite floor (carbon fibre and Kevlar over aluminium honeycomb). It featured pushrod front suspension, conventional rear suspension and ran on 16 in (406 mm) rims.

Given the pushrod operation, the inboard front spring/damper units were crossed over the scuttle to help make room for the cooler air channels feeding though the top half of the sponsons. The monocoque only formed part of the lower half of the sponsons while the fuel cell was centrally located in conventional fashion. The engine was carried semi-stressed via A-frames with a horizontal A-frame across the top of the engine bay. The transmission incorporated a five speed transverse Weismann transaxle which set the gearbox ahead of the cwp.

Three tubs were produced in 1985, although only two cars were built up. The second chassis phased in during the course of the season was to the same specification as the first while a major mechanical change for 1986 was a switch from Weismann to Hewland transaxle. The Bridgestone shod machine's Weismann transverse package had been stipulated by Electramotive. The Weismann transaxle looked good on paper: it included an inboard five-speed gearbox with easy and rapid access to the ratios and it had a good reputation in American road racing.

The Weismann gearbox did not sap power and had been used with success by Indy Cars but it was found wanting in the face of the output of the V6 turbo and the weight of a Prototype. Development of the Weismann package had proved too big a project and thus the team switched to Hewland's brand new VGC model, a conventional outboard gearbox which was run with a Salisbury clutch pack-type differential.

A sufficiently strong Hewland Prototype gearbox had not been an option when the car had been designed. Compared to earlier five-speed Hewlands, the VGC had a bigger differential case to accommodate a larger, stronger cwp. Electramotive found the VGC package

The Nissan GTP car dominated the IMSA Camel GT Championship in the late Eighties. The car was based on an original design by Lola, developed over a number of years by Electramotive.

tough enough for the job, unlike Sauber in Group C. Admittedly, it stayed clear of around the clock races until 1989 but after Daytona that year the transmission components, ''still looked good'', according to Page.

The switch from Weismann to Hewland proved ''a somewhat painful process'' according to Devendorf, ''but it was well worth it. The VGC alleviated a lot of stress – including to the staff and the driver!''

The VGC was less intrusive in terms of underwing space. Its installation involved modification to the bellhousing and the transaxle subframe to retain the correct suspension pick-up points. Although the gearbox was now outboard, the wheelbase remained at 106.5 in

(2705.1 mm) while the relocation of the gearbox weight behind the rear axle was not sufficient to markedly affect the handling characteristics. In theory there was a slightly higher moment of polar inertia, in practice this was hardly discernible. Better transmission reliability was much more obvious.

By 1987 Electramotive was running two cars on a regular basis, still the original pair of T810s from Lola although both had been rebuilt around replacement tubs and sported aerodynamic modifications by Suzuka, as described in Chapter Eight.

A major change for 1987 was from crossply to radial tyres, though crossplies came back during the season following a shunt. That shunt was caused by a

Electramotive specialized in sprint racing, not tackling the Daytona 24 hours until 1989. At Daytona the car ran as fast as everyone expected but further than most anticipated.

puncture but it prompted the conservative Bridgestone company to return to crossplies, to Devendorf's frustration. The GTP machine was a new area for Bridgestone in terms of tyre loading in respect of both engine output and downforce and it was not until the team switched to Goodyear radials for 1988 that the full potential of the package was realized, although a stiffer chassis was another significant new factor that year.

Devendorf reflects that: ''the Bridgestone crossplies were not competitive with Goodyears and on some tracks they would not work at all. The tyres obscured the real potential of the car in 1987.'' However, Goodyear recognized its potential and welcomed Electramotive into its fold for 1988. Testing commenced at Riverside in December 1987 with the new mandatory engine restrictor fitted. In cutting straightline speed, the restrictor cost at least 1.5 sec a lap. Nevertheless, with Goodyear tyres the car was a second a lap quicker than it had ever gone without the restrictor!

Says Devendorf: ''some handling ailments mysteriously disappeared. Goodyear and our car were made for each other.'' The switch to Goodyear implied some suspension changes but not a redesign. However, working with Bridgestone aerodynamic development had been following a programme to suit the available tyres and some revisions were made on that score. In particular, the Goodyear tyres could handle more downforce.

Likewise the Goodyear tyres could handle more power. With the Bridgestones, wheelspin had sometimes limited the amount of power that could be run. The tyres brought more grip and that in turn put a greater strain on the transmission.

During the course of the 1988 season the team switched to 17 in (432 mm) wheels, in line with Goodyear development. The stiffer new chassis for 1988 was a Harris-designed replacement that featured traditional rather than pushrod front suspension, the spring/damper units slung between the monocoque and the lower wishbone. The philosophy behind that change was the philosophy behind the entire GTP programme. The return to a simple, basic outboard system provided a much quicker spring change. That provided more track time in which to get the car right. The members of Electramotive Engineering were nothing if not practical racers.

Trevor Harris had started design work in 1987. Nissan USA had commissioned him to update the T810 design to meet the growing competition in IMSA, at a time when the Electramotive team was a force but yet the team to beat. He was not able to produce an all-new car, instead was given four months in which to modify the existing equipment. In view of the increasing downforce provided by the on-going aerodynamic development he specified a new, seriously stiffer tub. He saw the need for some geometry revision at the front, though the question of accessibility was

paramount while there was neither the time nor the money for a new rear suspension.

Thus, the 1988 Harris car was not a radical departure. Harris later reflected: ''assuming you have taken care of fundamental stiffness and geometry, aerodynamics have to be vital. You need the highest downforce with the lowest drag that can be achieved. And you cannot combine a high downforce car with a flexible chassis. Downforce and stiffness go hand in hand, and rigidity includes suspension links, uprights and mounting points.''

As we saw in Chapter Eight, the Suzuka modified aerodynamic package that the car was carrying these days was capable of generating three times its own weight at 200 mph – around 100 per cent more download than when the T810 had been designed. Harris provided an aluminium honeycomb tub that increased torsional rigidity by more than

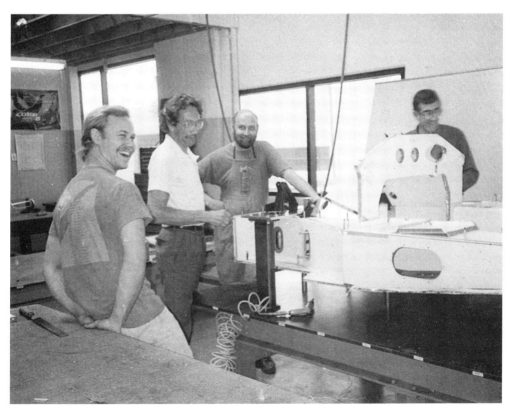

The later versions of the Nissan GTP had a monocoque designed by Trevor Harris (second from left) and produced in the Californian workshop of ex-Lotus engineer Jim Chapman.

100 per cent. With the new chassis the drivers found the car responded to alterations just like a good single-seater.

The much stiffer Harris chassis was produced in the Californian workshops of ex-Lotus engineer Jim Chapman and the prototype was first tested over the 1987-8 off-season. Says Don Devendorf, who left the driving to others in those days: "the Harris chassis was much more rigid in torsion and in bending. It was much better structurally in crashes and the local build meant that we had more control over quality".

A second Harris car was phased in for Lime Rock but this only went 50 miles before it was destroyed in a flip. Chassis 03 came on stream at Watkins Glen and both 01 and 03 went forward into 1989, 01 with ten wins to its credit. It then won Miami and Sebring 1989, and subsequently 03 started taking its turn in the winners circle. The model was ultra-competitive. IMSA tracks are often bumpy and range from street to speedway. Almost always the Nissan could be made to work well and rarely did it break.

The Harris monocoque had aluminium honeycomb for its floor and walls aside from the sponson flanks and top of central fuel tank which were single-sheet aluminium panels. The dash bulkhead was also aluminium honeycomb while the other bulkheads were machined aluminium plates. The base of the central fuel tank (at the back of the tub) was angled slightly upwards to accommodate the diffuser upsweeps. The tank carried an ATL 120-litre fuel cell, with three scavenge pre-pumps in view of an awkward shape.

The front mounting plate of the engine assembly was in a recess in the rear bulkhead and immediately ahead of it was the collector pump and a three-gallon (13.64 litre) engine oil tank, these items housed in their own enclosure within the tank. The fuel cell wrapped around this, was thus U-shaped in plan. The pre-pumps fed to a pump in each sponson which in turn fed the collector pot. The fuel was then supplied to the engine's fuel rail via an engine-driven Lucas mechanical pump.

The engine was supported by steel A-frames picked up by the bellhousing which bolted to the standard VGC case. Thus, although it was torsionally stressed it was not beam-loaded. The engine fed through an AP triple plate, 7.25 in (184 mm) gear-driven clutch (sometimes a similar Quartermaster item which was more readily available) to an essentially standard VGC gearbox. Some gears were Emco, otherwise all parts were standard Hewland issue, including the Salisbury-type differential. The driveshafts were Superboot, an Orange County supplier picked up via the team's Off Road operation which offered heavy duty, heat-treated, alloy steel shafts.

The key to transmission reliability was careful lifing of parts. Early in 1989 a carbon-carbon clutch was tried but the wear rate did not prove acceptable. The car retained the original cast magnesium upright design inherited from the T600 but this had been progressively modified for strength. Steel hubs were carried in an Electramotive ball and roller system, the ball bearings on the inside, the rollers on the outside.

Following Harris' work, the suspension was traditional front and rear. At the rear the spring/damper units were positioned outside of the tunnels, partially within the wheel rims, slung between the ends of a long transverse aluminium crossbeam and the lower N-arms. The spring/damper units were ahead of the wheel centres (behind at the front) and there was a single upper link, the N-arm providing track control.

Fox gas dampers rather than Koni oil dampers were employed from mid-1986. Fox was another Off Road supplier but its dampers formed the basis of the well known (in Indy and Formula Car racing) Penske dampers with remote chambers for ease of pressure adjustment. Damping was very important on the many bumpy IMSA circuits. Springing was via steel springs supplied by Rockwell of Indiana, well known in American racing circles. Significantly, TWR had to switch from its WEC titanium springs to stronger steel in view of IMSA's frequent bumps.

IMSA GTP cars tended to have to run softer than Group C and damping was more crucial. Greater wheel movement compromised the operation of the underwing but there was no point in scratching for every last kilo of downforce if the car could not be controlled over the bumps. The Electramotive team rolled out cars to be race winners rather than wind tunnel winners.

On the other hand, the term soft is relative and the springs run by Electramotive were of very high rate. There was a lot of wheel movement designed into the car – around 5 in (125 mm) – but typically only half of it was used, unless the track was very rough. The springs were not progressive rate and in view of the very high level of downforce generated could be as high as 5000 lb (2272.7 kg) just to keep the car from scraping on the track.

Unlike contemporary Formula One, Electramotive did not resort to droop restriction or pre-loaded front springs. Given the big tunnels it was less critical to keep the underwing at a consistent height and attitude. It was more important to ride the bumps well. The rival XJR had a very stiff front anti-roll bar and could occasionally be seen waving its inner front wheel in the air. Unlike almost any other Eighties race car, the Electramotive GTP had no front anti-roll bar.

''With stiff springs an anti-roll bar has little effect,'' says Devendorf. ''Without a bar we lack some adjustability but have independence of wheel movement. A front anti-roll bar promotes understeer. We found that taking the original bar off enhanced turn-in and we have developed it from there. The car had to be adjusted to compensate for the loss of some of the perceived advantages of the roll bar.''

Just as strange was the fact that the car ran with a stiff rear bar. In theory softening a rear bar enhances traction but Electramotive found just the reverse. ''Yes, it is curious,'' Harris reflects.

The 17 in (432 mm) wheels run from Mid Ohio 1988 were BBS three-piece magnesium-aluminium items, driven by six hub pegs, alongside aluminium disc

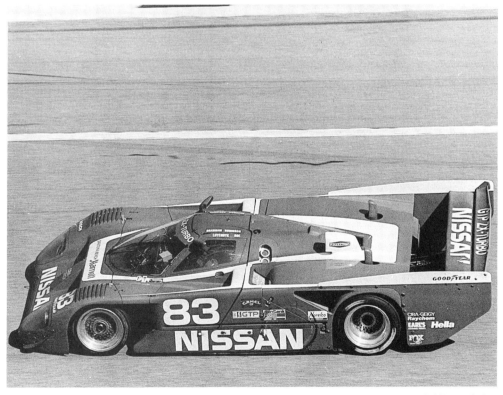

Nissan GTP at speed on the Daytona banking. This shot nicely shows off the purposeful lines of the car in its 1989 guise. Note the periscope intake for the single turbo.

bells. The brakes were 13 in (330 mm) cast iron with AP four-pot calipers, these having differential bores to avoid taper wear. The brakes were interchangeable front and rear which eased maintenance. Initially the team ran AP sphericone discs but these cracked too often and subsequently traditional curved vane discs were employed. Coleman curved vane discs were generally used, these similar to the familiar AP curved vane model. Coleman of Wisconsin was well known in stock car racing circles and provided a high quality product with the right availability.

In 1988 Electramotive evaluated Alcon curved vane discs and these provided a similar wear rate. That wear rate increased following the introduction of Performance Friction's new carbon-metallic pads at Portland in 1988. Originally Raybestos pads were employed – as per Porsche – but the switch was made to carbon-metallic following successful testing. The new type offered a good pad wear rate together with consistent performance and shorter stopping distances. However, they required very careful bedding. Since stopping distances were shorter, more heat was generated so they were harder on the disc, hence the increased disc wear.

Electramotive lagged behind TWR in the exploitation of carbon-carbon brakes.

This was essentially because the Nissan enjoyed better braking than the XJR-9. Further, weight was not a problem and carbon-metallic pads offered comparable braking distances to carbon-carbon. Rear brake cooling air was still collected via periscope scoops which protruded through the deck. Front brake cooling air was collected by a simple duct under the headlight. The distinctive nostril scoops collected air for aftercooler, oil and water radiators, the aftercooler and oil radiator on the right, water on the left. A transmission oil cooler was set between the wing support plates but there was no fuel cooler. Most of the coolers were made by next-door neighbour Alpha United, a firm known for its work for the aerospace industry.

The bodywork was advanced composite, mostly carbon fibre over Nomex honeycomb with some use of Kevlar, particularly where its wear resistance was important. The headlights were special Hella items when the car was run in a 12 or 24 hour race. The team made its own loom with some Raychem components and used Stewart Warner instruments with an MSD electronic tachometer. Usually the readings were good. The car was reliable, and it was fast enough to see off any competitor on the Camel trail in the late Eighties.

Chapter Sixteen

Nissan R89C/R90CK

When it came to the choice of constructor for its new Group C chassis, Nissan had straightforward priorities: the company would need knowledge of contemporary Formula One technology – particularly monocoque construction – and the freedom for unrestricted co-operation in the Prototype field. Nissan spoke to five possible partners early in 1988 but its target to have a car ready by January 1989 was a stumbling block for most. Lola could do the job, however, and fitted the bill perfectly. Not the least significant consideration was that Eric Broadley had never won Le Mans.

From the outset Broadley stipulated a carbon and plastic chassis carrying a fully stressed engine to achieve the stiffness he considered necessary in the face of the anticipated aerodynamic loading. Further, the engine would have to be packaged to meet Lola's underwing requirements, and as we have seen all of this involved a complete reworking of Hayashi's V8 turbo. While that task was duly completed in 1988, Lola missed some of its schedules and consequently the R89C did not emerge until March 1989. The major delay was the sheer number of man-hours involved in construction of the high technology tub, previous Lola Prototypes having had aluminium-based chassis.

The new Nissan was designed by Broadley assisted by Andy Scriven and the all-important aerodynamic studies were carried out at Cranfield using 25 per cent models. Lola had full access to the work done by Suzuka in California on the Electramotive GTP package but this was not directly relevant in view of the fact that IMSA races tended to be on tighter circuits and under Camel GT regulations fuel consumption was not of paramount importance. Thus, Suzuka's high-downforce package would not have suited the needs of contemporary Group C racing where fuel consumption considerations overrule aerodynamic download.

In terms of mechanicals the Group C car could not follow the Lola T600-derived GTP machine given the commitment to an advanced composite chassis. Further, the smoother circuits for which the car was designed offered potential to run the underwing closer to the track and at a more consistent ride height while front and rear rims were not required to be of the same diameter and thus the Harris-refined GTP suspension would have been inappropriate.

The wind tunnel investigation was assisted by the fact that Lola had a long relationship with Cranfield and consequently could expect its instrumentation to give reliable, accurate results. Further, Lola had developed a CAD/CAM system which produced highly accurate models direct from the design finalized on the computer screen. The model could then be altered by hand and put back on the microprocessor-

The Hayashi engine as it appeared at Le Mans in 1988 a turbocharged V8 of 3.0-litre displacement replacing the superficially similar engine seen the year before.

The Le Mans scrutineering hoist reveals the underwing of the Nissan R89C. Note the so-called bubble or indent between the front wheels and the tunnels rising either side of the engine.

controlled routing machine which would ''feel'' the new shape and feed that information back into the CAD system. The buck for the actual bodywork was made by the same computer-controlled process which ensured the clothing for both sides of the car was mirror-image and that it would be close-fitting.

As we have noted, the prime objective for the R89C design team was to produce a fuel-efficient Le Mans package from which a higher-downforce sprint package would subsequently be developed. The basic aerodynamic package that Lola came up with followed the lines of the TWR Le Mans cars, shunning a conventional two-element rear wing for a long-chord single-element wing at deck height, this seen by the air as a low-drag long tail and blending the over and underbody flows while scavenging the diffuser tunnels.

The underbody package was conventional aside from a muted bubble

The 1989 version of the Hayashi engine was produced to act as a stressed member of the chassis and had a 3.5-litre displacement. It gave a solid 800 bhp running to Group C fuel regulations.

and it was headed by a splitter unlike Suzuka's GTP underwing, although the use of a front radiator means that direct comparison should not be drawn. In view of 1989 Group C regulations the diffuser tunnels started behind the monocoque and followed the 1989 fashion of an 1988 style tunnel with a lid on it to keep

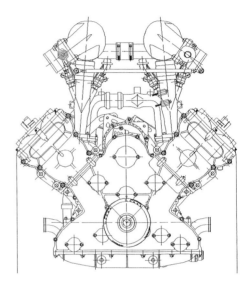

within the new mandatory maximum height. Ahead of the respective rear wheel the outer tunnel wall ran straight, there was that under-stated bubble between the front wheels while wheel sealing plates front and rear, side skirts and rear wheel covers were also employed.

The horizontal side skirt fitted a carefully sculptured recess in the lower flank of the sponson. In contrast, the rival TWR-Jaguar XJR-9 had a body width less than the mandatory maximum. Lola did not want the implicit loss of track width, in spite of the frontal area reduction to be won from the TWR approach.

The front radiator was mounted almost horizontally and was top-vented though a relatively narrow aperture flanked by the GTP-style nostril intakes for the mid-mounted aftercoolers and oil radiators. Air was ducted back through the top half of the sponsons to the coolers and to the compressors, then was expelled through the flanks of the tail, immediately ahead of the rear wheel covers. The resultant closed-deck lid, like the wheel covers, was clearly beneficial in terms of drag reduction. Evidently Lola did not accept the concept that exhausting air out through the deck was important in terms of enhancing the flow to the rear wing.

The stiffness sought from the chassis structure was not only to take the aerodynamic loading but was also seen as important to allow the suspension to do its job properly, to the benefit of tyre performance, particularly with regard to wear. Further, good rear suspension and adequate weight transfer were seen as essential in terms of getting the formidable torque of the 3.5-litre Hayashi engine onto the track. Dunlop was in the process of switching to radial tyres and Nissan ordered a relatively tall (high aspect ratio) version in 18 in (457 mm) front, 19 in (482 mm) rear diameters. The big rear tyre would give a long footprint to work well with a stiff chassis and high torque, the big front would balance it.

Further, the big front tyre would take a lot of energy input, an important consideration given that Group C cars tend to understeer. It would also avoid too much of a slope for the roll axis and

would accommodate a large diameter brake disc. Formula One cars ran 13 in (330 mm) diameter carbon-carbon discs: Nissan wanted a 14 in (355 mm) version for its heavier machine. The unusually high aspect ratio would give Nissan the tallest tyres in Group C. Nissan reasoned that if a radial is not cramped into too tight an aspect ratio it can have a lighter, cooler-running carcase. Further, the tall rear would provide some sidewall 'give' in the interest of traction, the tyre virtually wrapping itself onto the ground: an old drag racing technique.

Lola had a number of years experience of using advanced composite materials, in spite of the fact that this was the first sports car chassis from its Composites Division. The chosen material for the monocoque was carbon fibre over Kevlar honeycomb with Nomex honeycomb in areas difficult to shape. Further, Kevlar skins were to be found in some areas of high wear, while some aluminium honeycomb was employed in large flat areas – the cockpit floor in particular – for its crushability and ease of repair. Showing its experience of advanced composites, Lola incorporated a sophisticated combination of unidirectional and crossed fibres while an advanced carbon mould made for a very high quality product.

The monocoque provided integral front and rear and dash bulkheads with an additional aluminium diaphragm assembly helping support the front suspension. The rear bulkhead was of triangular section to form the fuel tank. The tub was produced as separate upper and lower portions which were bonded together, thus there was no problem of lay-up or of removal of the tooling as with a seamless fuselage. Under the driver's legs a transverse beam was incorporated in the cockpit floor and the front lower wishbones fed into this stiffening member.

The monocoque formed not only the central fuel tank but also the sponsons, aside from the section of the upper portion covered by the door, this having been cut away for cockpit access. Thus, either side of the door the cooler channel tunnelled through the actual tub. The monocoque also formed the section of the nose visible behind radiator vent and, above that, the cockpit section of the superstructure. An access plate in the nose revealed the spring/damper units. The monocoque ran as far forward as a tray carrying the radiator which formed the crushable nose box structure demanded by the regulations, the radiator itself being part of this structure.

In accordance with the regulations, the car carried a steel roll cage which was braced back to the engine. The hoop was fitted within the complex monocoque moulding which incorporated the windscreen pillars and the cockpit roof. A Triplex screen was inserted, this being toughened and laminated. Behind the monocoque, the diffuser section of the underwing was another very stiff composite structure in view of the downforce loading. The engine front cam cover mounts fanned out more than those of the Cosworth DFV for a wider spread of the load into the rear of the tub.

The bellhousing was cast magnesium with an integral 18-litre oil tank and it was designed specifically for the car. It was married to a standard VGC, with its

case machined to meet the requirements of the chassis. Aluminium plates were bolted on to support the rear suspension. The smooth flanks of the modified case were allowed to form part of the respective inner diffuser wall. This created a slightly wider tunnel, while the exposure of the case was in the interest of transmission cooling and permitted a smaller transmission oil radiator.

The transmission was fed by a 7.25 in (184 mm) triple plate gear-driven clutch, standard AP Racing Prototype equipment. However, away from Le Mans a carbon-carbon version was run. It was not possible to run carbon-carbon at Le Mans in view of the cooling effect of the long run down *Les Hunaudières*: the material hates low temperature, needing high temperature to attain a good co-efficient of friction and wearing too fast when over-cooled.

The five speed VGC was run with Hewland-issue gears and a March Ramp differential which was smooth and progressive in its action to the benefit of clutch and tyre wear. At Le Mans a spool was run since the team could live with the understeer it created; it was lighter,

The Nissan R89C ran low tunnels at Le Mans in 1989, the rear part of each horizontal. The wing was single-element with small endplates and was mounted low.

avoided heat build-up and would get a car home in the event of driveshaft failure.

The uprights were steel, fabricated by Lola for greater stiffness than a cast upright. Steel rather than magnesium was employed given the intention to run carbon-carbon brakes: the heat generated by carbon-carbon brakes is high enough to affect the strength of magnesium. The hubs were steel, running in Timken taper roller bearings and carrying the drive pegs. The driveshafts were Lobro with conventional cv joints.

Dymag one-piece magnesium rims were specified, these initially of 17 in (432 mm) diameter front and rear to suit the available stopgap crossply rubber from Dunlop. Widths were 13.5 in (343 mm) front, 15 in (381 mm) rear. The brakes were supplied by Brembo, initially 14 in (355 mm) diameter drilled Pioli discs run with single four-pot calipers. Cooling air was ducted to the eye of the disc through the upright, over the bearing section to keep the bearings well cooled. Periscope ducts collected air at the rear while at the nose the brake air intakes flanked the central nose radiator intake.

The suspension set the spring/damper units inboard – at the rear to clear the underwing – with pushrod operation front and rear. The front suspension employed conventional narrow wishbones while at the rear there was a narrow reversed lower wishbone and a wide-based upper wishbone picking up on the front of the upright plus an upper track control arm picking up on the back. The forward leg of the upper wishbone ran to the bellhousing.

The wishbones were steel fabrications except for the top front wishbone which was machined. Anti-roll bars were run front and rear while straightforward Koni oil dampers were located inside steel springs. The pushrods were steel operating steel fabricated rockers, these having a ratio close to 1:1 in view of extremely limited suspension movement. The steering was via Lola rack and pinion, mounted ahead of the suspension.

The bodywork, surprisingly, was good old fibreglass. It was recognised that a fair amount of modification would be required during the development programme and fibreglass was more adaptable than more advanced composites. Its use also helped overcome delivery schedule lateness. The weight penalty was acceptable given that the final product was comfortably within the weight limit. Cockpit cooling was promoted by an air outlet in the roof directly above the driver's head which bled the high pressure air within into a low pressure area above. This promoted a through-flow of air and if the ambient temperature was very high it was possible to tap a cockpit feed into the main air channels in the sponsons.

The water radiator was supplied by Calsonic in Japan, the oil radiators by Secam and the aftercoolers by Electramotive supplier Alpha United. The 100 litre fuel tank was by ATL. Varley supplied the battery, Lucas the lighting equipment and Smiths the standard instrumentation. The car also ran the Lola Pi system in sprint trim.

The micro-based Pi instrumentation provided a continuous read-out of engine speed with an override to warn of pressure or temperature beyond a pre-set threshold. The threshold could be re-set at the flick of a switch. The system also monitored the chassis via suspension G-meters and collected real time data, having a magic eye to recognise the start of a new lap. It could thus analyse cornering performance as well as acceleration and speed on the straight.

The wheelbase of the new challenger was 110 in (2794 mm) and it put 58-59 per cent of its 900 kg on the rear wheels, together with 68 per cent of its downforce in Le Mans trim. Following its first run at Snetterton it was shipped to Nissan's hot and very fast Arizona test track, reaching 380 mph, the fastest speed ever recorded by a Japanese car. The high-speed running suggested that there would be no Mercedes-style tyre failures on the Mulsanne while the heat provided confirmation that the cockpit and engine and brake cooling systems worked.

The car then made its Dijon début converted to sprint trim. This involved the substitution of larger volume diffuser tunnels (those run at Le Mans were not to the full permitted height, even under the new regulations) which started right behind the monocoque. The Le Mans tunnels started further back to shift the centre of pressure. There was also more front splitter and a two-element rear wing which was mounted higher than the Le Mans wing to act as a wing in its own right as well as an air extractor.

The switch to sprint trim increased downforce at 200 mph from 2400 lb (1091 kg) to 4000 lb (1818 kg) (downforce rising to 2900 lb (1318 kg) on the Mulsanne at 240 mph). At Dijon the car sported front tabs, these found to be more effective than extra splitter length. During the race it suffered windscreen blow-outs and subsequently the windscreen fixing was improved.

Another early problem was poor braking performance and in view of this, for Le Mans, the team eagerly adopted the Performance Friction carbon metallic pads used by the sister GTP car. The significantly higher co-efficient of friction of those pads stopped the car faster but they did not tackle the root of the problem which was in a restricted pedal ratio and excessive disc cooling. The pedal ratio was restricted by the room available in the pedal box while the wheel bearing and disc cooling provided by the air flow through the centre of the upright was known by Lola to be ideal for Formula One carbon-carbon brake applications. It proved too effective for use with cast iron: the disc was over-cooled.

At Le Mans the rear wing was at first found to be mounted too low: it had to be raised to bring the centre of pressure further back. Too much downforce at the front had been starving the rear end of air. The car that shunted had a wishbone punched into the tub and as a result of this an aluminium bracing piece was introduced for subsequent races.

A major change after Le Mans was a switch to carbon-carbon brakes (run for the first time at Brands Hatch), with which the car at last stopped well. Brembo supplied revised calipers to use with the carbon-carbon discs, while to ensure adequate cooling the rear wheel covers faded away. Further, for rear caliper cooling a duct was set into the underwing (beyond the driveshaft). It was important to supply cooling air to the calipers, mainly to keep the fluid cool.

The move to the planned larger diameter wheels cost a little in top speed, the necessarily taller front arches spoiling the airflow over the car at the cost of higher drag. The taller rear arches had less impact. More significant was the fact that the car had to be set up with its nose slightly higher, the new ride height compromising the operation of the underwing to a small degree. For these reasons Lola preferred the original 17 in (432 mm) wheels.

The bigger radials ordered from Dunlop were late arriving and the car was seen at a number of races with a mixture of radial and crossply rubber, neither in the tall size sought. The team switched from Dymag to BBS three-piece wheels to allow it to experiment with various tyre widths.

Aside from brakes and tyres, the key area of development in 1989 was the suspension. The major step was to increase wheel movement. The car was designed in accordance with contemporary Formula Car philosophy, whereby there was an almost solid front end with no droop – so the mouth of the underwing could not exceed ride height unless the car bounced over a kerb while the springs were pre-loaded – so there was no dip of the nose at low speed. The Nissan was not intended to run without droop but there was the facility to run pre-loaded springs while the maximum wheel movement at the front was in the region of one inch (25.4 mm).

This Formula Car approach was fine for maximum performance from the underwing but caused problems in the face of Prototype racing reality. A Prototype is almost twice as heavy as a Formula Car yet needs to be driven over a longer distance, with driver swaps and changing track conditions coming into the equation. Further, a Prototype has proper tunnels and is therefore less sensitive to the angle of attack of its flat-bottom area. The team found it was necessary to allow less restricted wheel movement to provide a driver-friendly supple ride. Thus, by mid-season the car was running 1.5 in (38 mm) bump, 0.5 in (12.7 mm) droop at the front with softer springs.

Further, there was a small front suspension geometry change for less anti-dive, the rear suspension was modified to reduce anti-squat and even promote a small amount of roll-on negative camber, and the roll axis was modified in the interest of weight transfer. In a nutshell, this allowed the driver to get onto the throttle earlier in a corner. All this suspension alteration further compromised the aerodynamics of the car but made the R89C a more practical racing proposition.

For 1990 the car was substantially unchanged, other than for a stiffer chassis structure. The nose form was slightly different in design as was the engine cover area but the latter change was not evident to the eye. The monocoque was made stiffer and heavier, primarily with a view to using the extra weight demanded by the regulations to increase the level of safety. Further, the transmission case was now a one-piece casting which offered greater torsional rigidity yet was narrower. That allowed wider tunnels which ensured more constant downforce from under the car together with a more stable centre of pressure.

The bodywork was now a mixture of fibreglass and carbon fibre, mainly fibreglass on the over-surface and still with a plywood splitter and with Jiproc to combat wear further back. Wherever possible, the internal dimensions of the monocoque were reduced to gain increased stiffness throughout the cockpit area while curved surfaces replaced right-angle joins. Improved serviceability was a major area of improvement: larger access holes were provided with careful design avoiding loss of rigidity. The spring/damper pick-up was also redesigned for ease of maintenance.

The modified tub and transaxle case left the R90C ''stiffer than a Formula Car'' axle-to-axle, according to Lola. The transmission internals were still VGC based but Lola introduced its own semi-dry sump modification. Not having the gears rotating in a bath of oil saved drag and weight. While the differential policy was unchanged, in the background was the development of a Nissan differential with ''an oil pressure factor'' – all other

information secret. A lighter yet stronger Nissan driveshaft was developed for Le Mans.

The suspension concept was the same but greater wheel movement was provided for – over 3 in (74 mm) at the front. During the blacker days of 1989 the team had gone so far as to try the car without droop and with pre-loaded springs at the front but the swing towards traditional suspension movement had been confirmed as the best compromise. This year there was some further adjustment of the roll axis to encourage weight transfer from the inner rear to the outer front wheel, putting cornering ahead of traction.

The suspension now had a reasonable amount of roll-on negative camber, this stopping the tyre tucking under. This was at the expense of static negative camber, although a little static negative was retained to avoid trouble under braking. The amount of negative camber at the front prescribed for 1990 was 0.75° static rising to a maximum of 3.0° under roll, with less at the rear to avoid the danger of the inner edge of the driven tyre overheating.

This season the wheels were Speedline while the TWR/Zytek developed infra red tyre temperature sensor was introduced, together with chassis ride height sensors. Also new was a 14.8 in (376 mm) diameter disc. For 1990 Nissan switched to AP Racing brakes. The British company employed the same carbon-carbon disc manufacturer as Brembo-Carbone Industrie – but offered a preferable back-up iron disc and new six-pot caliper. The 14.8 in (376 mm) diameter disc was ordered specifically by Nissan for the R90C in both carbon-carbon and iron guise.

The larger diameter was used in conjunction with the same width of rubbing area on each face but the fact that the caliper now operated on a longer radius meant that the brake could develop more torque. Further, it could pump more air for enhanced cooling, while at a given wheel rpm the rubbing speed was higher, thus more heat was put into the disc. Nissan aimed to develop a carbon-carbon brake package that could work at night and in the rain, with the potential to last 24 hours with no more than one change of discs, and then only at the front.

That task was spurred on by the Le Mans chicanes which meant that a driver would need good braking to keep out of trouble. Further, dealing with traffic under braking rather than acceleration would save fuel. In the days before the chicanes top speed was the most fuel efficient way to a quick lap: the chicanes put just as much emphasis upon braking. Of course, Nissan could have developed a big carbon-carbon brake with Brembo but it was felt wise to have the best possible cast iron back-up for Le Mans and in that respect AP's traditional curved-vane offering was to be preferred to Brembo's Pioli disc.

The curved-vane disc offered better structural integrity, a factor that had become important with the introduction of Performance Friction's carbon-metallic pads. The new pads offered comparable stopping power to the lighter carbon-carbon brakes but in so doing put an enormous strain on the disc. That strain had proved a little too much for the clever and extremely elegant Pioli disc.

Further, the new AP six-pot caliper offered more surface area for use with either iron or carbon-carbon discs, together with a more even distribution of pressure across the pad. With carbon-carbon, that in turn allowed the wear to be balanced between the pads and the disc to minimize time spent working on the brakes in the pits at Le Mans. Le Mans was always the major target for Nissan. It made a massive attack on the race in 1990, equipping no less than seven cars with factory-fettled VHR35Z engines.

Four were R90CKs, two apiece from Nissan Motorsports Europe and Nissan Performance Technology Inc, the latter pair run in conjunction with Ray Mallock Racing. Of the three older cars, one was run by the Le Mans team, one by Cougar Competition while the third was rebodied by Suzuka and – dubbed the R90CP – was run by NISMO. It had a new underwing and new nose and tail sections following work in the NPTI wind tunnel aimed specifically at Le Mans.

Carbon-carbon brakes were run only by NME and NISMO, the latter serviced by Brembo as were all the older chassis,

while NPTI opted for AP using six-pot calipers like NME but with iron discs and carbon metallic pads. Further, NPTI ran on Goodyear rather than Dunlop radials. The cars were all equipped with a spool and tended to be softly sprung to help reduce shock loading into the transmission. Nissan employed the VGC in essentially standard guise and this was felt potentially to be a weak link.

Further, running soft made the car more adaptable to changing conditions and more amenable to the often conflicting needs of three drivers while helping over the notorious bumps found at the first of the two new chicanes. Soft front and rear roll bars and springs of less than 2000 lbs (909 kg). were employed. The R90CK aerodynamic package followed some work by Lola specifically aimed at Le Mans but was closer to a regular configuration than in years past. The underwing was standard and there was more downforce, thus straightline speed was down while the handling was less spooky.

The fruit of Suzuka's work on the NISMO chassis was very impressive, the distinctive car from Japan timed as fastest of all at just under 230 mph while quick enough around the lap to take third on the grid, less than 10 seconds slower than the second-placed Brun Porsche. The revised circuit with the new chicanes was more than ever a power circuit and the rapid Porsche was running a very powerful qualifying engine prepared by IMSA specialist Andial in the USA. In the mid-Eighties GTP power outputs ran to over bhp.

The eye-opening speed of the 962C led Nissan to pump a lot of extra boost through the qualifying engine of its R90CK T car: unconfirmed reports suggest as much as 3.0 bar absolute was felt in the plenum. Given 3.0 bar in the plenum, we can expect the VRH35Z to have produced in excess of bhp at 7800 rpm even making an allowance for increasing exhaust back pressure. Nissan would only confirm ''over 2.6 bar'' and ''over 950 bhp'' but Hayashi admitted the output was nearer to the 1080 bhp being suggested to the author by Toyota engine designer Tsutomu Tomita than it was to 950 bhp. To be fair, he could not be much more precise than that since he hadn't ever run the engine at such a high boost level on the bench.

Did the Hayashi engine beat the Tomita 3.2-litre V8 turbo's 1989 record output of 1060 bhp? Tomita suspects it may well have done but we shall never know for sure since it has to be a close run thing. What was clear was the performance advantage of the super-boosted T car which required only one flying lap to clock a time that put it on pole by a convincing 6.4 sec margin. Equally impressive was the first day's pole time held by the lead NPTI car. It retained that time, set with a standard qualifying engine and little fuss for fourth on the grid.

Driven by Brabham/Robinson/Daly this Mallock-race engineered car ran on the lead lap throughout Saturday and took to the front soon after quarter distance. At that stage the NME pole car driven by Bailey/Blundell/Bracatelli lay sixth following a collision with a slower car while leading and a subsequent puncture. Meanwhile, the second NPTI car was well out of contention having lost two hours in the pits with a cooling system repair. Worse, the second NME car had not even made the start due to cwp failure on the warm-up lap.

Transmission trouble struck the pole car soon after midnight, at which stage it was back on the lead lap, and transmission trouble brought about its demise an hour or so later. However, the American Nissan remained at the front of the field, trading the lead with the fastest Jaguar through the early hours of Sunday. Alas, its fine run was ended by a split fuel cell. That left the R90CP as Nissan's main hope and although it had not sustained an impressive early pace it was running steadily. Indeed, it was only

a couple of laps down at half distance. A broken spring/damper mounting bolt cost time on Sunday morning then the loss of second, third and fourth gears in the final hour dropped the car from fourth to fifth place.

Almost all the cars met some form of transmission trouble and the delayed NPTI car was another to suffer a damper retaining bolt failure. It lost second gear and following a 15 min gearbox repair finished 48 laps down in 17th position. The only other Nissan finisher was the Courage car which required a one hr 15 min gearbox rebuild and suffered a host of other problems en route to 22nd position, 59 laps down. Engine problems afflicted only the Team Le Mans car which required a new ignition box early on and was eventually retired with ignition failure after a gearbox refettle. Overall, the race confirmed the highly competitive pace of the Lola chassis propelled by the Hayashi engine and there is no doubt that NPTI was ready to win when it struck its cruel fuel leak. The event also confirmed the reliability of the V8 turbo engine in its Z guise while showing the inability of the VGC gearbox to survive in the face of the engine's formidable output. The Nissan-Lola was the quickest car to the fuel at Le Mans in 1990 but it was too little developed to survive the rigours of a 24 hour race.

Ford-Lola Mk6, Aston Martin-Lola T70, Cosworth-Lola T600/T610: each car state-of-the-art in Prototype design but lacking an engine worthy of the chassis performance. The 1990 Lola offering had a worthy engine but still Broadley wasn't quite there. So near yet so far for the man who started the modern-style Prototype ball rolling with his 1963 car.

State of the Art

The Jaguar XJR-14

For 1991 FISA handicapped turbocharged Group C cars to the extent that only at Le Mans were they competitive. Elsewhere, the new breed of 3.5 litre sportscar ruled the roost and the TWR Jaguar XJR-14 demonstrated a huge advantage in the early races, its speed telling of advantages in terms of engine as well as chassis performance.

The heart of the XJR-14 was the Ford HB Grand Prix engine, victorious at Suzuka and Adelaide in 1990. Cosworth Engineering was at the sharp end of Formula One technology and with the Sportscar World Championship centred upon sprint rather than endurance races its expertise could not be discounted.

Both Daimler-Benz and Peugeot had engines designed by newcomers to the technology of 3.5 litre atmospheric screamers. Moreover, early in the season neither company had caught up with the pace of fuel development. Fuel can account for the majority of the gap between the 600 bhp estimated for the continental engines and the likely 650 bhp exploited by TWR. TWR apparently had the potent BP special brew, developed in 1990 and known to be worth at least 30 bhp at the top end.

Peugeot said that its supplier, Esso, was working on the problem whereas Daimler-Benz admitted that it had not managed to secure the right fuel contract. A situation that it planned to rectify before its home race at the 'Ring. Likewise both marques planned to shed weight – only the XJR-14 was down to the 750 kg weight limit – and to improve aerodynamics. The XJR-14 had a new and very effective approach to aerodynamics.

While the Peugeot and the Mercedes followed the basic 'Southgate' approach to aerodynamics, Southgate's successor at TWR, Ross Brawn, had gone a step further. The XJR-14 featured a two-tier rear wing, the lower tier of which virtually formed an extension of the diffuser roof. It was, nevertheless, at the level of the rear deck. In making the airflow across the body work in conjunction with a significantly lower rear deck, Brawn had taken advantage of the possibility for an improved superstructure shape given the post-Peugeot interpretation of Group C chassis regulations.

Prior to the coming of the 905, it had been assumed that a glass safety screen was mandatory: Peugeot got away with a more flexible plastic screen, establishing an important precedent. The 'bubble-type' plastic moulding that became accepted practice permitted a narrower superstructure of purer teardrop form and this in turn allowed provision of a low rear deck without significant separation of the airflow.

The lower tier of the Brawn wing situated at deck height was reminiscent of the rear wing of Southgate's XJR Le Mans package. As we have seen, in its original guise, that package set a long chord wing just above and behind the roof of the high diffusers and no higher than the deck. There it blended the flows from the deck and from the diffusers, acting both as an extension of the deck and as an extension of the tunnels.

Brawn's lower wing acted in the same manner, blending the flows and bleeding air from the higher speed flow over the deck down into the diffuser exit channel, thereby promoting the scavenging of the underwing. Those who had tried this set up in the tunnel told us that diffuser action was enhanced 'a lot'.

However, some designers felt that the low set wing really ought to be considered as an extension of the diffuser tunnel, which arguably made it illegal. Like the plastic screen, it all came down to interpretation of the regulations and like Peugeot, TWR set a precedent. Perhaps it had already done so with Southgate's 1986 Le Mans car.

Brawn's lower wing tier/diffuser package was cleverly detailed to maximise the potential of the underwing. Between the diffuser roof – typically almost horizontal at the maximum permitted height, aft of the rear wheels – and the rear deck was a low passage through which air escaped from the engine bay while the aerofoil section and its positioning had been carefully chosen to optimise interaction with the underwing.

Moreover, the regulation height diffuser/low deck/low-set wing package left the upper tier of the rear wing to be set as high and as far back as possible, thereby enjoying relatively clean air so as to work to maximum effect. Of course, the majority of the car's overall downforce came from the lower-tier scavenged underwing; the upper tier could be seen as a 'trim tab'.

The underwing form of the XJR-14 took advantage of the combination of the short HB engine and an inboard gearbox location, the car's bespoke transaxle extending rearwards no further than the cwp. With careful shaping of the tunnels to avoid air separation, this permitted exploitation of a larger tunnel volume behind the cwp. According to a designer who had modelled this approach in the wind tunnel, the gain was highly significant.

Another innovation was to be found at the front of the XJR-14. Although the Southgate-style underwing had held sway since the mid Eighties, as we have noted, it had never been found possible to combine adequate downforce at the nose with the best possible lift:drag ratio. Further, the large expanse of flat belly had tended to make the underwing highly pitch-sensitive at the expense of poor turn in. Thus, Group C cars had tended to lack grip at the front, a problem often magnified by the implications of running a heavy engine package.

The XJR-14 had a nice light engine, mid-mounted radiators and a re-thought nose form. In essence, Brawn started the flat area of the underwing at the front wheel axis rather than with a splitter. Ahead of the front wheel axis the traditional nose package was missing; in its place was a wing with an adjustable flap.

Shades of the first ever Prototype of the modern generation, the 'lobster claw' BMW-March. That car, of course, had full length tunnels behind its nose aerofoil. In the case of the flat belly XJR-14, the net result was a less pitch-sensitive underwing – following the Tyrrell high nose principle – and a Group C car that evidently turned in like a Formula One car.

In essence, Brawn had applied Formula One thinking to a Group C car and at the time of writing (mid season 1991) the jury is still out. A shorter, less pitch-sensitive underwing was surely a plus and it might be that the ratio of the length of the flat bottom area to the length of the diffuser area was improved. Further, the lower profile of the front wing might well have provided an enhanced feed for the underwing.

On the other hand, some said that merely squashing a car hard to the track with bags of downforce could promote the astonishing turn in demonstrated by the XJR-14. Eighties Group C cars ran with perhaps 4500 lb downforce at 180 mph. In 1991, without fuel restrictions to consider, drag was of less consequence and the going rate was above 6000 lb downforce at the same speed. Consequently, the car was pressed harder to the track at a given speed and with the right springs and pre-load was glued down through a wider speed range.

Was the XJR-14 nose wing really a step forward, or merely – as some suggested – a device that an ex-Formula One designer could feel comfortable with? Certainly, the XJR-14 nose wing – even if it did not work as a pure wing – ran with its flap element typically at a very, very steep angle of attack.

We are given to understand that a front aerofoil situated behind the tip of the nose of a prototype will invariably need to run at a steeper angle of attack than one outrigged ahead since it will not meet a 'horizontal' airflow. Running a flap as steeply as that of the XJR-14 is surely not in the best interest of the overall flow across the body? On the other hand, it is unlikely that the XJR-14 front wing ran in stall. It was suggested that Brawn had, to a degree, been able to separate the front flap 'spill' from the crucial over-body feed to the rear wing package. Nevertheless, in this case, what you saw must ultimately have been what you got and the air shovel on the front of the XJR-14 did not impress rival designers. It must have added a lot of drag.

Even then, the XJR-14 did not appear to be rid of the dreaded curse of understeer, though with its overall high level of downforce it experienced understeer at a very high level of grip. With the sort of grip available to the XJR-14 driver, he could commit to a corner at an alarming rate of knots, in view of which mid corner understeer was to be much preferred to mid corner oversteer!

Overall, the Brawn approach clearly offered a highly effective underwing and put less pitch sensitive front and (high) rear wings in clean air where they could both add consistent downforce and offer the flexibility to adjust the car's overall aerodynamic characteristics through easy flap angle alterations. On the other hand, the high front flap angle that always seemed to be necessary cannot have been good for the overall lift:drag ratio. On balance, Brawn had introduced a gust of fresh thinking that had set his rivals reeling. The XJR-14 was clearly a major stride ahead of the opposition as the new era got underway.

Silverstone, 14 May 1991, Warwick/Fabi win ahead of the Mercedes-Benz C291 in the British WSCC round, driving the new Jaguar XJR-14.